How to tell a PRINCE

from a FROG

Law enforcement techniques
for knowing who you're dating

by Christine Kerrick

How To Tell A Prince From A Frog
Law Enforcement Techniques for Knowing Who You're Dating

COPYRIGHT ©2012 Christine Kerrick. All rights reserved. No part of this book may be reproduced in any form without written permission from the publisher.

ISBN - 978-0-9786687-1-6

Text, illustrations and cover design by Christine Kerrick

Published by Christine Kerrick Images

www.christinekerrick.com

Christine Kerrick is not a licensed counselor, lawyer or medical practicioner. This book is not meant to provide legal, psychological or medical advice. Do not go off of any of your medications if you're not supposed to. This book is for entertainment purposes only.

All works cited in this book are © and/or ™ by their respective owners.

All content, with the exception of the works and references cited, are the opinion of the author, and not of the authors of the works cited here. Cited authors do not share the opinions stated herein.

Printed in the United States of America

Christian/Self-Help/Dating

*For all the princesses who may need a reminder
of how special they are.*

Contents

Acknowledgements
Introduction

Part 1 – How To Tell A Prince From A Frog 19

   Chapter 1 – How To Tell A Prince From A Frog 20
  - What is a Frog?
  - Frog For All Seasons
    The Narcissist, The High Roller, The Moocher, The Manchild,
    The Fighter, The Golddigger, The Liar, The Know-It-All,
    The Critic, The Sympathy Monger, The Ice Man, The Double Agent,
    The Charmer, The Spiritual Superstar ('Extra-Strength' and 'Lite')
  - What is a Prince?
  - Diagram of Integrity
  - Diagram of Foolishness

   Chapter 2 – The First Type of Frog: The Bull Frog 25

   Chapter 3 – The Second Type of Frog: The Poison Frog 29

   Chapter 4 – The Lie and Its Side Effects 55
  - Anatomy of a Lie
  - When Is It Ok To Lie?
  - Manipulation
  - Froggy Verbal Behavior

   Chapter 5 – What Deception Looks Like 81
  - Body Language
  - Eye Contact
  - Linguistics
  - Internet Cons
  - How To Protect Yourself
  - Psychic Payday

   Chapter 6 – The Devolution of Courtship: Dates vs. Mates 97
  - Love and Other Drugs
  - 'Relationship'
  - Table: Courting vs. Dating
  - Why Marry?
  - Why Living Together ≠ Marriage

Chapter 7 – The Date (a.k.a., 'The Interview') 111
- Your Preparation
- The 'Interview'
- Asking Questions
- Listen
- Listen To Your Gut
- Clues That Demand More Investigation
- A Word About Judging
- How To Attract a Frog
- How To Attract a Prince

Part II – Why Women Ignore Their Red Flags 135

Chapter 8 – Red Flags.. 136

Chapter 9 – Why Women Miss Red Flags... 140
- Family Conditioning – Raised by Wolves
- Princess In The Pot: Cultural Conditioning
- Miss Fix-It
- Compassion
- Girl's Gotta Have It
- Everyone Else Likes Him

Chapter 10 – Breaking the Pattern... 165

Part III – Your Identity... 172

Chapter 11 – Identity Theft: Reestablishing Your Value 173
- One of a Kind
- Sorely Insecure
- God's Girl
- Fitting In or Standing Out
- Consequences of Insecurity

Chapter 12 – The Mirror Lies.. 192
- Mirror of Achievement
- Mirror of Self
- Mirror of a Man
- Mirror of Popular Culture
- Mirror of Opinion
- Mirror of God's Word

Chapter 13 – Self Esteem 202

Chapter 14 – A Masterpiece 211
 - What Is Confidence?

Chapter 15 - R-E-S-P-E-C-T 217
 - You Can't Reward Bad Behavior
 - Signs That You're Losing Yourself in a Dating Relationship
 - What About Girlfriends?
 - Frogettes

Chapter 16 – Your Seven Pillars 227
 - Organizing Your Life: Achieving Balance
 - Mirror of Self
 - Mirror of a Man

Chapter 17 – The Perfect Relationship 244

Chapter 18 – Healing, Post-Frog 247
 - Safety Precautions - If you are not in danger/if you are in danger
 - What Not To Do, Once Your Relationship With The Frog Is Over
 - Healing Steps
 - Are You The Friend?

Helpful tables 261
 - Gifts
 - Groceries
 - Goals
 - Putting a Timeline To Your Goals

Devotions 270

Epilogue: Happy Endings 273

Acknowledgements

There are many people I could thank for this book coming into existence. My family and friends, of course, who stood by me not only as I wrote it, but when I wanted to put it down and forget it. Most importantly, I am grateful that I lived through some of the experiences which pushed my limits. There are no better friends in the world than mine who have given me words of wisdom, inspiration and friendship when I most needed it.

I would also like to thank the many women who contributed stories to the book. You know who you are. Because some of these women are still in danger, and others have healed from their experiences and have moved forward in their lives, their names are not mentioned here, but their sacrifice of time and dredging up memories so other women can be helped are appreciated.

I would also like to thank the law enforcement officers, deputies, and federal government employees who helped with their experiences, training and willingness to try to help women by taking time with me in my research.

Thank you most to God, who is always there for me, and who is the Author of love and adventure. I am looking forward to Him writing my love story...and yours!

Introduction

The concept of the handsome prince has been around since time began. Women everywhere dream of landing that wonderful, handsome, charismatic, kind, guy who makes mothers swoon and wedding planners drool. The reality is that all of us, at some point in our lives, have dealt with a Frog; i.e., a dangerous man.

In the stories, a princess kisses a frog in hopes that he transforms into a prince. With rules like that, we should all be guaranteed that if we stoop down into the dirt and kiss one of these warty creatures, we, too, would be rewarded with Mr. Tall, Dark and Handsome. The problem with using this fairy tale model in real life is that we are still left with a frog and maybe even a few warts. Many women don't know they are trying to live by the fairy tale idea until they kiss their Frog, let down their guard and let him further into their lives than they should before truly knowing him. When the Frog breaks their hearts, steals their money and does anything else worthy of a country song, a woman is shocked and hurt. Some stories end worse, with women battered or murdered, all because they did not recognize a Frog, or because they did not leave when the red flags started waving.

Most of the chapters of this book contain stories from women who have been hurt by Frogs. Their stories are cautionary tales to the woman who may have a Frog cross her path in the future. The intent of this book is not to blame women or to bash men, but to allow us to open our eyes, recognize traits and character flaws in certain men which are in our best interest to take as warnings, determine why we would ignore those flaws, and their red flags, and learn when and how to flee.

You may see some points and truths more than once in this book, but I felt the need to reiterate them in order to anchor them into the reader's mind.

When I began my research on this book, I must admit my focus was on these men: cons, sexual and emotional predators, and manipulators. However, as someone once said, "It takes two to tango." What I include in this book are those of us who, for whatever reason, have tangoed with the wrong partner and, having seen or felt something wrong, ignored those signs and refused to stop the dance, to our detriment. Please understand, again, this does not include unwilling victims, such as women who are raped or otherwise assaulted. Some of the dating relationships in this book have included rape or assault, but these examples begin first with some kind of relationship—friends, dating or business—in which the woman sensed something was wrong but chose to stay. In each case, a woman saw red flags but ignored them.

How To Tell A Prince From A Frog is divided into three parts:

Part One covers the definition of a Frog. No book of mine would be complete without cartoons to lighten the mood, drive home some important points and of course, to entertain. Biblical references may offend some, but are necessary for truth. If you are offended, keep reading. I'm guessing you picked up this book because your dating life—and maybe life in general—isn't turning out the way you thought it would and nothing else has worked. This book is not the Bible and is not a substitute for God's infallible word, but it is based on the Bible's wisdom. It is a book I wrote to try to help women skip my mistakes and those of other women out there, to be safe, and to hang on until that Prince comes along.

I have used examples of Princes (men of integrity and character) from the Bible so you can see what a man of marriage quality looks like in an easy-to-understand way. There are Frogs in the Bible too, and I outline the character traits that make them so. In addition, I put Frogs in a police lineup cartoon in Chapter One. I did this because many of us have grown up thinking some wrong behaviors from men are acceptable, or that righteous characteristics are boring; i.e., the 'bad boy' is more desirable than the 'good guy', even if he's run over our heart with his Harley again and again. When you have had your heart stomped—and all of us have—shouldn't you go for the guy who treats you like the precious creation of God that you are? Yet many times women accept behavior which even a snake would find repellent.

In **Part Two**, I address this issue of why we consider bad behavior acceptable. I researched the reasons we let red flags slide under our radar. Maybe a man is behaving in a charming and above-board way, but something still is not right. Our red flags start waving, but we ignore them again—why? It is important to know that we can have all the information on deception detection and bad character we want, but if we are not willing to use it, it is the same as jumping off the Titanic and not taking the life preserver because our flawed thinking says: 'the water can't be that dangerous'. A psychologist cited in this book says: "There are no victims, only volunteers." If we are adhering to all of the steps listed in this part of the book, and if we have good female friends who can hold us accountable, there is no reason to have to be hurt by a Frog again. If dating Frogs is a constant, repeated action, however, it is necessary to address the issues that lead us to do so, like I did, and arrive at a solution which changes things. It is not pretty, but it is important to face your own weaknesses and learn why you are drawn to Frogs. Your quality of life, your joy and mental health depend on it. I will show you one inherent cause of these flaws in you as a woman.

In **Part Three** I talk about identity. You didn't drag your tail up onto some foreign shore at the beginning of time and decide to become a biped with a Y-chromosome. You were God's idea—a masterpiece, and you have a purpose. There is an enemy of your soul who longs to destroy you, restrict you and depress you to the point where you are joyless, hopeless, ineffective, and in constant turmoil. The unfortunate truth is that sometimes we help this enemy along by not knowing the truth about what miraculous and loved creations each of us are. When we know without a doubt how much God loves us we have joy and fulfillment. For the first time in our lives, when we relinquish the fear that kept us bound, and walk forward into the promised land of what we were created for, we are safe. We do not need a man to carry us along, tell us we're beautiful, or to assuage our insecurities with any other superhuman support men were not designed to give. The secure woman who knows the identity God gave her is a blessing to a man and has something to offer him, just as he does her.

For the insecure woman who is looking for her worth in a man or being 'in a relationship'—an inaccurate and undefined term in itself—she will forever be sucking the life out of what could be a potentially great mate. She could also be attracting Frogs to her who can smell her fear and are more than willing to act on it.

This section outlines the innate and unchangeable value of who you are, how get the most out of your life whether there is a man in it or not, and most importantly, how to get to know the One who knows you inside and out and cares about who you marry.

If you do not believe in God or have chosen to live by your own rules, you can still benefit from this book, but you will not get the benefit and all-encompassing joy that comes from a relationship with your Creator, or the gift of living in Heaven forever. If you are a Christian who has moved away from God, you may come to realize what living by your own rules has cost you.

Although this book is written from a female perspective regarding men, there are women out there who are equally as 'froggy' and dangerous as a man. While it is true that certain women can be just as immoral and criminal as the dangerous men in this book, their numbers are not as great as the men who manipulate and con. Statistics and veteran police detectives who have helped with this book attest to this fact. Whatever the reason is that people choose the path of hurting other people for their own gain, one thing is certain: you, being the decision-maker in your life, have the final say in your own safety. There are some dangers you cannot prevent. By knowing the signs of a manipulator, recognizing when someone is trying to infiltrate your life with an agenda using covertly aggressive tactics and by noticing the faults in yourself which may prevent you from moving away from a deceiver, you can prevent much of the pain you would have experienced letting these Frogs into your life. This book is helpful for anyone who wants to better understand the 'mode of operation' of a manipulator, male or female, and who wants to change the dangerous, repetitive habits in themselves in order to live a fuller, more productive life. It will also help you to see the *sin* (i.e., 'missing the mark': an archer's term) in your own life and get rid of any Frog characteristics in yourself that hurt other people.

In compiling this book, I have interviewed women who have been hurt and defrauded by men who wanted something from them for their own gain. These men used covert manipulation in one form or another to get what they wanted. Some of the women left before experiencing much loss, and only their pride was hurt. Some were crushed or lost money and some were physically abused. There is no better teacher than experience, but sometimes learning from others' experiences without having to go through that story ourselves is much less painful—if we are willing to listen. I added to these findings the stories from of veteran law enforcement officers and deputies, some of whom deal with white collar crime, some with child and sexual predators and all of whom have seen the common thread of human selfishness coupled with manipulation in the criminals they deal with. There have been countless articles about cases of manipulation and cons ending in terrible ways. I also drew on my own experience interviewing witnesses using the cognitive approach I learned at the FBI Academy's Forensic Art Lab. This significant step in determining if a person was a 'good' witness, or, if (s)he was telling the truth, had seen the crime and/or had a good view of what went on, was essential in arriving at the truth not only for detectives but for me, the forensic artist.

The most important research I did was in the Bible, where our loving God has outlined the way we should live to have the most peace and joy possible in life. There are all kinds of t.v. shows, radio programs and self-help books that try to right the painful wrongs people have experienced. If you have a problem with your car, you look at the manual. Simple, right? Wisdom is found in the one who invented wisdom—God. You can try taking shortcuts or going to other sources for so-called 'wisdom', but it always falls short. People usually try to find answers to suit their own desires. I've done it. We run ahead of God's timing, or think that the rules don't pertain to us, opening ourselves up to danger. This brings us out from under God's protective covering.

Considering the fact that there are things we as women—and all of us as humans—can do to guard our hearts, purses and lives from these people, shouldn't we know all we can about how they operate and, more importantly, how to get our own hearts more in line with God's word so that recognizing right and wrong comes as second nature?

The last chapter of the book approaches the sensitive subject of a woman's healing after she has been hurt by a Frog. Many times women repeat their actions, dating Frogs because they have either anesthetized their pain or jumped into a rebound relationship. This section stresses why it is so important to experience the pain, learn from it, forgive and be real—with yourself and with God.

This book does not discount a woman's desire for a husband, but focuses on what she needs to do to be marriage material for a good man—a Prince, and how to recognize that man when he comes around. She must also recognize the Frogs who may flock around her for what they are. She must be secure enough in her 'already-value' to let them go; even if they are handsome and charming. She must be busy doing what she is wired to do while God works out His amazing and wonderful promises for her. There are sheets at the end of this book which will assist you in organizing your life and being prepared when God's blessings come your way.

My hopes in writing this book are not to highlight and stigmatize the kind of man who hurts women, or to put all men in this category. While the media denigrates men, father figures and men's masculinity, the Bible defines men as having a special place in the world as leaders, protectors, conquerors, fighters, providers, builders, teachers and more. With God, a man can accomplish everything he is wired to do and, in the process, reveal more about our good and wise Creator. This is the kind of man a woman wants. Somewhere along the line women have settled and put up with men who are the opposite. Maybe by taking back our own minds, realizing who we are in Christ, not putting up with bad or dangerous behavior and being safe and secure enough to wait for God's best, women can cut off the supply of desperation and attention to certain men who have not realized their identity in Christ. Perhaps these men will see this decision and be spurred on to be better than who they are.

Part One

How To Tell A Prince From A Frog

Part 1

Chapter 1

How To Tell A Prince From A Frog

The tears never seemed to end. The tightness in my chest refused to let up. Again, again, again I had gotten involved with a man who had ripped my heart out: a Frog...possibly King of the Frogs. As I lay paralyzed with not even the will to turn on the t.v. for distraction, I wondered how I had missed all the signs of what he was, and why men seemed to be so horrible. I wanted to be married, but the road between 'husband' and 'psychopath' seemed to be fraught with land mines and psycho Frogs.

It is tempting, when your heart has been broken, to lump all men together into the 'jerk' category. You want to make sure everyone knows he's a jerk by stapling a sign with that name to his forehead...kind of like flashing your lights to oncoming traffic to warn other drivers of a speed trap. But the fact is, all men are not jerks. The fact is also, all of us—men and women—behave like jerks at some point. It's part of being human. *"No one is righteous—not even one. No one is truly wise; no one is seeking God. All have turned away; all have become useless. No one does good, not a single one."* – Romans 3:10-12

Another fact: many of us women can purposely blind ourselves to men who have become used to behaving this way or, as I like to call them, Frogs. But that is another chapter.

After being involved with a particularly poisonous Frog in my life, I saw the difference between the 'not-yet-ready-for-matrimony' (or, in many cases, not ready to be out on his own unsupervised) Frog, and the downright dangerous Frog. The first kind of Frog usually hits on women to try to get sex, and has no plans for any future with her. The second, more dangerous Frog has indentations on his forehead from banging it against the walls at the institution…or maybe it's where his horns used to be.

I don't believe the saying: 'you have to kiss a lot of frogs before you meet your prince'. Contrary to the sport sex lifestyle our culture preaches, we were not designed for revolving door dating- or sex-relationships. In showing you how to spot a Frog when you encounter one, I want to help you keep your heart intact so you can give it all, with as few scars and baggage as possible, to your Prince.

Like a cop, observation and the ability to deduce from evidence—also known as *critical thinking*, are necessary to know what you're dealing with when faced with a dude who seems like The One. Then you will have the truth you need to make a decision to stay or leave the situation.

What is a Frog?

The Frog population can be pared down to two kinds: the **Bullfrog** and the **Poison Frog**.

The Bullfrog is a guy like my friend Dave*. Dave is single, owns a white box of a house that serves as a 'catch-all' for his musical instruments and art supplies. Like some guys, he doesn't think much about his living space. He also thinks nothing of being out with one woman and openly checking out others as they saunter past whatever table he occupies with his current catch-of-the-day. Dave is harmless, unless you set your sights on him as a mate and think he is going to change for you and have eyes only for you. Dave is a decent friend. He is friendly to people and encourages them when they're down, but presently he's not quite cooked enough to be husband material.

The Poison Frog is more cunning and purposeful in his goals: to get something from you without regard to your welfare. He is an outright manipulator. He is usually a textbook example that psychiatrists use on talk shows. That would be a man Jaimie once knew, named Travis:

*All names have been changed to protect everyone.

"I met Travis at a video rental place near my apartment in college. He was extremely attractive and asked me out. One time we went out and he tearfully told me stories of women who had treated him badly. I kind of felt bad for the guy, but just the same, wanted him to 'suck it up'. His emotional display set off some red flags and I wasn't sure why, but I wanted to be compassionate, so I did nothing about it.

One morning a burglar broke into the apartment my roomate Jen and I lived in and stole a few things. Jen and I were understandably nervous after that. We found out the burglar was a crack addict, when he was arrested a week later. He confessed to burglarizing our whole block to support his habit. He had gained access through all the roof decks. Some of our coworkers from the record store where we worked stayed overnight in the livingroom in case the guy came back (which he tried to do a couple of days later, before the arrest).

I told Travis about the burglary. He came to our apartment. I let him in and he pulled me into the bathroom and showed me a 9mm semiautomatic he'd brought to 'defend me' should the guy come back. Needless to say, my red flags were waving like departing passengers on the Love Boat, but again, I did nothing about the situation until a few days later on our roof deck. That night up on the deck, Travis told me he actually worked at the video rental place down the block and had gotten my address and phone number from their records to track me down. He had been watching me at my job for weeks. I didn't want to know any more. He needed to be gone."

Not all Frogs are so forthcoming with their creepiness, but each has his own modus operandi for getting what he wants. Each Frog also has a particular desire he wants to satisfy. The goals can be sex, money or control. The more tenacious cling-ons may want other things, like your time or sympathy. He may lie about who he is presently and act deceptively going forward to get you, or he may hide a questionable past from you in order to get these things from you.

You can usually spot a Bullfrog pretty easily. They're the non-committal types who would sooner commit hari-kari on themselves with a butter knife than wear the circulation-stopping wedding ring. They can be the party guy or the 'friend' or play numerous other personas. Some will be honest and lay the truth on the line: that they're just not into you, but they will still hang out with you as long as you let them, until something better comes along.

The Poison Frog travels further under the radar. He is on assignment and would have a PhD. in deception, if there were degrees for it. He wields his intrigue like a scalpel and has no problem doing whatever he must to dismantle your life. That is, unless you know what to look for.

There is some overlap between the Bull- and Poison Frogs, but, again, they are both Frogs. You don't need to have anything to do with either one.

Part 1
Chapter 2

The First Type of Frog: The Bullfrog

I like to call the Bullfrog the 'Frog Lite', but he is no less dangerous, should you get your heart too involved with him. While lying is a deal-breaker (and if you don't consider it one, you should) there are other deal-breakers worth mentioning that would classify a man as a Frog. The following is a list that may signal a man's need to become more mature. One common thread is the lack of ability to sacrifice and think of the woman's well-being before he thinks of himself—or, the inability to be selfless. Kids, as they grow, should move out of their natural self-centeredness and become more others-centered as adults. Frogs haven't grown out of their self-centeredness. They are not out for your best interest.

This list is taken from women's actual stories. Men with these characteristics can change, but it's not your job to make them change or to hang around waiting for them to do so.

1. **The Rat Collector.** Does your potential mate have a rat living in a terrarium on top of his fridge? Does he have tarantulas named Stella and Archimedes who continue to escape from their box? If this is not a deal-breaker for you and you have your own fridge-dwelling rat or adventurous arachnids, that's fine (although tarantulas are cannibals, so you may want to keep them apart). But if the guy is dead-set on keeping his precious pets and letting you take a back seat, you might want to move on and consider someone ready for a grown-up relationship with a human being.

2. **The Collector.** Once I dated a guy who had bundles of newspapers and magazines stacked to the ceiling of his house. They actually hid the walls of the place. You probably could have knocked down the

walls from the outside and the roof would have remained where it was, resting on top of the periodical stacks. It had been years since the inception of the internet, and the guy did have online access, but he decided walls of newspapers were better 'because he may want to read them sometime'. The strangest part was that when someone tried to break into his house one night, rather than fix the lock, he moved some of his stacks to block that door 'so the intruder couldn't get in next time'. I pictured the criminal bursting in like the Incredible Hulk, sending years of L.A. Times crashing to the floor. I think the issue here wasn't what my ex collected, but the fact that this guy's bulb had dimmed long ago. The newspaper 'walls' were just the clue. That first trip to his house was pretty much the end of things.

CHOLO HAD HIS REASONS FOR NOT WANTING TO GET MARRIED.

3. Living at mom's house. If he lives with his mom, it had better be for one of these reasons:

1) He's taking care of her.

2) He's in an interim stage of moving/buying a house or otherwise getting back on his feet after a setback—and that interim stage shouldn't last for more than a year or so if he's dating you. Economic trends have lengthened this time on the average, but my point is that if he's been living with mom for ten years, watch out.

3) If his mom is living with him. If, rather than putting her in a home, this guy has enough heart to let his mom live with him, he's a keeper. Of course, be sure he doesn't fall into the 'Man Child' category, but if he doesn't, this is a good guy.

4) He's working out family issues

5) He's saving for a house.

On the other hand, there are some reasons for living with mom that should cause red flags. Living at home is a red flag if:

1) he says it's more convenient to do his laundry there because his mom is nicer to him than the people at the laundromat, and she doesn't starch his shorts,

2) he's there because it looks better to his parole officer,

3) he's there so she doesn't have to worry about where he is,

4) he says he likes her mashed potatoes and meatloaf better for dinner than the circus peanuts and Twinkies he's used to,

5) he says he doesn't want to deal with bills,

6) he says the people who are looking for him would never find him there,

7) he says his cartoon shows look so much better on her minivan-sized t.v. screen,

8) he says it's more convenient to see his kids when his baby-mama brings them over for his mother to watch,

9) he says his mom's house has more room for him to sleep than his car does,

10) he says his landlord wouldn't let the band practice in his apartment,

11) he says she has a bigger basement where he can hang lights and spread out his 'crop'

Maybe you've noticed that most of these reasons center on the man's living situation. You may not think much about where your potential mate lives now, but if you marry this man, you're going to live with him. And if you live with him, you'll be sharing in many of his habits, as he will yours.

Part 1
Chapter 3

The Second Type of Frog: The Poison Frog

Types of Poison Frogs are as wide and varied as some of their amphibious namesakes. Just as there are creatures like carpenter frogs, green tree frogs, squirrel frogs and pig frogs (don't get me started on that one!), there are some names our human Frogs can be given by some behavioral characteristics they bear. One general characteristic of all of these men is that they are manipulators and will use any and all means in their bags of tricks to get what they want from you. They fall into divisions depending on their MO, or, modus operandi (the way they get what they want); and their goal (power, control...you):

A Frog For All Seasons

1. The Narcissist

Like the personality disorder, it's all about him. You may pick up on this right away if he talks incessantly, either about himself or about anything related to him. He won't let you get a word in, or if he does, the conversation circles back to where he wants it to be: whatever he's interested in. He may be a little more covert if a previous girlfriend has told him about his self-focus. In this case, he may give the impression of catering to you, but his natural way will show itself in time and you will see through his apparent care for you to the true motive of keeping you around for personal reasons—himself.

He may be a Narcissist if he:
- is selfish, and does rude things, like not holding the door, walking ahead of you, or considering his time and himself more important than you,
- uses the pronoun 'I' too much in sentences, steering the conversation back to himself,
- acts concerned, curious or otherwise interested in you, only to have license to talk about himself. There is usually a pattern to this. This is not give-and-take conversation. Once he has listened to you for a short time at the beginning of the conversation, he goes back to talking about himself. He interrupts constantly, increasing speed and volume until you acquiesce. Wrestling him off of his royal selfness onto another subject is like trying to pry your arm from a pitbull's jaws.
- He also shows low self worth through bragging or being defensive,
- needs attention, will sulk if he doesn't get it, and will manipulate to get it,
- tells tall tales of accomplishments and potential accomplishments,
- needs emphatic and repeated reinforcement, or
- can't empathize with others (though he can mimic the emotions).

2. The High-Roller

There are two scenarios for this guy. Either he really has the money and is using it to get you, or he doesn't, is living beyond his means, and is 'priming' you in order to con you. In the latter case, you see his generosity and how he pays for you, so when he doesn't have his wallet with him or occasionally has you get the check at dinner, you don't think much of it...until he tries to get you to sign for a loan, give him your bank account info (he's already given you his, saying he 'trusts you'), or asks for a large loan because his money is 'tied up'. This guy eventually wants the big score: cleaning you out and leaving, or cleaning you out after marrying you, or marrying you and milking you while he goes to visit other pastures. Ask yourself three things: 1) Does this man have a financial need or emergency or something that would make him chase money? 2) Does he have a time deadline for getting this money? 3) Are you an opportunity for him to get that money? These are some indicators economic crime investigators use to identify fraud.

He may be a High Roller if he:
- waves money around, acting unconcerned with the prices of things
- likes to be seen spending in front of people
- talks about money and 'deals' he plans on doing, whether real or imagined (dealmakers with integrity don't broadcast it),
- may have been involved in a scam or financial deal that went bust,
- shows low self worth by bragging about possessions or name-dropping
- has Narcissistic attributes, as mentioned previously, or
- is very concerned with his appearance.

3. The Moocher

He comes over to your house and helps himself to your food, your remote, and your sofa. He gives the appearance of just being relaxed with you and can easily become a habit, but he's using you until something better comes along. He is easing his boredom and satisfying himself with a counterfeit relationship. Because you like the attention of having a man around, you don't mind. He won't take you out anywhere or go do anything with you because, to him, you're not someone in whom he finds a worthy investment. He doesn't have to be poor to do this. I knew a woman who was out of work. A moocher she knew made 30 dollars an hour at his job, yet came to her apartment, watched t.v. during work hours and helped himself to her sparse groceries. Activity like this won't end until you get tired of being used or until he meets someone else with more channels and a bigger dish.

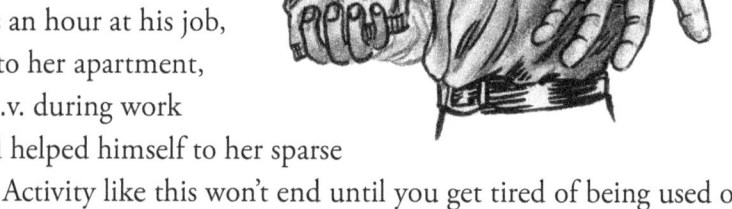

He may be a Moocher if he:
- has been living in his parents' basement way too long,
- makes you feel like you have a child—and you're not sure when you acquired him because you don't remember giving birth,
- drains your time with long, emotional stories,
- uses your remote control and sofa more than you do…and you're not even married to him,
- uses 'forced-teaming' approach to use your resources, like appearing at your apartment asking if 'we' have any milk, or what 'we're' having for dinner tonight,
- stops asking to use your resources after a while and just assumes and takes what he wants,
- asks you to cover the dinner bill more than once, citing that he forgot his wallet, or
- is always borrowing money from you.

4. The Man-child

This guy wants a mom. He may even jokingly call you 'mom' when you do something to care for him. He resents your doting, but is fighting the desire he has for the mom he either never had or who never gave him what he needed. If his mom is still around, he's more than in contact with her—he's either living with her or letting her make most of his decisions. She controls him, because he allows her to. He's not man enough to tell his mother that his life is his own. His decisions are helmed by her and, as a result, so are yours. If she has passed on, you may be the replacement. If she is still around, you may be looking at a marriage where you're his 'second woman'.

He may be a Man-child if he:

- has Moocher attributes,
- slips and calls you 'mom', or just acts like your son anyway by expecting you to make dinner, plan events, wash his clothes, deal with unpleasant people or circumstances for him and other duties,
- takes no responsibility for his life, the evidence being a sloppy living space, unpaid bills and shifting blame for his circumstances,
- buys or does whatever he wants, without considering the consequences,
- is high-drama and throws tantrums to manipulate you into doing his will,
- has no plans or goals for his life,
- expects you to take care of the day-to-day essentials like a secretary or a mom would,
- spends his paychecks on video games, action figures and Comicons on a regular basis (I can say that: I've sold my art and comics at Comicon and I've seen some of these guys there.), or
- looks to you to plan the evening, the week, and his life.

5. The Fighter

With this one, again, it may not be apparent on a first date, but rest assured that this man's true nature will show itself, usually when his high view of himself is threatened or his goal is jeopardized. He may show irritation at a waiter or other service person, perceiving inadequate service as a blow to his pride. He may speak badly about someone from his past— a boss, an ex or friend. You may even be an ignition for him if he envies a talent or possession of yours, or if you are more intelligent or financially stable than he is. When the arguments begin, you may think you're crazy. You may notice that you don't argue with anyone else like you do with this guy. You may even believe what he says or implies about you because of the conviction he puts into his words, and because of the importance you have given him in your life. But this is another controlling technique to put you down and keep you corralled and bound so he feels superior, which was his goal.

He may be a Fighter if he:
- makes a big deal about going to the gym, how much more he presses than other guys, or talks a lot about going to the gym, with little follow-up,
- has a bad temper and you feel like you're on eggshells around him,
- starts arguments, and possibly fights, with waiters, people in traffic and others,
- talks about fighting, and how he wants to 'destroy', 'crush', or do harm to a boss, competitor or enemy,
- speaks negatively about other people, especially men who he perceives are better, more talented or more powerful than he is,

- grabs, swats, tickles you or otherwise touches you against your consent or to the point where he dominates you (this is called assault) or throws things at you,
- believes the world is wrong and he is right, or
- hits you, even once.

6. The Golddigger

And you thought golddigging was only a woman's game? This guy is looking for you to support him. He may give himself away by showing Moocher tendencies, or he may keep his cards close to his chest until the big score. If he doesn't play the obvious Moocher role, he may talk a lot about the things he dreams of owning or the places he dreams of traveling, while waxing poetic about the 'company he will own someday' or the 'big deal he's working on' so you don't get suspicious. He sees something in your life he can take: money, if you have it; future money from a talent you possess; your impending inheritance or even just your compassion and good work ethic—things as foreign to him as wings on a pig. Presently he will have no means vocationally or financially of realizing his dreams or goals, nor is he able to support you in such a grand way. Because he is convincing, you may believe him (but hopefully not!). He may be a waiter with no college education who wants to own a global company, or someone constantly involved in 'get rich quick' schemes and multi-level marketing schemes. Ask yourself: Did Bill Gates get where he is today by lounging on the sofa all day watching ESPN?

He may be a Golddigger if he:
- is always on the lookout for a 'get rich quick' scheme, calling it an 'investment',
- has High Roller attributes,
- forks out money to you initially and later gets you to fork back,
- jokes about wanting you to buy him things and the money/success of others,
- has low self worth, shown by how he talks down about others or boasts about himself,
- takes note of the nice things you have and makes comments like, 'Wow, must be nice to have a _____ like that',
- expects you to buy him things, whether or not your income is higher than his, or
- uses charm to disarm you.

7. The Liar

While lying is a common thread in each of these categories, this guy is in deep. He has a whole other life. Don't write off the strange, inexplicable feelings you have. Those red flags are there for a reason. Strange phone calls he receives, text messages, and having to go somewhere suddenly at night are indicators. He may prime you to accept these activities, saying he doesn't want you acting 'wifey' toward him by asking who's calling or text messaging him. He's feeling you out, and if you acquiesce and keep your questions to yourself, he knows he can do his dark activities right in front of you for a while...until his secret life comes out. He tells you not to be silly and uses affection to try to convince you of his veracity. If he does come clean, don't believe him when he says 'I was forced to lie because I love you so much. I won't do it again'. This leopard doesn't change his spots. Check out the chapters on detecting deception for how to spot physical and verbal signs of deception.

8. The Know-It-All

He doesn't, which is all the more reason he will try to prove that he does. He may belittle you or highlight the times when you are wrong. Sometimes you may find yourself thinking that he thinks you're stupid, but you can't put your finger on why. Pay close attention. No one can make you feel inferior, but when a man is attempting to cut you down to his size, he is showing his low self-worth. You won't be able to engage him in verbal combat to prove who is smarter; it will lead to an argument. You won't be able to back down and be less than you are; he will treat you like a doormat. You were not meant to be less than God made you to be, and the right man will revel in and admire who you are.

He may be a Know-It-All if he:
- likes the sound of his own voice,
- tells people things he thinks they didn't know, whether they wanted to know or not,
- interrupts you often,
- is opinionated,
- rarely, if ever, gives praise,
- often knows 'factoids' and not actual truth; memorizes headlines instead of engaging in critical thinking, or
- exhibits signs of low self worth, such as putting you down or pointing out your mistakes.

9. The Critic

The soles of your shoes are made of eggshells with this one. You may find some 'Know-It-All' characteristics in him, too. You are constantly trying to do better and be better, but it is not enough. As with all of these personality traits, there may be something here that feels familiar from your past, but it is not healthy. There is no such thing as someone being 'gifted' to criticize. This trait comes from someone who wants to control, who was criticized as a child, or who resents your success, brains or some trait in you. You may hear, "Let me tell you what you did wrong back there," or, "I'm just trying to teach you so you'll be a better person." Let God's word, a teacher, a pastor or life experiences teach you. Your date may unknowingly teach you something or may just want to show you something he discovered, but he will not harp on you constantly about your shortcomings to make you a 'better person'. He will like you the way you are.

He may be a Critic if he:
- has Know-It-All attributes, but focuses his 'knowledge' on you,
- is pessimistic,
- has low self worth, which is shown in his criticism of you (which, in his mind, elevates him),
- points out what you do wrong/could have done better,
- analyzes your words, tells you what you should have said,
- explains that he is 'teaching' you or 'making you a better person', not criticizing you, or
- puts down others behind their backs.

10. The Sympathy Monger

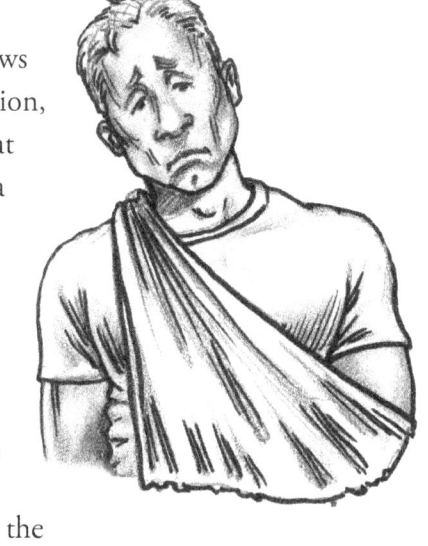

A man with this characteristic knows he can con a woman who has compassion, as most women do. This is most used at a time when he is conning or has run a con and then needs someone on his side to vouch for him. Enter you: the new girlfriend, who sympathizes with his plight, and shares his woe that 'everyone is against him'. Gifts and flattery suck you in, but go only so far, so he must engage your heart to use as a weapon against an ex-girlfriend or the people who are onto his previous lies or cons. This is a powerful weapon for a manipulator, especially if he uses a woman who has not yet learned to live by truth rather than emotion. He knows that when her emotions lead, he is steering a ship that is his for the taking. An emotion-led woman will not hear the truth when her man is 'in pain' or 'being tormented' by an old girlfriend or ex-friend or business associate, because she believes emotion is truth. He knows this and plays her like a piano at Mardi Gras. What better way to get what he wants than to preemptively strike and become the victim, endorsed by the new girlfriend at his side—you! This is called vilifying the victim. He assassinates the character of a previous mark, or someone who was onto him, so people are primed to judge in his favor. Many special interest and political groups use this tactic today. They play the victim to deflect focus from the fact that their goals are dangerous. The opposing side loses favor with the unquestioning masses, no matter how righteous those who oppose the 'victims' are. People are easily moved by emotion and stories...ask Hollywood.

This tactic prevents the Sympathy Monger's opposition from being able to say anything without looking like the bad guy...or girl.

He may be a Sympathy Monger if he:
- accuses others of having done him wrong,
- tells you how badly his life is going, or other stories of woe,
- always complains about what little money he has or how bad his circumstances are because of a certain person or people,
- is emotionally dependent on you,
- drains your time with emotional stories,
- has low self worth, shown in putting others down, or
- is pessimistic.

Many times this tactic fails if someone starts asking questions or presses the Sympathy Monger for details, and if those details are checked out. More often, he doesn't have solid facts, events and times to back his story up, as we will see in the *What Deception Looks Like* section.

'The first speech in a court case is always convincing—until the cross-examination starts!' – Proverbs 18:17 (The Message)

10. The Ice Man

This man usually has his eye on someone or the idea of someone other than you, is separated (by the way, 'separated' still means married!), is 'healing' from a past relationship (his own words) or is otherwise emotionally unavailable but, for some reason, still feels nothing wrong with spending a lot of time with you. You may feel like the two of you click, and, because he tells you he isn't looking for a relationship right now but he still hangs around, you may ignore his words and choose to look at his actions—after all, he still wants to be around you, right? You think, *maybe he is just saying that, but really does want a relationship with me*! But beware: in this case, he means what he says. Don't let his apparent interest fool you, even if he gets affectionate. More accurately, he wants a place to spend time, the no-strings comfort of a woman, and/or sex with no commitment. Because boundaries are laughed at by so many in our culture, and because a woman is convinced that it's okay to spend hours upon hours with a man and actually believe she doesn't bond with him, it is the woman's heart which gets stomped while this Frog goes to play in yet another pond.

He may be an Ice Man if he:
- can mimic emotion, but for some reason it is not convincing to you (you'll see more of this in the *Facial Expressions* section),
- is 'not ready' for a relationship (which means he's not ready for a relationship with you. Sorry. Take this as truth.),
- makes sure the relationship stays status quo, pushing away any talk of the future you want with him, but making sure you stay hooked for his purposes,
- gets late night texts and/or calls from someone whose identity he refuses to reveal (or he does reveal her name, and you put up with that),
- texts you for a late night meeting so he can try to get his 'needs' met,
- isn't too concerned if you tell him you're going to date someone else,
- contacts you sporadically (basically, when he's bored or out of options),
- charms you enough to keep you around but never commits,
- is focused on his own goals, or
- is selfish/self-absorbed.

11. The Double Agent

You may be dating this guy, or start out with him on a professional level. But he's got a whole other agenda. You may even have met him at church, thus lowering your guard, but just like walking into a donut shop doesn't make you a cop, walking into a church doesn't make him an angel. This double agent has his own covert operations going on.

Whether it's the excitement of a forbidden affair with someone's wife, or with two or more women at one time, or a whole other group of friends he hangs with who are involved in illegal activities or drugs, somehow he hides it. And part of  the excitement is that he's got you on a string and you know nothing about what he does. He may even drop obvious hints you won't get until it's all over. That's another part of the thrill for him. Beware when he isolates you or doesn't introduce you to his friends or family, or if he won't go places with you, especially in public, unless it's well off the beaten path of his usual haunts. He may even be married. When you get the feeling that you're a secret to the people in his world, run, don't walk, to the nearest surgeon and have this scaly appendage removed.

He may be a Double Agent if he:

- shows clues of deception in face, voice and body language (see the *What Deception Looks Like* section),
- exchanges late-night texts he tries to hide from you,
- makes frequent last-minute changes in plans,
- disappears from your presence after receiving a call or text, giving a wide variety of excuses for doing so, which usually involve work,
- is selfish with his time, seeing you only when it suits him,
- is hesitant about being seen in public with you,
- gives you enough charm and attention to make you stick around, or
- may exhibit signs of stress from his double life: acne, hair loss, irritability, sleeplessness.

In all of these cases, if you're unsure of the integrity of the man you're involved with, and see evidence of any of these characteristics, test things out. A good idea is to offer to go to dinner at your married friends' house—wise, stable friends who have discernment and are out for your best interest. A Prince won't mind putting himself out there and being under your friends' microscope in order to get to know you better. Your friends, especially your girlfriend's husband or brother, will usually be able to spot something out of the ordinary that might give you a clue that all is not well…that is, if you're willing to listen.

12. The Charmer

This silver-tongued devil will have you at 'hello'. He doesn't need to be dressed well because his talent lies in his gift of gab. An obvious charmer will use flattery to soften you up. A pro will use subtle compliments, looks, even innocent touches. One technique he uses is gazing into your eyes while he listens to you, as if you're the only one in the world who is speaking. This doesn't necessarily have to be a romantic gaze right away, but you will walk away feeling like queen of the world.

He may be a Charmer if he:

- flatters your appearance, personality or scathing wit—often,
- uses pet names for you like 'honey', 'sweetie' or 'babe' easily,
- has an inordinate number of female friends (and not many male ones),
- seems to be an intent listener, hanging on your words and not taking his eyes from you,
- appears to be exactly what you need,
- reminds you of a salesman, convincing you and 'selling' you his point of view, or himself,

- pushes physical intimacy, forcing a physical bond that will likely cloud a woman's judgment—which is something that works to his advantage,
- teams with you quickly, showing he is 'in your corner',
- he gives you a subtle challenge by telling you how other women missed the mark with him, or did something bad to him, counting on you to take the bait and be 'better', or
- ends your dating relationship one of two ways: actively, launching insults and abuse, making you think you never knew him…(because you never did!) or passively, shrugging and saying you were 'the best thing that ever happened to him', while he moves on.

Listening, complimenting and thinking you are the greatest woman in the world are fine—over time. But this guy wants things quickly. His fast flattery will ring hollow with you. The Charmer seeks out needy women who have experienced some kind of trauma, whether in a dating relationship or family situation. They can pick up on this through the same visual and auditory clues you use to determine his motives. They use touch and/or sex because it's a drug for a woman who is lacking self-worth or who has been abused. This emotional stroking is not free; there is something he wants and once he gets it—or once you're onto him and boot him—parting will be anything but sweet!

13. The Spiritual Superstar

This guy comes in two sizes: *Extra Strength* and *Lite*. But make no mistake; the 'Lite' version is no less dangerous simply because of his subtlety. The Extra Strength Spiritual Superstar uses the words 'Praise God' with the frequency of reality t.v. show turnover. He attributes everything to 'The Lord', mentioning the Lord in ways which people may not have thought: 'I lost one of my sneakers and the Lord found it for me' or 'The Lord told me to order a salad instead of a burger' or, the one that should really raise a red flag: 'The Lord told me to tell you to [*insert the Spiritual Superstar's desire here*]'. They are the fringe of churchgoers and are usually held up as examples by non-believers as to why they don't want to go to church.

The Spiritual Superstar - Extra Strength:

A woman told me a story about a man who approached her at church and gave her that kind of 'thus sayeth the Lord' quote. He told her, "The Lord told me to tell you that you're going to be my wife." The woman was taken aback. "That's funny," she whispered, pointing to the pulpit at the front of the church, "because that's my husband preaching up there."

If God 'tells' a man something the guy says he must tell you, God should have impressed that same thing on your heart. The man's words should be a confirmation, not breaking news to you. The latter is how cults are formed. Putting your brains into another human's hands or group of humans' hands is irresponsible and dangerous (That includes politics.). God always speaks directly to a person about guidance when they ask him. But many women don't spend enough time reading their Bibles to know this. Most of these guys are aware of that.

Extra Strength   **Lite**

They simply act like they're chumming off the side of a bridge for fish, seeing which ones will bite. At some point, a predator reasons, his line will work on a woman if he just keeps dumping.

The Spiritual Superstar - Lite:

This guy has actually been attending church for a while, whether it's yours or another one. He may be recognized by the pastor, so he uses that to his advantage. He is seen around the church campus. He is more subtle, thus more dangerous. He may duck into a home Bible study occasionally to check out the female prospects there. He has the 'appearance of godliness' at first, with all the seeming kindness and helpfulness every girl wants, but this guy will have an agenda. Frogs always do. He has become good at putting on sheep's clothing and trotting under the radar to wreak havoc on the flock. These men possess one or more of the attributes listed here:

'Don't be naive. There are difficult times ahead. As the end approaches, people are going to be self-absorbed, money-hungry, self-promoting, stuck-up, profane, contemptuous of parents, crude, coarse, dog-eat-dog, unbending, slanderers, impulsively wild, savage, cynical, treacherous, ruthless, bloated windbags, addicted to lust, and allergic to God. They'll make a show of religion, but behind the scenes they're animals. Stay clear of these people. These are the kind of people who smooth-talk themselves into the homes of unstable and needy women and take advantage of them; women who, depressed by their sinfulness, take up with every new religious fad that calls itself "truth." They get exploited every time and never really learn.' – 2 Timothy 3:2-7 (The Message)

From this list, you may think you are looking for a monster or a guy in a trench coat with shady eyes and a shadier disposition, but the danger comes from this sort being able to hide behind charisma, charm and enough scripture to sound like a Christian. Jim Jones and Charles Manson used this kind of allure to twist the minds of their followers to do their bidding. Both claimed a kind of tie to religious things, which they used as a tool for manipulation. These manipulators went to extremes to get carry out their plans. I was amazed when I read that Jim Jones sold monkeys door to door to fund his church[1]. Some Frogs will go to great lengths to get what they want.

Whether it is an aspiring cult leader or a Frog in a Prince costume, you can know a manipulator by the fruit of his life. Does his life produce love, joy, peace, patience, kindness, goodness, faithfulness, gentleness and self-control? Or does he show these characteristics:

'…loveless, cheap sex; a stinking accumulation of mental and emotional garbage; frenzied and joyless grabs for happiness; trinket gods; magic-show religion; paranoid loneliness; cutthroat competition; all-consuming-yet-never-satisfied wants; a brutal temper; an impotence to love or be loved;

---

1 - Lattin, Don. "How spiritual journey ended in destruction." San Francisco Chronicle. 18 November 2003.

divided homes and divided lives; small-minded and lopsided pursuits; the vicious habit of depersonalizing everyone into a rival; uncontrolled and uncontrollable addictions; ugly parodies of community...'

– Galatians 5:19-21 (The Message)

The word of God protects people from deception. That is the point of this book—and of God's book. To know the Bible is to know Him, and He cannot lie.

The most important thing to remember if you are dating or have been deceived by a Spiritual Superstar is this: he is NOT a reflection of the one true God. Jesus Christ loves you and does not lie, cheat, try to control you or in any other way hurt you. Don't walk away from God because of what one fringe Frog did. God still has a plan for your life and by the Spiritual Superstar/Lite being gone, God has opened the path for something better.

This man may be a Spiritual Superstar if he:
- attends church but is divisive and speaks badly of members of the congregation or of leadership,
- claims to know the Bible, but twists scripture to suit his own opinions, or quotes it out of context,
- appears to be filled with peace when it suits him, but is not consistently peaceful, especially when troubles come,
- carries a Bible as a fashion accessory, not as a means to know God,
- is involved in frenzied church activity, with no time to connect one-on-one with anyone (thus keeping people from seeing his true colors),
- has no close male friends, or
- has lots of female friends.

Any one of these attributes is a cause for concern on its own. Many Spiritual Superstar Frogs have been responsible for people leaving or avoiding church. Fortunately God is bigger than these guys, and can heal a woman's heart and woo her back to Him. Knowing these signs can help you steer clear of these Frogs.

There are other, general signs that something isn't right with the guy you're dating:

- Erratic moods (can signal drug use or mental instability)
- Rage (can signal drug/steroid use, but even if not, RUN!)
- Irresponsibility with money, perpetual and considerably more debt than just a house and car
- Starting any sentence with 'If you loved me you would'
- Excessive social time on the phone or texting every day all day
- Hitting you at ANY time
- Stories he tells of how he abused other women (this is usually a test to see how you react, to see what you would put up with)

What Is A Prince?

You may have noticed by now that Princes and Frogs are not born, they are made. I'm not going to go into the intricacies personal responsibility here. We are all responsible for our own actions. The fact is, behavior shows what is in the heart of a man, and it will tell you whether your man is a Prince or a Frog.

My best friend Nikki has a couple of favorite Bible verses about men. One is, 'Man is of few days and full of trouble,' from the book of Job, and the other is 'All men are liars', from the same book. She is quick to jokingly point out that the text only mentions men, not women. She knows the true translation of both the words 'man' and 'men' means 'mankind'; i.e., men and women, but it's something she likes to kid about. At least I think she's kidding.

It's easy for an unmarried woman to give up and believe all men are Frogs, but I have personally seen some Princes; some married, some single, but the latter not single for long.

You can ask 100 women what makes a good man, and you will get 500 different answers, ranging from looks to bank account balance to sensitivity to any number of descriptions they've imagined would make the perfect 'Mr. Right'. This used to confuse me, because I would meet good-looking men who were charming, but soon I would see that they were ugly on the inside. It's like the commercial where the gorgeous guy on the beach approaches some sunbathing women. The women smile, he flexes his muscles, then opens his mouth and speaks and out comes a Woody Woodpecker voice. Kinda ruins the image, because no amount of bulging biceps and nice tan could keep them from laughing—or hide the truth.

When I started reading the Bible and saw the characteristics of its famous, though flawed, characters, I began to understand the difference between a man with merely good looks and charm and one with strong character. When I looked at the text in 1 Corinthians 13 and changed out the word 'God' for 'Love', wanting to get a more personal view of God—considering God is love, I found I could also I substitute the words 'My Ideal Man', where 'Love' is. This allowed me to create a litmus test for what a Prince's life looks like:

'[My Ideal Man] is patient, [he] is kind. [He] does not envy, [he] does not boast, [he] is not proud. [He] is not rude, [he] is not self-seeking, [he] is not easily angered, [he] keeps no record of wrongs. [My Ideal Man] does not delight in evil but rejoices with the truth. [He] always protects, always trusts, always hopes, always perseveres. [My Ideal Man] never fails.'
– 1 Corinthians 13 (parentheses mine)

Of course a human man cannot meet these conditions perfectly, only God can. But it is a good start in seeing the difference between a Frog and a Prince. These characteristics have one thing in common: the subversion of 'self' in the one who loves, with the intent of putting the other person (the loved one) first.

I have a couple of married friends whose book I illustrated. He is a chef and his wife is his 'girl Friday'. By their own admission they have a great marriage. It's not perfect, but they work on their marriage, and it shows. They are Italian, which may be the reason they make their own pasta and create a multi-course spread for dinner on Sundays. They are warm and giving people. I believe some of the main ingredients in this successful marriage are the husband's willingness to admit when he's wrong, his wife's willingness to let him be wrong without berating him, and their willingness to look at the marriage as a team effort instead of playing the blame game when things go wrong. In short, they work together, doing what it takes to keep the team strong.

A movie star smile and a fat bank account may float things for a while, but nothing replaces kindness and others-centeredness (i.e., love) when you are considering the lifelong commitment of marriage.

While lots of women seek out charm, charisma, good looks, money and other temporal features in a husband, couples who have been married for a while say that what is most important about their spouses and their answers have nothing to do with looks, power or money. A couple of single women have already figured this out:

"When I meet a man now, I ask myself, 'Is this the kind of guy who would give me spongebaths and help me to the bathroom if I ever had cancer?' It sorts out a lot of the losers." – Andrea

"I always picture my future kids as being like the guy I am dating. Sometimes, if I get chills, I know this is not the guy for me." – Jaymie

"I know that when my husband travels for business, I don't have to worry. We didn't have sex before we were married. He never pressured me. I know he has self control. We have a wonderful sex life, but I know that when he goes to do his job, the same boundaries are in place that we had before marriage, so that he doesn't let himself get into a situation we'll both regret. He is an honorable man." – Britney

The Wise Woman

A diagram of integrity

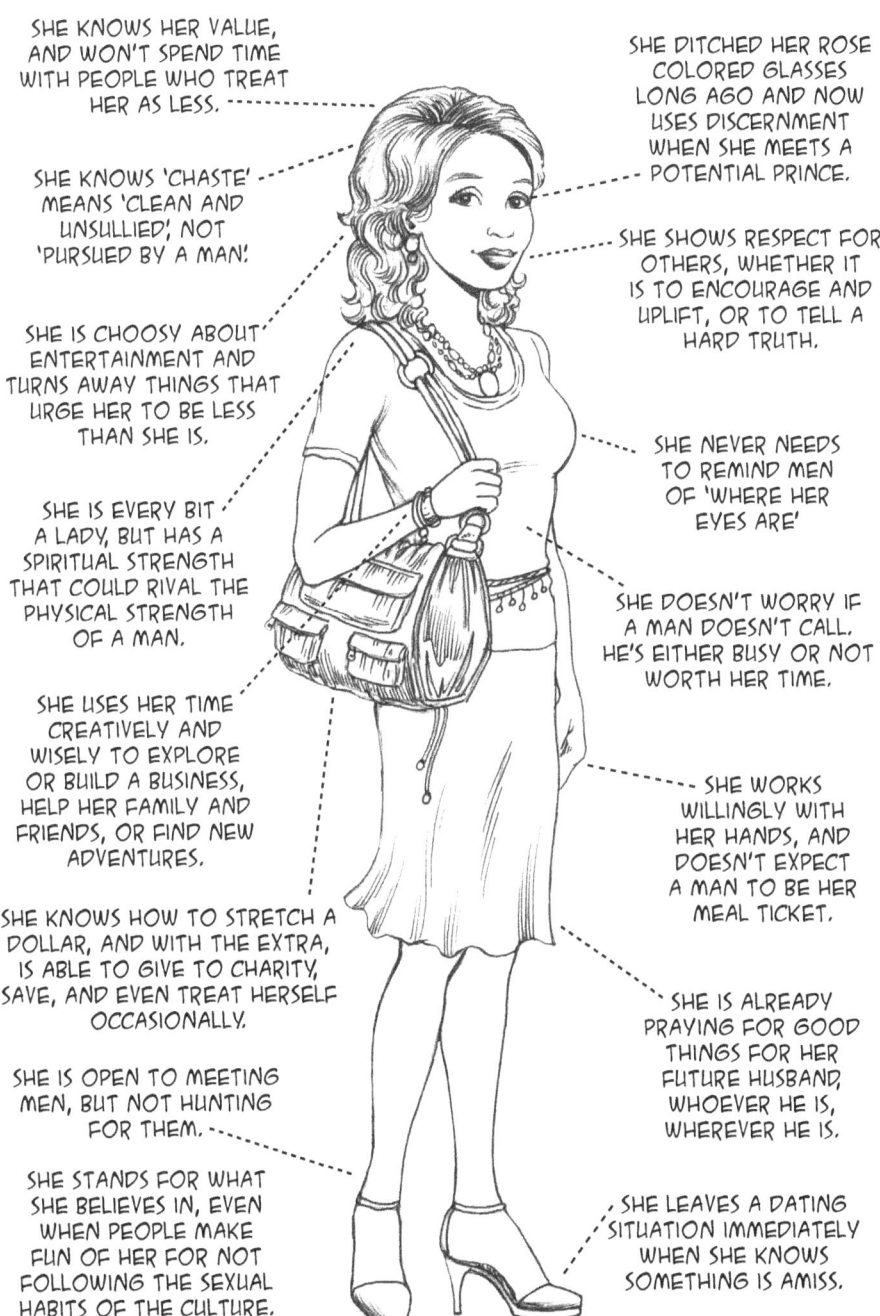

- SHE KNOWS HER VALUE, AND WON'T SPEND TIME WITH PEOPLE WHO TREAT HER AS LESS.
- SHE KNOWS 'CHASTE' MEANS 'CLEAN AND UNSULLIED', NOT 'PURSUED BY A MAN'.
- SHE IS CHOOSY ABOUT ENTERTAINMENT AND TURNS AWAY THINGS THAT URGE HER TO BE LESS THAN SHE IS.
- SHE IS EVERY BIT A LADY, BUT HAS A SPIRITUAL STRENGTH THAT COULD RIVAL THE PHYSICAL STRENGTH OF A MAN.
- SHE USES HER TIME CREATIVELY AND WISELY TO EXPLORE OR BUILD A BUSINESS, HELP HER FAMILY AND FRIENDS, OR FIND NEW ADVENTURES.
- SHE KNOWS HOW TO STRETCH A DOLLAR, AND WITH THE EXTRA, IS ABLE TO GIVE TO CHARITY, SAVE, AND EVEN TREAT HERSELF OCCASIONALLY.
- SHE IS OPEN TO MEETING MEN, BUT NOT HUNTING FOR THEM.
- SHE STANDS FOR WHAT SHE BELIEVES IN, EVEN WHEN PEOPLE MAKE FUN OF HER FOR NOT FOLLOWING THE SEXUAL HABITS OF THE CULTURE.
- SHE DITCHED HER ROSE COLORED GLASSES LONG AGO AND NOW USES DISCERNMENT WHEN SHE MEETS A POTENTIAL PRINCE.
- SHE SHOWS RESPECT FOR OTHERS, WHETHER IT IS TO ENCOURAGE AND UPLIFT, OR TO TELL A HARD TRUTH.
- SHE NEVER NEEDS TO REMIND MEN OF 'WHERE HER EYES ARE'
- SHE DOESN'T WORRY IF A MAN DOESN'T CALL. HE'S EITHER BUSY OR NOT WORTH HER TIME.
- SHE WORKS WILLINGLY WITH HER HANDS, AND DOESN'T EXPECT A MAN TO BE HER MEAL TICKET.
- SHE IS ALREADY PRAYING FOR GOOD THINGS FOR HER FUTURE HUSBAND, WHOEVER HE IS, WHEREVER HE IS.
- SHE LEAVES A DATING SITUATION IMMEDIATELY WHEN SHE KNOWS SOMETHING IS AMISS.

The Prince
A DIAGRAM OF INTEGRITY

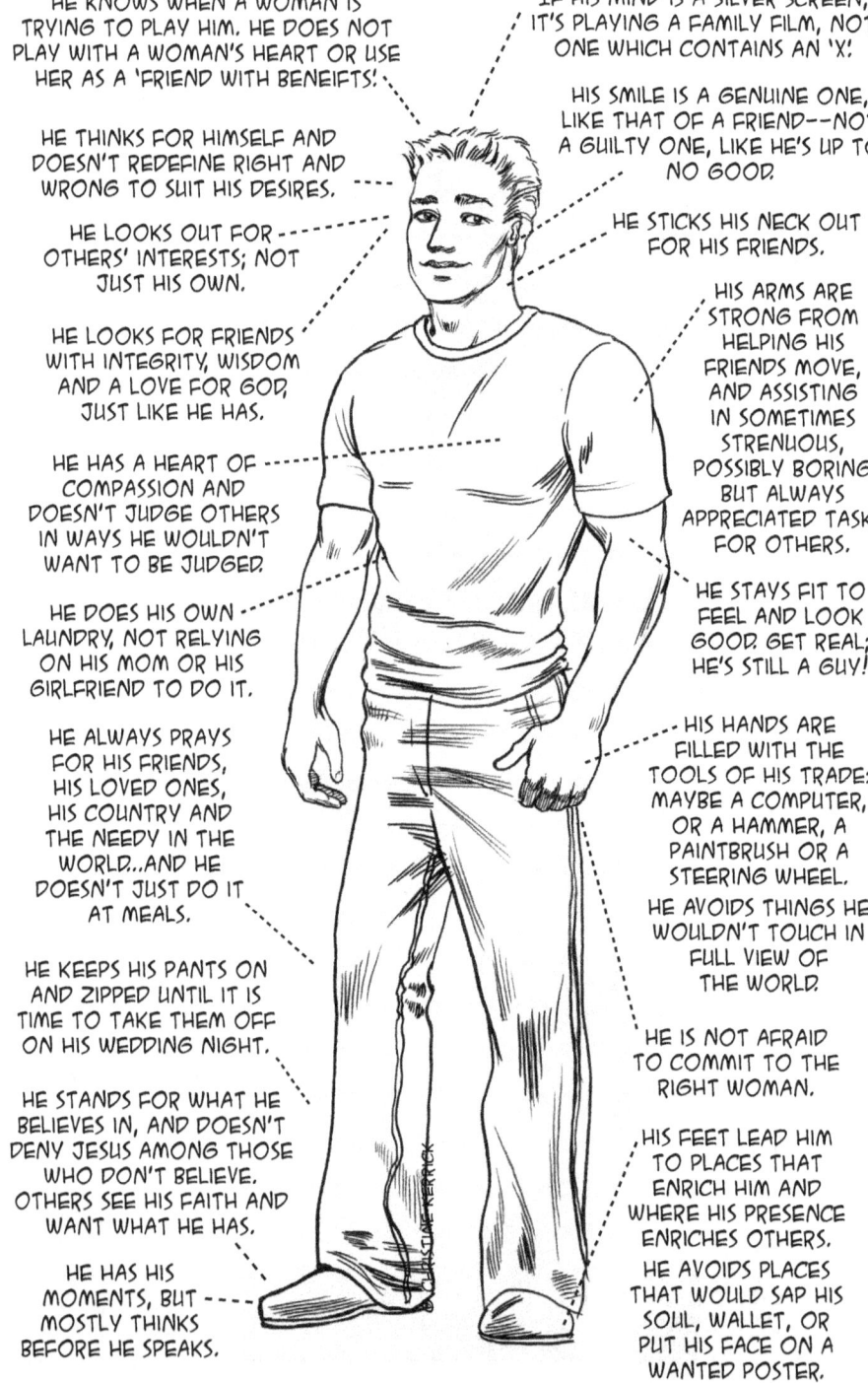

- HE KNOWS WHEN A WOMAN IS TRYING TO PLAY HIM. HE DOES NOT PLAY WITH A WOMAN'S HEART OR USE HER AS A 'FRIEND WITH BENEIFTS.'
- HE THINKS FOR HIMSELF AND DOESN'T REDEFINE RIGHT AND WRONG TO SUIT HIS DESIRES.
- HE LOOKS OUT FOR OTHERS' INTERESTS; NOT JUST HIS OWN.
- HE LOOKS FOR FRIENDS WITH INTEGRITY, WISDOM AND A LOVE FOR GOD, JUST LIKE HE HAS.
- HE HAS A HEART OF COMPASSION AND DOESN'T JUDGE OTHERS IN WAYS HE WOULDN'T WANT TO BE JUDGED.
- HE DOES HIS OWN LAUNDRY, NOT RELYING ON HIS MOM OR HIS GIRLFRIEND TO DO IT.
- HE ALWAYS PRAYS FOR HIS FRIENDS, HIS LOVED ONES, HIS COUNTRY AND THE NEEDY IN THE WORLD...AND HE DOESN'T JUST DO IT AT MEALS.
- HE KEEPS HIS PANTS ON AND ZIPPED UNTIL IT IS TIME TO TAKE THEM OFF ON HIS WEDDING NIGHT.
- HE STANDS FOR WHAT HE BELIEVES IN, AND DOESN'T DENY JESUS AMONG THOSE WHO DON'T BELIEVE. OTHERS SEE HIS FAITH AND WANT WHAT HE HAS.
- HE HAS HIS MOMENTS, BUT MOSTLY THINKS BEFORE HE SPEAKS.
- IF HIS MIND IS A SILVER SCREEN, IT'S PLAYING A FAMILY FILM, NOT ONE WHICH CONTAINS AN 'X.'
- HIS SMILE IS A GENUINE ONE, LIKE THAT OF A FRIEND—NOT A GUILTY ONE, LIKE HE'S UP TO NO GOOD.
- HE STICKS HIS NECK OUT FOR HIS FRIENDS.
- HIS ARMS ARE STRONG FROM HELPING HIS FRIENDS MOVE, AND ASSISTING IN SOMETIMES STRENUOUS, POSSIBLY BORING BUT ALWAYS APPRECIATED TASKS FOR OTHERS.
- HE STAYS FIT TO FEEL AND LOOK GOOD. GET REAL; HE'S STILL A GUY!
- HIS HANDS ARE FILLED WITH THE TOOLS OF HIS TRADE: MAYBE A COMPUTER, OR A HAMMER, A PAINTBRUSH OR A STEERING WHEEL. HE AVOIDS THINGS HE WOULDN'T TOUCH IN FULL VIEW OF THE WORLD.
- HE IS NOT AFRAID TO COMMIT TO THE RIGHT WOMAN.
- HIS FEET LEAD HIM TO PLACES THAT ENRICH HIM AND WHERE HIS PRESENCE ENRICHES OTHERS. HE AVOIDS PLACES THAT WOULD SAP HIS SOUL, WALLET, OR PUT HIS FACE ON A WANTED POSTER.

The Frog
A diagram of foolishness

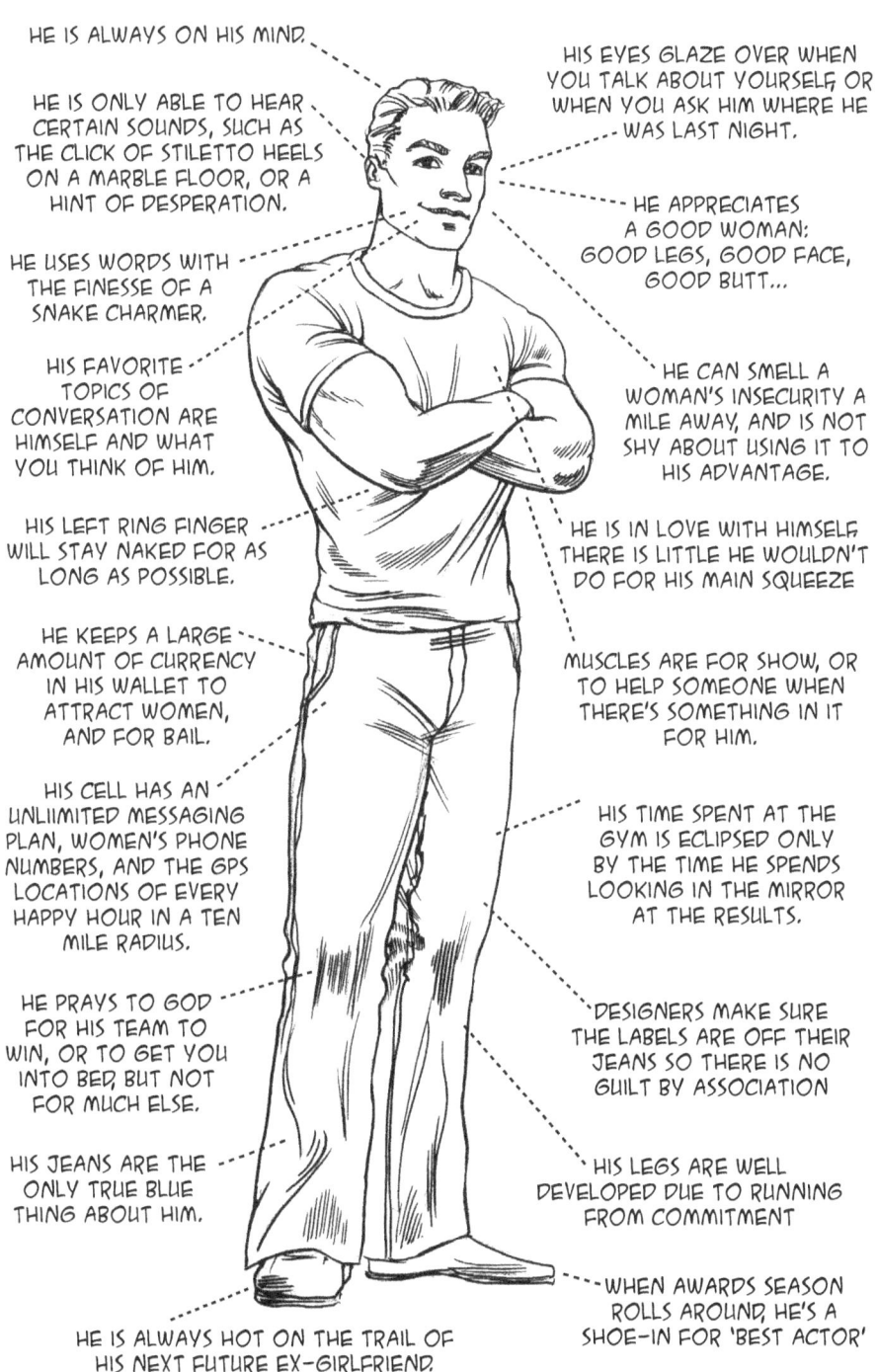

- HE IS ALWAYS ON HIS MIND.
- HE IS ONLY ABLE TO HEAR CERTAIN SOUNDS, SUCH AS THE CLICK OF STILETTO HEELS ON A MARBLE FLOOR, OR A HINT OF DESPERATION.
- HE USES WORDS WITH THE FINESSE OF A SNAKE CHARMER.
- HIS FAVORITE TOPICS OF CONVERSATION ARE HIMSELF AND WHAT YOU THINK OF HIM.
- HIS LEFT RING FINGER WILL STAY NAKED FOR AS LONG AS POSSIBLE.
- HE KEEPS A LARGE AMOUNT OF CURRENCY IN HIS WALLET TO ATTRACT WOMEN, AND FOR BAIL.
- HIS CELL HAS AN UNLIIMITED MESSAGING PLAN, WOMEN'S PHONE NUMBERS, AND THE GPS LOCATIONS OF EVERY HAPPY HOUR IN A TEN MILE RADIUS.
- HE PRAYS TO GOD FOR HIS TEAM TO WIN, OR TO GET YOU INTO BED, BUT NOT FOR MUCH ELSE.
- HIS JEANS ARE THE ONLY TRUE BLUE THING ABOUT HIM.
- HE IS ALWAYS HOT ON THE TRAIL OF HIS NEXT FUTURE EX-GIRLFRIEND.
- HIS EYES GLAZE OVER WHEN YOU TALK ABOUT YOURSELF, OR WHEN YOU ASK HIM WHERE HE WAS LAST NIGHT.
- HE APPRECIATES A GOOD WOMAN: GOOD LEGS, GOOD FACE, GOOD BUTT...
- HE CAN SMELL A WOMAN'S INSECURITY A MILE AWAY, AND IS NOT SHY ABOUT USING IT TO HIS ADVANTAGE.
- HE IS IN LOVE WITH HIMSELF, THERE IS LITTLE HE WOULDN'T DO FOR HIS MAIN SQUEEZE
- MUSCLES ARE FOR SHOW, OR TO HELP SOMEONE WHEN THERE'S SOMETHING IN IT FOR HIM.
- HIS TIME SPENT AT THE GYM IS ECLIPSED ONLY BY THE TIME HE SPENDS LOOKING IN THE MIRROR AT THE RESULTS.
- DESIGNERS MAKE SURE THE LABELS ARE OFF THEIR JEANS SO THERE IS NO GUILT BY ASSOCIATION
- HIS LEGS ARE WELL DEVELOPED DUE TO RUNNING FROM COMMITMENT
- WHEN AWARDS SEASON ROLLS AROUND, HE'S A SHOE-IN FOR 'BEST ACTOR'

The Unwise Woman

ANOTHER DIAGRAM OF FOOLISHNESS

- SHE DOESN'T HAVE TO THINK FOR HERSELF BECAUSE FRIENDS, DATES AND MEDIA DO IT FOR HER.
- SHE IMAKES MOST OF HER DECISIONS USING SOCIAL NETWORKING SITES, MAJORITY OPINION OR A MEDIUM.
- HER EARS HEAR WHAT SHE WANTS THEM TO HEAR. 'HER' TRUTH TRUMPS ACTUAL TRUTH.
- SHE HANDLES MONEY LIKE A BULL HANDLES CHINA. FIRST COMES THE MALL THEN COME BILLS, IF THERE'S ANY CASH LEFT.
- LIFE IS A COMPETITION BETWEEN HER AND OTHER WOMEN. WHILE THE OUTSIDE OF HER LOOKS LIKE NEIMAN MARCUS, HER INSIDES LOOK LIKE A THRIFT SHOP.
- SHE USES HER FEMININE WILES TO ATTRACT MEN, NO MATTER IF THEY ARE SINGLE OR MARRIED.
- SHE IS RARELY AT HOME AND IS OFTEN OUT HUNTING FOR A GOOD TIME, A GUY OR SOME OTHER KIND OF EXCITEMENT. IT IS DIFFICULT FOR HER TO BE STILL. THE COFFEE HELPS WITH THIS.
- SHE IS IN LOVE... WITH HERSELF IT'S ALL ABOUT HER, AS LONG AS YOU LISTEN TO HER, COMMENT ON HER AND FOCUS ON HER, THINGS WILL BE JUST FINE.
- SHE COVETS WHAT SHE SEES AND JUDGES BY APPEARANCE. HER MOTIVES FOR LOOKING GOOD ARE SO THAT OTHERS WILL THINK HIGHLY OF HER. SHE JUDGES OTHERS THE SAME WAY.
- SHE HAS A TURBO-POWERED MOUTH WHICH WORKS TWICE AS FAST AS HER EARS.
- GOSSIP, BACKBITING AND COMPLAINING ARE THE NORM FOR HER. FLATTERY GETS HER WHAT SHE WANTS.
- MONEY IS TIME, AND SHE SPENDS THAT ON HERSELF TOO.
- SHE SPEAKS THREE LANGUAGES: VISA, MASTERCARD AND AMERICAN EXPRESS.
- THIS GUY'S ANGRY BECAUSE HE'S JUST AN ACCESSORY. HIS MISTRESS HASN'T YET UNDERSTOOD THAT HE'S A GUY DOG AND SHOULD NOT HAVE A BOW IN HIS HAIR.

Part 1
Chapter 4

The Lie And Its Side-Effects

"Help, LORD, for no one is faithful anymore; those who are loyal have vanished from the human race. Everyone lies to their neighbor; they flatter with their lips but harbor deception in their hearts. May the LORD silence all flattering lips and every boastful tongue— " – Psalm 12:1-3

Lie - 1) 'a false statement made with deliberate intent to deceive; an intentional untruth; a falsehood. 2) something intended or serving to convey a false impression; 3) an inaccurate or false statement.'[1]

We have all lied. I've done it. Presidents have done it. You have done it. If you say you haven't, you just did, because everyone has lied. Congratulations. Now you can call yourself a liar. The difference between a man of integrity and a 'lifestyle liar' is that if the person of integrity lies, he comes clean when he does. He is not afraid of telling the truth, and does so in love…because it is best for everyone.

The man who lies as a second (or first) language is dangerous. He doesn't trust God to give him what he desires, but grabs for it with his own grubby hands and tries to control every circumstance with his plethora of prevarication. He doesn't care how this affects you. He has no problem living as a lifestyle liar. For the sake of simplicity, we will address the lifestyle liar simply as a 'liar'.

Liars are not new. The only thing that has changed in thousands of years are the liar's clothes but, rest assured, the little black heart of the liar still beats with the desire to deceive his prey so he can achieve his goal, whatever it is.

---

1 - http://www.dictionary.com

Notice the word 'boastful' in the scripture above. Liars—and criminals—have enough pride to think they are smart enough not to get caught. Some even know that if they get caught eventually they believe they can talk their way out of the lie. They believe they are above what is right and above respecting you.

Here are some real lies men have told women:

- "I'll call you." (If he means it and does it, good. This statement refers to the man who uses it like 'see ya' and has no intention of doing so.)
- "I've never felt this way about anyone before." (except for the last woman he knew…and the one before that…)
- "You're the most beautiful woman I've ever met."
- "I would never do anything to hurt you."
- "I have a brain tumor and I just need to be on my own. Let's be friends."
- "I didn't show up because I was tired. I pulled over to the side of the highway to catch some zees."
- "There's a ghost in my house. I have to take care of that tonight." (No kidding.)

I reiterate: liars are not brain surgeons, but for every lie, there is a believer. A man who wants to be with you will not manufacture excuses not to be with you.

Anatomy of a Lie

Where there is a lie, there are other deceptive practices. Lies are verbal, whether they are told, or are truth omitted. Deception comes across verbally and non-verbally. The lie is only one in the Frog's vast arsenal effective for getting something from his prey without the prey knowing it… unless you know what to look for.

Lies, all lies.

"A small lie, if it actually is a lie, condemns a man as much as a big and black falsehood. If a man will deliberately cheat to the amount of a single cent, give him opportunity and he would cheat to any amount."

– E. H. CHAPIN, *Living Words*

A statement is either true or false. Good liars—if they can be called good—know to stay close enough to the truth to make their case convincing. This works in your favor, because you know now where to focus your line of questioning. No liar, if pressed, can keep up the lie without either slipping up or losing control of visible indicators of stress out of fear of exposure. The motive and agenda of the one speaking the untrue statement determines if it is a lie or misinformation. I feel the need to say that because somewhere along the way in this culture a black-and-white lie has devolved into subjective grayness…or, in many cases, 'little'ness and 'white'ness.

I have no idea who invented the concept of 'the little white lie', or when it came about, but I used to use the term myself. I used it when I wanted something and didn't want to be honest about getting it. It was just easier to say, 'Actually, I need to work tonight,' than 'I just don't feel like going out tonight,' and risk offending one of my friends. I know, it's not like capital murder, but it bugged me. I felt like I was not being myself. I knew I was doing something wrong, even though it seemed like a small thing. God had said not to lie for a reason, and I wondered what would happen if I did just tell the truth for once. After I popped out a 'little white lie', I felt dirty, like I was deceiving the person to whom I was speaking, and like I was selling myself short. I got annoyed at people for (I believed) making me have to lie, and I started resenting myself, too. So, I decided to challenge myself. I didn't put a time limit on it, but I decided from then on to tell the truth. If I lost friends or job opportunities, then I lost them. It was one of the most freeing things I had ever done.

I wondered how many things I had avoided by using my lie/excuses which could have either made relationships richer or which could have separated me from people who were a drain on me. No matter how people want to define lying on blogs, talk shows, or at the water cooler; no matter what the trend is, withholding or twisting the truth is lying, and there are no degrees to it.

So what's the big deal about lying? Everyone does it and usually there's no harm done. Why should I be concerned about this?

When I worked for a local sheriff, he addressed a group of new cadets. He said, "Throughout your career you will experience problems. Be it family, alcohol or drugs, or anything else, come to me or someone else here and we will help you. One thing, though: if you ever lie to me, you will be immediately fired." That wasn't word-for-word, but it was something I remembered. The Sheriff considered lying worse than almost any offense, short of murder (though the roots of selfishness are the same). The reasons?

- It is morally wrong. Even in our culture of situational ethics, lying still retains its definition and its results.
- Lying disrespects its recipient. People become a means for the liar to get what he wants, rather than valuing people for who they are, trusting God, working hard and then letting the chips fall where they may.
- It takes away the victim's chance to make an informed choice in a matter, leading them to make decisions they may not have made, had they known the whole truth.
- It alters the value of communication.
- It ruins the liar's reputation, once he is found to be a liar.
- It hurts the liar because he must now remember all the lies he's told, which creates worry, stress then anger.
- It makes the victim question her ability to judge.
- It erodes the liar's integrity, the more lies he tells.

Lying puts the liar before everyone else, regardless of the consequences to others. 'All liars' are among those listed as being cast into the Lake of Fire in Revelation 21.

There is a story of Jacob, grandson of Abraham, who deceived his blind father Isaac in order to steal his firstborn brother Esau's blessing. The blessing of the firstborn was quite valuable and afforded its recipient authority, power, lands and inheritance. Esau's younger brother Jacob put on a goatskin so he could pretend he was his hairy brother. He served his father stew and received Esau's blessing from Isaac. Decades later, Jacob got a taste of his own medicine from his own eleven sons when they sold the second-to-the youngest, Jacob's favored son Joseph, to slave traders. They covered their crime by slaying a goat, putting its blood on Joseph's favorite coat which was handmade by Jacob, and telling him his beloved Joseph was dead.

God allowed a goat, older brothers and a favored son—three of the things he used to deceive his own father—to be used to send a message to Jacob. Jacob had taught his children well. Lies do come back to the liar. They are like spiked boomerangs. Whether it is a case of hurting the object of the lie, or that the liar is simply discovered later as having told the lie, it has a power of its own, as all our words often do. Lies hurt, and yet people still find a way to excuse their own. Think of someone who has lied to you. Do you trust them now, knowing they lied to you? What do you think of them? What do you believe they think of you? Can the rift in your relationship be healed? Maybe, but there will always be doubt there.

Many of the stories told by women in this book show the destructive nature of lying. Consider Beth:

Beth's Story

"I moved to Alabama to start a new job at a church in May. I met Joe my first week there. He was also working at the ministry. I wasn't necessarily attracted to him at first, but he pursued me like the hero in a romance novel, telling me how beautiful I was, emailing me, talking on the phone for hours.

As I look back, I realize the first email was a red flag. He told me he was 10 years younger than me. I overlooked it. He charmed me, using emoticons, then the words 'princess' and 'I love you', but writing the latter backwards. I thought it was strange and kind of forward. He was moving too fast. I responded in a guarded way, and didn't address his advances. I allowed the relationship to continue.

Nearly two months after we had met, he began talking about marriage. I wanted to seek the counsel of people at my church and pray. I told him he needed to do so as well. I knew I wasn't focusing on my relationship with the Lord like I should have been, so my discernment wasn't sharp. I heard Joe speak 'church talk', like scripture, telling me things he was praying about and other church-related subjects. He was manipulative. I went home to Pennsylvania in July, saying we needed time to pray and seek counsel on how we should proceed with the relationship. We agreed to have no contact during that time.

Joe's grandmother passed away one day and he called me, hysterical. We were back in contact now. He said that a pastor in Orange County, CA did her funeral and that her Catholicism had been 'controversial' in that church. Everything with Joe was controversial. He said he had to move too, which added to the drama. He kept me close by saying things like 'I need you' and 'You're the kind of woman I need.'

I was wrestling with the decision. I knew I needed to trust God in this situation. The 'grandma passing' had distracted me. The counsel I received from the pastor was: 'don't rush into anything', but I didn't heed. Instead, I returned to Alabama a few days later.

Joe said he needed help finding a place to live, and had to go on interviews to Boston and other places. He asked me where I wanted to live, including me in the decision-making process of his life. He was going to drive from California to Boston, with a stop in Alabama to see me. When he stopped in Alabama, he spoke to me again about marriage. I hadn't received any kind of confirmation from the Lord that this was what I should do, but I was open to discussing marriage. My heart was guarded from his charm, but I loved the idea of being married to a missions-oriented doctor. He asked me to marry him that July, and even had a ring. I accepted. Later I recalled the method he used to ensure a 'yes' from me:

He made it hard for me to say no, involving others so it was public. I was so worried about what others thought. Immediately, I called my family. My mom was upset—she hadn't even met this guy, had only talked to him on the phone. My mom worked in security at a major airport and is close to the sheriff's department and FBI there. Mom called my brother Mark, who is suspicious by nature. She also talked to one of her deputy sheriff friends. Mom thought this all sounded too good to be true.

Over the next couple of days I discovered that a missions team from my church in Pennsylvania was coming to Alabama. I got to meet with one of my previous supervisors and his wife. They did a premarital counseling session with me and Joe. The counselor said he saw no red flags, but suggested we go through premarital classes.

Joe left and flew to Boston for an interview. While he was gone, my brother Mark got a hold of his cell number, called and said he knew who Joe was and that he'd better leave me alone or he'll pay him a visit. Joe called me two hours later, in a panic because of my Mark's call. He told me not to speak to my family. I asked him why and he simply said he was coming back. He was hysterical and screaming, saying Mark had called and threatened his life and accused him of not being who he said he was.

I told him not to come back because it wouldn't solve anything. I called Mark, puzzled about his actions toward Joe, and learned my mom had a police officer do a background check on Joe. Because his name was unique, it made it easier for them to confirm he wasn't who he said he was. Joe had multiple identities, ages and addresses. One name was a female name, which was linked to the same social security number.

Another red flag was raised when a female volunteer at the church thought something didn't ring true about Joe. The volunteer searched his name on the internet and came up with a story from a news channel: he had been arrested in a foreign country because his roommate had called the cops saying 'the guy living with her had stolen her credit card and bought stuff'. At the time, Joe was arrested and held, then released until the court hearing. He found some good Samaritans to put him up. The good Samaritans learned he was planning to flee the country. Authorities found him with a female passport and ticket to Texas. He was arrested. A physical exam showed that he was female with a partial sex change. He had been living as a man for six years.

The volunteer emailed the story to her organization, questioning their background check process because men are supposed to room with men and women with women. The organization emailed me. Because I didn't want to assume the worst about someone who claimed to be a Christian, I addressed Joe directly. He explained away the story, saying he had never been to the country where this happened, that the event with the roommate happened in California and it was an ex-girlfriend who did all of this; more drama. He said this was retaliation; that the ex-girlfriend had paid someone to put this story out. He volunteered to mail me copies of his passport as proof, and said the stamps for that country weren't in the passport. He did this even though I hadn't asked for any kind of proof.

Joe let time go by and finally sent the passport copies to me, along with some gifts. The copies looked official. When my brother returned with the background check, Joe said someone had stolen his identity. Joe said he would go to the Social Security Administration and basically blame someone else. Because I had been through identity theft, I thought I could help.

After my brother and I spoke, Joe told me he wasn't 28 but 38. One of the fake names came back as the same one from the Google story. This was one of the major red flags for me. What were the chances of the two names being the same? One girl from my Pennsylvania church's mission team had a dad who was a private investigator and former Secret Service Agent. The girl had access to background checks. I told my counselor all of this. The counselor called the California pastor who supposedly had done Joe's grandmother's funeral. The pastor said he had not conducted the funeral.

I realized now I needed to do a lot of research—it consumed me. I discovered so many things that I was ashamed and shocked about, when I should have just given him the boot. I had access to his email. This had been one way of roping me into his life: giving me email access to his account. I found records of emails sent to girls on Yahoo personals. I discovered he had lied to all of them. He told them his grandma had died 4 months before the date of the passing he had given me. Joe had told the girls he lived in my big house, was wealthy and didn't know what to do with himself.

I told Joe I couldn't marry him because of all the false pretenses, but I didn't heed the warnings of the now-obvious deception and I continued to talk to him, uncovering lies. I admit should have 'left bad enough alone'.

The extent of the deception was overwhelming. I was trying to understand, but couldn't. I should have let God reveal the truth, not searched for it on my own. In searching for the truth, I compromised my integrity by *going through those emails, searching his wallet, etc. I did things that were not Christ-like because I was hurt and couldn't believe this was happening. Looking back, I would have changed how I handled it. I learned a lot about the whole situation, and I only regret how I had handled it, that I didn't listen to God and that I rushed. Now, I think: what was the rush? Joe had created urgency to have a relationship and get married and I had helped. I wasn't getting God's best. I wasn't even getting a man!"*

Two months passed from the time Beth met Joe in May until he asked her to marry him in July. The last conversation between them was in February of the next year. At that time, he was still desperate to get her back. Joe called one of Beth's ex-boyfriends and others in her life, essentially stalking her. He applied to a discipleship camp in the Islands in an attempt to show her he had changed. The counselor who had advised Beth heard one of the leaders responsible for the camp's application approvals lean toward approving Joe's application. The leader questioned Joe on everything. Joe lied to the leader about Beth, saying she had told everyone about him and his past.

In weeks following, Joe threatened her so much she felt she needed a restraining order. Beth told him others from Alabama knew his story, so any one of them could have said something. She told him never to call or see her again or she would have him arrested. She got prank calls and texts then, in December of that year, got a call from him on her birthday. Afterward, a woman called Beth's cell asking where Joe was. Apparently Beth was listed as his emergency contact. The woman was his employer and said Joe was working in Research and Development at Mass General in Boston and had not shown up for work for a while. To this day, Beth has not heard anything more from Joe.

Beth's story, while involving heartache, could have ended worse, but it started with little lies. Little 'white' lies about ages and dates. Lies are never what they seem. Like icebergs, the little ones are merely harbingers of a bigger danger under the surface.

When is it okay to lie?

In our modern world of situational ethics, some people define truth by whatever fits the situation. Usually this belief system is for the benefit of the one adjusting the truth. This book is not about arguing one person's right and wrong with another. Right and wrong is laid out in God's word. In the book of Joshua, Rahab, the prostitute, lied to protect the Israelite spies who came to spy out the land. She was rewarded by being included in the Messianic line, which ended with Jesus.

It is okay to lie to save someone from physical harm or death. Corrie Ten Boom, a famous Dutch Christian, hid Jews with her family during World War II. Because of her work in protecting the Jews, she was honored by the state of Israel who named her 'Righteous Among Nations', was knighted by the Queen of the Netherlands and had a women's home named after her by King's College in NY.[1]

People who say they 'had to' lie about anything else usually mean they 'had to' so they could get what they wanted, or wouldn't get caught in an immoral or criminal act: it is pure selfishness.

Manipulation

Frogs lack the strength of character and integrity to think past what they want at the moment. Whether it is money, you, attention, power, time, or a thrill, the Frog must resort to underhanded tactics to get what he wants, without you knowing he is doing it.

Manipulation is not the same as lying. Manipulation is the game. Lying is one of the plays.

There are many techniques used by a manipulator to make him appear to be what he is not to get you to do something for him or to get something from you. That is a manipulator's goal. A manipulator—a covert aggressor—has grown practiced at hiding his aggression and concealing his motives. There are a few ways a manipulator manipulates:

1. Lying - Lying is verbal deception. It is like painting an illusionary picture. The liar shows what he wants you to see. He takes away the choice of his victim to make an informed decision. A liar may be involved in something morally wrong while he pursues the victim for a relationship or money, all the while knowing the victim would never put up with his sin.

2. Flattery - *'to praise or compliment insincerely or effusively; to gratify by falsification' (dictionary.com)*

'A lying tongue hates those it hurts, and a flattering mouth works ruin.'
– Proverbs 26:28

One time I reconnected with an old classmate on a social networking site. I remembered him from high school, but we hadn't talked a whole lot. He was quick to tell me 'I miss you' and how beautiful I was. I got a little excited, but the first series of communications ended abruptly and my heart stung a little. I realized I was getting a little too enamored over this newfound 'friend' and, after a few weeks of not hearing from him, I wrote him off. Weeks later another message came: more 'I miss you' and telling me how my beauty went further than my hair and face, etc. He asked if he could call me again, that maybe we could talk that night. I liked his seemingly old-fashioned approach to contacting me. After my history with the previous man I'd been involved with taking up almost all my time on the phone with multiple calls a day, this man was being respectful. But the night he said he would call, no call came. I thought something had happened to him, but saw his presence more than ever on the social networking site. He had termed himself 'cyber-challenged' yet suddenly he was all over the site, responding to everyone, playing the site's little games and taking its tests; everything but contacting me. When I talked to two male cop friends, both said he was using flattery to keep me hooked...to 'keep me on the line'. They said he was 'making the rounds', doing with other girls what he was doing with me. My cop friends said that when he was bored he would contact me, and when he was okay, he was onto other things. Again, I had let flattery hook me, but this time I had guarded my heart and put a stop to it before my emotions had become truly engaged.

3. Aggressive threats - Child predators are notorious for making aggressive threats, like threatening to kill their victim's parents, should the child tell an authority what the predator is doing. Other threats of this type are those of physical harm, or, in the case of an employee, the threat of termination, should the employee not do the boss's bidding. They are always tinged with anger, whether it is subdued or overt.

4. Passive threats - These kinds of threats may come with a kind tone, a pleasant face and an all-around passive demeanor. But, like a Venus FlyTrap, they should never be taken to mean the manipulator is the victim's friend. When a manipulator's secret is at stake, his statements may sound like this: "You know, you've told me some sensitive information, too. I'm sure those people would be hurt if they knew such-and-such.". Or, when seeking to get money out of a victim who is reluctant to cosign his loan for a large amount, he may say, in a condescending way: "I know you get nervous about your money." This technique is especially successful with victims who are people-pleasers.

5. Financial - When a manipulator controls the victim's money, it can be difficult for her to escape the situation. This manipulator may even reinforce his physical control of finances by telling her she will never be able to earn a living; that he will make sure she doesn't work in a certain industry, or threaten to smear her reputation so she cannot get work. Sometimes, when children are involved, the mother doesn't even think of escaping due to concern for the kids.

6. Big talk - Just like the get-rich-quick schemer, this technique is used many times on potential business partners, investors or customers. By talking about future earnings, products, and their names in lights, the

manipulator sells a bill of goods without actually possessing it in hopes of gaining the victim's money and/or participation. This is not limited to business, however, and can be used on women who want to see that a man is 'going somewhere' with his life.

7. Vilification - This looks like someone who tries to garner sympathy, as shown in the 'Sympathy-Monger' type, earlier. There is nothing more effective after the manipulator has deceived someone and been caught than for him to hunch his shoulders, take on a pained look and give a non-comprehending shrug to his accusers, saying he 'doesn't know why (the victim) would say that'. He will try to make his victim into the villain. He may also make up a situation or lie about an event and say 'I don't know why she would do that to me'. The focus is now on his pain, on his victim's supposed 'betrayal' of him, and not on his dirty deed. He knows, at this point, that fighting back or accusing the victim will make him look like the bad guy he is, so he opts for getting people onto his side using sympathy. He knows they will not even question his emotional appeal and will fly to his side to support him. His most powerful ploy is to speak kindly about the victim so he appears blameless. People operating on emotions will fall for this. Wise ones who ask questions and think critically won't. Sometimes he will use his next victim, such as a new girlfriend, as a weapon against the former victim, considering that the next victim does not yet know him or his ways. But changing the players does not change the game, and the new girlfriend will soon see what the last one already has.

8. Crocodile Tears - This could fall under the previous category, but is a stand-alone manipulative maneuver. There are times when the manipulator will cry—even sob—in an attempt to solidify his reversed role as 'victim' and further convince an audience using this emotional appeal. Whether it's his new girlfriend or authority figures who are accusing him, he will cry and may say that he has been 'wronged' by the victim, but has 'changed'. There is an easy way to identify real tears from manufactured ones. The manufactured tears, which come from 'worldly sorrow' say, 'Oh, darn, I regret getting caught'. The real tears, or 'Godly sorrow' say, 'Oh, God, I hurt You and others and I'm going to do my best to change, no matter how long it takes'. Look and listen. A repentant person; that is, someone who wants to turn his life around and change may or may not cry, but will:

- **appear truly humble.** He will not talk about being humble, but will simply be humble. He won't be so quick to speak, and his words will be filled with grace and benefit of the doubt, not leaping in constantly to give his opinion.
- **take the blame.** Before repentance—or turning in the opposite direction from one's wrongs—happens, a person must take responsibility for what he has done. He wants peace, which only comes from acknowledging the truth to those he has wronged, but especially to himself.
- **apologize.** Someone who has wronged others should feel the heavy hand of conviction on his heart, and should want to make things right. He will want the slate clean; whether he is afraid the wronged party will react well or not. He will know that, with God's strength, he can apologize and at least do his part, even if the wronged party reacts badly or shuns him.
- **be concerned with others' feelings or pain.** He will realize the effects of what he has done and acknowledge others' pain before his own.

A man who wants to manipulate you with crocodile tears will:

- **focus on himself.** He will lament, saying, "I've been betrayed"; "Why did she do this to me?" As a third party listening to this man, you may find yourself resenting and having bad feelings toward the person or persons who apparently hurt him. But do you have the whole story? If most of the recounting of his story is about how he has been wronged, and not about how he did wrong and hopes the other person will forgive him, he is not repentant.
- **blame the victim.** "She seduced me"; "I didn't have a chance/choice" or "I had to fudge the numbers". There are only a few situations in which you don't have a choice in life, among them: being born, being

assaulted, physical disease, and the time of your death (excluding suicide). Everything else involves choice; it's just a matter of whether you want the consequences. *'No temptation has overtaken you except such as is common to man; but God is faithful, who will not allow you to be tempted beyond what you are able, but with the temptation will also make the way of escape, that you may be able to bear it.' –1 Corinthians 10:13.* The Frog had a choice—he just wanted his fun without reprisal.

- **not apologize.** This would be admitting he did wrong, and would fly in the face of his pride. He may offer an apology with a 'but you' clause. For instance, "I'm sorry I did this, but you put me in that position." or "I'm sorry I hurt you, but you knew I wasn't ready for commitment." This is a manipulator's perfect 'out' so he can have his cake and eat it too.

- **use the tears often.** He won't cry in front of you often enough for you to get suspicious, but, especially in the beginning of this new relationship, he may try to secure his position as victim by tugging at your heartstrings. This may taper off into heavy sighs and dramatic pauses when the previous situation of which he is accused comes up.

- **say he's "changed".** I have a friend who struggled with drug addiction and other illegal activities for years. We started as roommates. She said she was a changed person when we first met, and told me about the drugs and illegal activities from her past. About a month later, my new friend went back to the drugs and illegal activities again. Upon coming back into my life a year later, she said she'd changed and 'things were happening' and, basically, she talked a lot. She was arrested again and disappeared for a while. I wondered how she could say she had changed but obviously hadn't.

  Thirteen years later, after hearing of her time in and out of jail here and abroad, I saw her face to face and got to talk to her. She didn't tell me she had changed. She didn't have to. The glow on her face and her quiet excitement at her new job said enough. Her confident, quiet demeanor and not even a mention of the past told me she had changed. To this day, she continues to thrive and grow where she is, happy, married, drug-free and at peace.

The moment a man wants to come back to you and say 'I've changed', red flags should go up. He is convincing you. Selling you. Someone who has changed has no interest in convincing you, only in living the new life he has decided to adopt, telling you about the things which are happening in his life, and asking about you. Saying 'I've changed' is like saying 'I'm humble'. Chances are a person doesn't even know when they've changed. My friend didn't, and was delighted when I told her I could see she had.

'Let someone else praise you, not your own mouth—a stranger, not your own lips.' – Proverbs 27:2

9. Isolation - This is a form of control that does not allow the victim the freedom or contact with others to 'fact check' or have accountability with anyone outside the relationship. The manipulator uses a variety of verbal tactics to keep her isolated. He says that he wants her 'all to himself'; that 'they both have lots of work to do if they're going to be successful'; that he is bored with what's going on in the outside world and wants to 'focus' on whatever task he has made up, or that 'no one needs to know our business'. In each of these cases, the manipulator wants either to control the victim by forming a bond of attachment, or keep the victim from being out from under his spell so she can think for herself and put things together. There is almost always a sexual thread to this kind of manipulation.

10. Love Bombing - Derived originally from a 1978 speech by cult leader Sun Myung Moon, the term is defined by Margaret Singer in her 1996 book, *Cults in Our Midst*:

'As soon as any interest is shown by the recruits, they may be love bombed by the recruiter or other cult members. This process of feigning friendship and interest in the recruit was originally associated with one of the early youth cults, but soon it was taken up by a number of groups as part of their program for luring people in. Love bombing is a coordinated effort, usually under the direction of leadership that involves long-term members' flooding recruits

and newer members with flattery, verbal seduction, affectionate but usually nonsexual touching, and lots of attention to their every remark. Love bombing - or the offer of instant companionship - is a deceptive ploy accounting for many successful recruitment drives.'

It is also an effective tool used by a manipulative man to ensure the loyalty and favor of an unaware and/or needy woman. Sometimes the compliments and 'love' will not appear obvious; a good manipulator knows not to overkill, but when you find yourself depending on or playing toward getting compliments or attention from him, be careful. A healthy relationship depends not on one party needing to feed the other's need for love and attention, but both parties being already well-adjusted and esteeming themselves in a healthy way so they are grounded enough to receive compliments. Those compliments and adoration should not be their life-blood.

You may not be able to tell the difference between a man's genuine affection for and desire to get to know you and 'love bombing', but time will tell. Revert again to the scripture *'Keep your heart with all diligence, for out of it spring the issues of life.' – Proverbs 4:23*. You are the only one in charge of your welfare and safety. If the affection, verbal or otherwise, seems rushed and urgent, beware. If his speech leans toward wanting something, even if he doesn't say he wants it from you, stay guarded. There is no rush to move ahead, and a righteous man will appreciate and value your caution and will show his own good true colors in time.

Another way this is seen is when an adult befriends a child; usually one who is longing for a family or who has family problems or rejection issues. The child is 'groomed' for an abusive sexual relationship, human trafficking and/or prostitution.

11. Wearing down - A manipulator will keep you in a constant whirlwind of drama. This man will keep things exciting, calling you and pursuing you, wanting to spend large amounts of time with you, taking you out to dinner, text messaging or phoning. You will find yourself trying to take naps because of the inevitable late nights out or just staying up. Your personal time and time with friends will be shoved aside to accomodate him. This technique has been used by many enemy nations to brainwash prisoners of war. When you are tired and worn down, you are not as alert and are more open to suggestion and manipulation than when you are sharp. Don't be surprised later in the relationship when you feel relaxation and peace when he's not around. Don't be surprised either that you like it.

12. Rationalization - A manipulator will try to convince the victim or other party that what he's done was either necessary, unavoidable or important to his, the victim's, or someone else's welfare. Even an intelligent person may fall for this, and doubt his or her accusation of the manipulator, which is exactly what he wants. Again, there is always a choice.

13. Diversion - You may find, in confronting a manipulator, or even gently trying to keep him on the subject of what he did, that he will use a diversion tactic. This is an attempt to get you off the subject of what he did wrong. Whether it's accusing you of something or moving on to another subject altogether, you may find yourself losing your train of thought or wondering what your point was in the first place. Fear not. You're not crazy. The manipulator has gotten his way. An effective tool against this is to remember your first question or accusation. Many people don't do this because they allow the Frog to pull them down the rabbit trail, not knowing who they were dealing with in the first place. Once you suspect you've been diverted, keep the main thing the main thing, no matter how tempting it is to answer a secondary argument. If necessary, say, "We'll talk about that in a second. Let's get back to the question I asked about what you did yesterday."

14. Guilt-tripping - Knowing that others are conscientious and reasonably compassionate, the manipulator plays on these positive character traits by fooling the person with a conscience into believing she is lacking in some area, has hurt him, is contributing to his failure or is making him appear to be a bad guy. He will do this with subtlety, so she truly believes she either needs to be "better", or is just simply a "bad person". This form of control is powerful to people who do not know their own weaknesses and who want to help someone who seems to be having a hard time. It is virtually impossible to show this behavior to a third party, because the manipulator knows the victim will look like the 'bad guy' for seemingly kicking him when he is down. This is often used along with the 'vilifying the victim' tactic, before the victim is onto him.

15. Shaming - This is another control tactic and form of dominance, which plays on other weaknesses of the victim. All it takes is for the victim to mention her weakness, or for the observant manipulator to pick up on it, and he is off and running with a subtle barrage of words that feed into that fear. A woman concerned with her weight may hear: "You'd better go easy on those cookies." or, when looking at a thin girl in a magazine or on t.v., say simply, "That's my ideal woman" or "She's beautiful." A woman who is concerned about her age may hear: "I know you're getting older and you want to be married..." or he may mention 'cougars'; a strange term for older women seeking younger men. If a woman is insecure about how she appears to others, this is ripe fruit for a manipulator. Any number of techniques can come into play here, from the 'teaching' position he puts himself in to criticize her, to outright scolding her for saying something that didn't meet with his standards.

16. Serving - A manipulator will play the servant role, looking as if he is helping someone's cause or giving of himself, but this is a mask used in order to get his own agenda met. Again, this is a difficult action to mark, because who wants to look like the bad guy and assume someone is volunteering with ulterior motives? But his sin will find him out. It is not your job to judge/condemn, but to judge/discern, and when you discern that this man is serving for some other reason than why he should be, mark him in your mind. If he appears on the scene to serve you; i.e., to help you with a project, fix things around your house, help solve problems, be aware. Why is he doing this? Is it out of the goodness of his heart? After a time, does he expect you to reciprocate? Time will tell, but in the meantime, guard your heart.

Froggy Verbal Behavior

I talked to men about what they meant by some of the things they commonly say to women to 'let them down easy'. The consensus was that when they didn't want to tell a woman outright that they just weren't gelling and there was no future for them together, they made excuses. One man said that there are men who will say, outright, "I'm just not interested/attracted," etc. and who will be direct with the truth that the dating relationship won't go anywhere, but for the rest (most guys) they opt for the 'soft' approach. The excuses make it easier for the guy using them, but will drag you along in hope, if you let them. Let's take a look:

The Excuses (a.k.a., 'The Pushbacks')

1. "I'll call you" - As we mentioned before, some guys use this as a parting sentiment, like 'Later' or 'See ya'. So when he says "I'll call you," and then he doesn't, just write him off. That's right. In this case, he doesn't mean what he says. If you call him, thinking that maybe he 'got busy' or 'is shy and needs some encouragement', and he does go out with you, you've set the tone for the relationship. You chase him and, inevitably, he will run away. If he doesn't call when he says he will, don't take it personally. You're too fabulous to worry about a guy who can't even keep this simple promise. I used to get all caught up in this "I'll call you" statement, checking my cell, waiting by the phone with butterflies in my stomach. Not only did some of these men not call, but they went and married other women. When he says he'll call and he doesn't, it's his cowardly way of pushing you away and letting you down 'easy'. Do yourself a favor: get off the merry-go-round first and step away from the phone so you don't have to hang in there 'til the bitter end and get your heart stomped anyway. If he does call, great! You've gotten on with your life anyway and didn't stop everything for him. Go out with girlfriends. Write that book. Take that trip. If he doesn't call, he will fade from your mind and leave room for your true Prince.

2. "I love you" - If he's about to ask you to marry him, this is fine. If it's a week or two after you've met, run! He's either lonely, bored or needs a green card. He could be joking, too, but a guy you should avoid is one who shoots his mouth off with this phrase without having commitment to you in mind. Beware, too, if he says this during an emotional moment. Usually it is to try to have sex with you. Contrary to our culture's belief, true love does wait.

3. "I'm just not ready for a relationship" - Run! He means what he says, and there's nothing you can do (or should want to do) to change his mind. More accurately, he is saying he is not ready for a relationship with you. All of us have been with guys who say they 'aren't ready'. Some of us have seen them propose to the next woman they date, or someone they had already known before us. Take my word for it: no amount of 'hanging out', helping him with household chores or projects, or using your feminine wiles will change his mind. You are just prolonging the inevitable.

4. "I'm praying about our relationship." - This is one the Spiritual Superstar loves to use. It is another push-back. When a man wants to be with you, he lets nothing stand in the way. A Godly man will pray about the relationship, but he will do so in secret or with a trusted male friend. If a future is not to happen between him and you, he will not drag things on by telling you this statement. A man who uses this phrase as an excuse to create distance between the two of you for an indefinite amount of time is not serious about having any kind of future with you.

5. "I'm busy/have a lot of work to do/have a deadline…" - Another pushback. You have to discern with this one. Obviously, we're all busy. Saying this once in a while is expected. But when it becomes a lifestyle, especially in the early stages of a dating relationship, he is creating distance. Don't try to fill it. He is either focused on work to the degree that he doesn't have room for anyone in his life, is using it as a 'soft letdown' because he doesn't see a future with you, or is lying and is using work as an excuse for other nighttime activities. Be especially suspicious if he doesn't have a job (stranger things have happened).

In all of these cases, excuses and the actions of backing away are indicators that there's nothing happening on his end that makes him want to pursue you. Usually a Bullfrog will use any or all of these phrases and actions until you get the picture and give up, or until he is cornered and finally does come clean.

On your end, you can make a decision just to exit, or just tell him you want to pursue a courtship with someone who can give the you the time you need, that until then, you want to free him—and yourself, up for other possibilities. You don't want to do the "Where is this going?" question, which will shut him down, but just give him the space he apparently needs—just be prepared for him to take that space and leave. If he does leave, you have saved yourself lots of pain and time. You decide what you want to put up with: a 'maybe' man who gives you the feeling he's not really 'into it', or a future Prince, who will chase you until he catches you?

If you think withholding information as a pushback is less serious than outright lying, consider Gretchen's story:

"I met him online on a very reputable dating site. He was an attractive Chinese man and we seemed to have a lot in common. His English on his profile was broken, but I skipped over that, making sense of what he was saying. He contacted me first and we messaged back and forth, then we emailed. I was coming up on a trip to New York City, where he lived, so I suggested we meet. What could go wrong in a city of millions of people? Besides, I knew New York like the back of my hand. I felt safe meeting him at my hotel.

He came off as shy and sweet when I saw him waiting in the lobby, even bringing me a fresh flower in a beautiful, small cannister. We walked around uptown a little, and then went to a nice sushi dinner. It was a little hard to understand him, but I really worked on it. I was having a nice time and he seemed very interested in me. He didn't hold the door for me but asked what I believed about a man paying for a woman's dinner. I told him if it was a date, I expected at least the first time for him to pay. And yes, I wanted the door held, like he should for anyone. After that, he seemed to 'turn on' his chivalry. Whether it was fake or not, his attentiveness and kindness softened my heart.

I guess my first red flag was when he said he believed in having sex before marriage. It was something I didn't believe in, and I told him so, but we continued the evening. He was expressing great interest in me; not in a sexual way, but like a schoolboy in love. The next morning we met for breakfast at a local diner. He seemed to stumble over what he wanted to say, not because of language, but he was trying to ask me what would happen if things didn't work out. I told him, if they didn't, they didn't, but we should at least try. He seemed unconvinced, and I told him if he didn't want to see me again, that was ok. He seemed more interested then, especially after I told him I liked him for who he was.

I went to the meetings I needed to go to that day across town and he picked me up at my building. We went to dinner and he seemed excited again to be with me. After dinner, as we walked, he got quiet and I sensed the trepidation in him. I thought: He must be really shy! The next day we went to dinner and the pattern continued: excitement at seeing me, then pulling back. During one of the 'excitement' times, he said he wanted to be my boyfriend. This was after three days of knowing him! I told him it was a little soon, and he said he didn't understand why, if two people got along, why they wouldn't date exclusively. I couldn't answer him on that one… we'd both said we had the goal of being married, and I personally was not a serial dater. Although getting hooked into a dating relationship at that early point made me extremely uncomfortable. I let him push me into it.

On my last night in the city, we went and sat at by the river. He said he didn't know why we couldn't be married soon. I almost choked on my water. The sun was setting over Manhattan and he took my hand, saying he wanted to buy me a ticket to China to meet his family. That made me very uncomfortable, this man who I'd known now for five days.

I left New York and he offered a ticket back up for the next weekend, as well as paying for a hotel for me near his apartment for the weekend. He actually came down on the bus to where I lived, paid for my bus fare up to the city and had bought tickets for both of us so he could ride the bus back down with me to drop me back off in my city. I had never had anyone be so thoughtful—especially riding up and back with me each way! Before the trip, he called me multiple times a day, excited about 'us' and keeping me on the phone. I told him I really wanted to take things slow. I was beginning to feel not only that this was too fast, but that there was something else going on here.

The second trip to New York, 'we' didn't fare as well. I pushed back again regarding marriage...I needed a little more than nine days to know someone! With that statement, he said he had told me everything I needed to know about him...how much more time did I need, he asked? Did I think he was lying in telling me who he was? At this point, I remembered he said he came from a family of lawyers. That was what our conversations were turning into: cross-examinations. He also became less attentive and kind. Obviously, the chivalry had been an act.

He said he didn't want a big wedding, but just to go to the Justice of the Peace. He also said (BIG red flag) that he didn't want to break any promises to me, so he couldn't promise that he could remain faithful. This became a big 'thing' between us. I told him that, while no one knows what the future holds, and we all hope we can be faithful, that we needed to make that promise to the other person, then put up hedges of protection along the way so we wouldn't be unfaithful to one another. He said that Americans placed too much emphasis on law and on vows.

Americans?

I wondered about his choice of words and then asked him if he had his citizenship. He said no, he didn't. Ah! That did clear things up. I knew what he was after. I never brought it up, but I understood now the rush to the altar—or, in his case, to the government desk.

He beat me to the breakup when I got home, and started an argument on the phone, saying I was 'hard to get to know' and I 'tended to lie'. Now I knew something was really wrong with him. When he asked me what we should do about us (apparently he didn't want to do the breaking up), I said that maybe it was better if we didn't see each other anymore. He asked me if I wanted us to remain friends, or never to speak again. I told him we weren't enemies, but that I needed time to myself (if only to figure out what this speeding car was that had just hit me!). He asked how many days I needed. I told him and at the end of those days, he called. He was a little colder, which made me sad, but I reminded myself that God had someone who wouldn't rush me and with whom I would get all green lights. And, who wouldn't need a green card! I haven't heard from him since."

Part 1
Chapter 5

What Deception Looks Like

"Understand that the tongue can conceal the truth, but the eyes—never!"
– MIKHAIL BULGAKOV, The Master and Margarita

Law enforcement has almost made detecting deception a science, but it is not perfect. Still, it is a fact that the human mind was not created to be comfortable deceiving. Because of this, the human body displays physical evidence, which is more reliable than verbal behavior. Non-verbal behavior accounts for more than three-quarters of total human communication. The breakdown is as follows: 55% non-verbal, 38% tone of voice and 7% actual words.[1]

Pathological liars, or people who lie in order to achieve a goal, may be so practiced at lying that they don't show immediate signs of deception. Some people are sociopathic or psychopathic, feeling no compunction about the lies and manipulation they commit.

You don't need to be a police officer or detective to be able to know when someone is lying, but the following list helps cut to the chase when you are confronted with a possible Frog.

Lynn had red flags about a man she had become involved with at work. She couldn't place the feelings, which manifested as a knot in her stomach and stress, but thought the knot was because he told her he was interested in her only for help on their work project. As Lynn continued working with him, the red flags and stress continued. She was trying to keep her mind on business, and this man even scolded her for showing signs of her feelings for him. She thought she was going crazy, because she didn't think she was showing any such signs and, in fact, was working very hard to keep her mind on the project and away from any possibilities with this man. After months passed, and after

[1] - Borg, John. Body Language: 7 Easy Lessons to Master the Silent Language. Prentice Hall life, 2008

he had turned around and used her sexually, he told her he had been involved in an adulterous relationship with his best friend's wife for years. When she asked why he hadn't told her this long ago, he simply said she 'couldn't have handled it'. In effect, he had taken away her freedom to decide whether she wanted to have a business relationship—or anything else—with an obviously immoral man because he knew she wouldn't have done so, had she known the truth. Sneaky little Frog. Tricks are for kids.

In this chapter, we'll look at the physical signs or, as gamblers call them, *tells*. Learning to see some of the *tells* in any of these three groups makes it easier to put things together when something does not feel right. Seeing any of these tells individually does not indicate with certainty the person is lying to you; these tells could be signs of nervousness or insecurity. It is the timing of these clues, combined with the baseline (or normal, usual) behavior of the man that should put you on your guard and make you reassess the situation.

Body Language

Any cop will tell you there is no 100% foolproof method of telling whether or not someone is lying. It is also not possible to tell by one indicator that someone is lying. These indicators must be used in tandem and with a baseline of 'usual' motions and words a person uses, to arrive at a conclusion that someone is not being truthful. There are physical reactions the human body cannot suppress when faced with the stress of fighting against telling the truth. They indicate heightened emotion. These reactions should be taken as clues to tell the interviewer/cop/Princess to dig deeper and to beware: things are not as they appear. Sociopaths and those not guilty about lying can hide some of these but, again, anomalies will show themselves if you learn and get used to observing these things.

A note about guilt: These indicators may be present due to guilt from self-doubt, but that will show in the person's baseline. In other words, if he is shy or insecure, he may always avoid eye contact or always appear fidgety or always show any of these other indicators, but these actions will be consistent. They key for you is to determine what these baseline characteristics are so that when an anomaly—an inconsistency—appears, it sticks out like a mouse in a punchbowl.

Body

There are several of these physical reactions police notice when questioning someone about a crime. You should be aware of them, too. They usually happen right after a question you ask or a comment you make. Following is a list of typical deceptive body postures:

- slouching
- lack of interest
- general stiffening of the body, especially straightening the shoulders and slight tilting back of the head to a straight position, as if the person is waiting to be slapped; stiff, controlled movements
- not facing front; facing or tilting to the side
- defensive posture: crossing the arms in a folded gesture can be a relaxed position for some men, but is indicative of protecting oneself; placing something (a book or other object) between the two of you.
- runner's position; as if he is about to take off; also shuffling, tapping and swinging or arching of feet. This signals a desire to escape the 'interview' or the question.
- in a chair, leaning back after a question is asked
- crossing and uncrossing their legs - crossing the ankles is an indicator of withholding something.
- head and body slouch
- anxious; erratic and rapid posture changes; rubbing and wringing of hands; pinching, scratching, stroking and picking; pulling nose or earlobes; hair straightening or twirling, licking lips, difficulty swallowing; nail inspection, biting or chewing; knuckle-popping, drumming of fingers; leg bouncing
- they appear calm, but in a false, forced way. They seem like they are in motion, but are still, controlling themselves.

Hands

- In their peripheral vision, police often watch, a suspect's hands. When they see the hands clench, it's on. This clench is usually followed by a swing of the suspect's fist against the cop. A watchful cop knows the clench and reacts before the assault.
- The up and down motion of the Adam's apple signifies a gulp; an unconscious sign of emotional anxiety, embarrassment or stress. This may also show as the subject clearing his throat.
- Sweaty palms; wiping sweat from brow or neck are deception cues which happen with increased heart and breathing rates, indicating stress in polygraph tests. This could indicate nervousness and not deception, but would still give cause to probe more in search of the truth.
- Palm-up or shrug indicates deception.
- grooming gestures: adjustment of clothing or accessories; dusting, lint picking, thread pulling; winding of watch or adjusting jewelry
- supportive and protective gestures: Head or chin on hand; hiding of mouth or eyes; hiding of hands or feet

Contrast this with truthful body language, where the subject sits or stands upright, his body is open and relaxed, he leans forward on occasion, is frontally aligned with the interviewer and casual posture changes.

Facial Expressions

- When he searches your face for signs of skepticism, he's trying to see if you're 'onto him'. You may feel like you're under a microscope. Don't mistake it for interest! Interest will look different; like a warm, unguarded expression. The eyes of a deceiver will be sharper, and the expression may last only for a second or less.
- Red or rosy face comes from shyness, anger or shame. It can also appear as a sign of actual or possible defeat. Pallor (paleness) is associated with extreme fear or anger. These come from an increase in adrenaline in the face of a threat.
- false smile: Normally the zygomatic smile, so named after the anatomy at the outside of the eye, makes the outsides of the eyes crinkle into

crow's feet while the mouth curves upward. In a fake smile, or polite smile, the lip muscles stretch sideward, not up, using the risorius muscles, with little upward curl and no crow's feet.

- micro-expressions: barely perceptible but definitely noticeable facial movements, such as a twitch of the mouth, darting or widening of the eyes for a millisecond
- Covering the mouth indicates lying or withholding information.

When you are asking questions—essentially *interviewing*—know that facial expressions in response to your questions provide clues into identifying the emotional state of the suspect.

Eye Contact

Normal eye contact is usually maintained between two people conversing 30-60 percent of the time. Eye movements can be very telling when trying to detect deception, if observed after one of your questions or statements.

- 'Flashbulb' eyes can be almost imperceptible. They appear like a reverse flutter of the eyelids, or it can be a longer, dramatic widening of the eyes. This normally shows up in intense emotion, such as anger or fear.
- A blink or twitch of the eyes; sometimes a barely-noticeable flutter, after a question, indicates discomfort with the question and/or with answering it truthfully.
- Avoiding eye contact or averting their gaze is also a tell. Truthful people tend to look at you longer than deceptive ones. A pro will hold your gaze for an unusually long time, trying to sell you on his innocence. You will know the difference when you sense something is 'off'.
- A glance at the interviewer after she brings up a subject indicates interest in that subject.
- A normal person's blink rate—the rate at which they blink their eyes when they are at rest (not engaged in conversation)—is 10-20 blinks per minute. Talking increases the blink rate to 20-25. The rate increases to 30 to 50 for someone speaking on t.v. because of the stress of doing so.[1, 2]

1 - http://www.ncbi.nlm.nih.gov/pubmed/9399231
2 - http://www.social-engineer.org/framework/Psychological_Principles:_Eye_Cues

In the final interview video with Ted Bundy by Dr. James Dobson, Bundy's blink rate was astronomical as he answered questions about how pornography led to his murderous lifestyle. At many points, his eyelids were closed as he was answering. He was either lying or extremely uncomfortable talking about the subject; I don't know what Bundy's baseline expressions were, but something was not normal there.[3]

- The subject's eye movements may even appear stiff and not free.
- Dilated pupils indicate interest in the subject presented.

Linguistics

Linguistics is the science of language including, among other things, syntax and phonetics. Verbal *tells* will show themselves several ways. Characteristically, verbal behavior clues will show as more controlled than non-verbal symptoms; i.e., the person will seem stiffer when answering or speaking. You must always weigh the verbal cues—how words are said and which words are used—in light of the nonverbal clues you observe.

Truthful people:
- answer questions with direct and specific words: "I lived in Paris for five years working on my bachelor's in foreign languages."

Deceptive people:
- avoid realistic words: "I lived in Paris for a while."
- answer after a pause or may fail to answer. They try to redirect your attention in an attempt to hide the realization that they did not answer the question.
- minimize issues
- answer with a question: "Why would I take their money?"
- may answer too quickly, even stepping on your words

> *'He who answers a matter before he hears it, it is folly and shame to him.'*
> *– Proverbs 18:13*

- may repeat the question, in an attempt to buy themselves more time to think up an answer, excuse or alibi
- may forget facts or have a rehearsed answer
- may use complimentary or flattering words to appease. On the other hand, a deceptive person may turn the tables and try to accuse or ask you pointed questions, to get the focus off of them.
- may change the subject
- may question or challenge facts or information
- may try to 'hard sell' you on their answer, not considering that their answer is good enough to stand alone. He may speak excessively to try to convince you.

'But let your 'Yes' be 'Yes,' and your 'No,' 'No.' For whatever is more than these is from the evil one.' – Matthew 5:37

- may not use contractions
- avoid direct statements or answers
- speak in a monotonous tone
- may leave out pronouns (he, she, it, etc.). JonBenét Ramsey's parents referred to her in a note as 'the child' instead of using her name or 'she'
- may give "other answers", for example,

    Q: "Did you steal that car?"
    A: "I don't even drive."

    Q: "Did you take the last brownie?"
    A: "I don't even like brownies."

    These subjects are answering truthfully but the answers they give are not addressing the actual questions.
- use humor and sarcasm to avoid the subject
- tend to over-explain or give multiple excuses, for example: "I can't come tonight because I need to work on my project. I'm tired, too."

When someone is accused and is deceptive, they will act differently than someone who is innocent:

1. "Joe, why would she say you did this?"

Deceptive answer: "I don't know why she said I did that." The answer is emotional, and there is no denial of what happened.

Truthful answer: "I don't know, but she's wrong. I didn't do that." The answer is a straightforward denial and challenges the accusation as false.

2. "Joe, can you think of any reason why someone would accuse you of this?"

Deceptive answer: "People don't like me." There is no denial of being a suspect. The accusation is thrown back at someone else.

Truthful answer: "No! People know me and know I wouldn't do that!" The truthful person rejects the idea of being guilty of the event.

3. "Did you ever think about doing that, even though you didn't actually do it?"

Deceptive answer: "No, not seriously—I didn't want the fallout." This is not a direct denial.

Truthful answer: "No way! Never!" This is a direct denial.

4. "Can you tell me why you wouldn't do something like that?"

Deceptive answer: "You just regret it; you could lose a lot." or "It's against the law." The answers are in the third person.

Truthful answer: "I wasn't raised that way. That's not the kind of person I am." These are first-person answers.

You can notice deception not only from what is said, but how it is said, such as an answer given with shortness or an attitude, a higher-pitched voice than normal, monotonous tones, mumbling, fast-talking or muddled sentences.

Given the fact that some of these signs occur in people who may just be insecure in themselves or speaking to someone, it is important to weigh all of the indicators —body language, eye contact, facial expressions and linguistics— together. That, along with your own red flags, will show you when someone is being deceptive. Someone who may be nervous or insecure in a certain area of his life, but who is truthful, will have his lack of confidence fall away as he talks to you.

This is why it is so important not to drink alcohol on a first date. You need all your senses sharp. Alcohol colors everything happy and fuzzes your judgment. It also pulls down your walls, making you have much more grace and leeway in your discernment than you should have. Stay straight and sensitive to your surroundings and your company. Be sober as a judge, because that's what you will be doing: judging (discerning) words and actions.

Internet Cons

People can be anyone they want online. That fact, coupled with the access to information, makes a woman searching for love on the internet more of a mark than ever for nefarious men.

Anyone who asks for money over the internet, who is not a verified merchant and/or who has initiated first contact, should raise a huge red flag. Hopefully most people delete the emails from Nigeria or London sent by a dignitary whose money is 'held up' or the ones from the kind but grammatically-challenged woman who just wants to help starving kids. But it is the next tier of internet con who should give you pause: the one you know...or, who you think you know. Just because you have begun conversing with a man even from a reputable dating or social networking site does not mean you know him. Just because it seems like he 'opens up' or tells you things 'close to his heart' does not mean those things are true.

Please keep in mind that by opening your heart, personal life or any personal records to someone online or by sending them money, you could be on a path to ruining your future—financial and otherwise. The physical dangers of not being aware of who you are corresponding with may seem distant, but it is very easy now for someone with little information to know more about you than you thought possible, and to follow up on that. Considering the massive count of people who are conned online, people still trust others they don't even know when there's a perceived promise of a life different from and better than the one they have:

A 54 year old woman named Jana* said she met a man online who 'said all the right things'. She figured that not a lot of men would want to be with someone like her, a woman who was older and looked after a child. Drawn in by his romantic talk, she sent the man money, and never heard from him again. His last known location: Nigeria—a place out of which many internet money scams operate.

These cons are known as '419 Scams', referring to an article number of the Nigerian Criminal Code.[1]

I had my own experience with the Nigerians. I was trying to sell my laptop. I put an ad on Craigslist and got a bite, which seemed too good to be true. The woman wanted no negotiation on my price, and she said she would pay $95 to have me ship it to her cousin outside the United States. The email address contained an American name. The catch: once I sent them the shipper's tracking number, they would send the money through (a reputable pay service...we'll call them ABC).

Big problem. Of course, once I would have shipped the item and given them the tracking number, they wouldn't need to send the money. I got trickier versions of this from scammers who cut and pasted ABC's logo and stock photos into an email saying ABC was 'holding' money due me from these people. On checking the url, it was not 'abc.com', but 'service.com', featuring ABC's name. Being the bold and justice-seeking person I am, I wrote a sternly-worded email to them, saying I knew they were cheating me and would have to account to God for their actions. I would bet more than one person is sitting in Nigeria with a nice laptop computer—but it isn't mine. I ended up selling it to a guy who was moving to teach English to school kids in Southeast Asia. I met the guy in person in a crowded Starbucks and got cash. We were near a computer store, so if he

*Name changed
1 - travel.state.gov/pdf/international_financial_scams_brochure.pdf - Feb 28, 2007

had wanted to check the integrity of the computer, he could have done so. In the end, both of us left happy.

There are all kinds of internet scams.

- At the very least, you won't be conned out of anything but your time. There are men who will chat you up, get you hooked for weeks or months and end up disappearing. A control tactic? A sick joke? It could be a fantasy, they could be married, or just suffering from office boredom. You'll probably never know which is just as well.

"I AM A CONSERVATIVE, SPORTS-MINDED MILLIONAIRE SEEKING A SIZE 2 BLONDE"

"I AM A SIZE 2 BLONDE SEEKING A CONSERVATIVE, SPORTS-MINDED BUSINESSMAN."

- Bride scams offer brides—and sometimes grooms—from other countries as well, and some are reputable (if ordering a spouse like a pair of shoes online is reputable), but, again, when they start asking for money, log off! Note for men: just because you're corresponding with a Russian babe named Tatiana doesn't mean she's not actually a Siberian iron worker named Josef! These can also be opportunities for human sex trafficking. Again, it should go without saying (yet still needs to be said), never ever travel to another country to meet someone you don't know. If you do travel internationally, never hand over your passport to anyone. American passports—especially military—are highly prized. You can be detained for days if you don't have it with you. Carry a copy of your passport, keep a copy with a friend at home, email yourself a scanned copy, and keep your original safely hidden or on your person.[1]

- One of the most alarming hunters on the internet is the child predator. But don't think that keeping your child away from the computer keeps him or her safe from these bottom-feeding Frogs. They look for single moms in order to get close to their children. A police detective who works with child predators tells me these men have girlfriends who swear the man 'wouldn't hurt a fly' and 'that he's changed' even though they're on parole for that very crime. My detective friend is called to many houses where this crime has happened multiple times to the surprised girlfriend's child.

- A disturbing story comes from California in 2006 where a man named Raymond Merrill thought he had found 'the one' online. After corresponding for a time, he bought her expensive gifts, then went to meet her in her native Brazil to make wedding plans. When he arrived, her real boyfriend helped her tie him up, drug him and drain his bank account of $200,000. Raymond's best friend had told Raymond he saw red flags, but the lovesick man hadn't listened. Fortunately the couple were caught, but only after taking the life and life savings of an innocent man and burning his body.[2]

- Letting down your guard to a faceless person can also cost you your freedom, too, as in the case of a woman who tried to cash a check from a new online 'friend'. His check was bogus and she spent 3 years in jail. You can't get into this kind of trouble if you don't take the bait.

1 - Visit http://travel.state.gov/ for more travel safety tips.
2 - cbsnews.com; The Seattle Times, Nov. 1, 2006 article by Kim Curtis and Stan Lehman

But how can you spot these people? Here are more detailed clues you may see:

1. Check out the integrity of the dating sites or companies you are using. If they are free, they are probably not very discriminating and are allowing all kinds of Frogs into membership there. But, don't let your guard down just because the site is reputable. If you can have access and are able to create a profile, so can Frogs.

2. Beware of anyone who asks for money. This is obvious, but some people still fall for it.

3. Beware of someone who says they love you too quickly. While this should be an alarm in real life, online you know a person even less. Two truthful people may 'feel' like they're in love online, but you don't truly start to know a person until you experience being with them in person and see their body language, facial expressions and speech patterns in a range of situations. It's not what they tell, it's what they show. You should wait until you meet in person to expect to hear the 'L' word, and even then, not at the first meeting! Give it time.

4. Professionally photos of themselves: nice, but is that really them?

5. Emails that repeat things they've already said, misspell your name, call you by another name or use no name at all or keep it impersonal could be sent by someone who has several email 'relationships' and is cutting and pasting into an email.

6. His 'come-ons' may be:

- His girlfriend just left him and he just needs someone to 'talk to'
- He's divorced and depressed
- He caught his wife or girlfriend cheating and wants a 'nice' girl like you

How to protect yourself

1. Keep a paper trail with dates and time stamps when you first start getting to know someone if you think there is potential for

a relationship. An additional folder in your emails with the man's name should suffice.

2. Keep as much of your personal information secret as you can. No one needs your social security number or your home address. If you're pressed for any personal information, end the correspondence. Even if a person offers you his or her information, know that it could be an attempt to lure you into giving yours out. Resist the temptation. No good will come from it.

3. Keep control of the correspondence. Keep communication short—no marathon or long emails. Never let yourself be rushed or otherwise pressured into someone else's will. Remaining a mystery who's not always available to a man is attractive. It can also protect you from cons who don't want to put time in to pursue you.

4. Don't get sucked into communication with someone who contacts you first (of course, this doesn't include membership-based dating sites, but keep your guard up, even so). You make first contact; especially where money is involved, such as with credit card offers or banks.

5. Ask for anything that will help you to discern a person's identity. If he asks for a picture from you, ask for one from him first. A good technique is to ask the person to take a picture of himself using his webcam or digital camera holding up a piece of paper with your name on it. If they can't do this, it's a scam. If they say they can't get a camera, run. If they're on the internet, there are ways of getting a camera. Most computers have them built-in now. All cell phones do. There's also video chatting. Lack of technology is not an excuse.

6. If you see red flags, flee! Many crime victims cite, as part of their unfortunate stories, 'I just knew something was wrong, but…'

7. Don't be overly paranoid. Polite caution is good. A righteous person will respond and satisfy your curiosity. An unrighteous person will resist or use a control tactic to 'guilt' you into avoiding identifying who s/he is. Once you feel your fear, anger or irritation rising at the uncertainty of who this person is, flee.

Psychic Payday

People use the internet for money scams and claim to be psychics, according to a consumer fraud reporting site.

A psychic, like a manipulator who is already reading you, is sizing you up the moment you enter her parlor. She knows you have some kind of a need, even if you are acting like you are there 'just for laughs'. She knows you need a 'wise' word from this person. The entire experience; the candles, the decor, the lighting, is designed to draw you in—like a seduction. But the psychic is not the only one to be blamed here.

Just like the woman who hears what she wants to hear from a manipulative man, the seeker who approaches the psychic formulates in her mind a truth around what the psychic says. Most likely, through your body language, your words and your answers to the psychic's questions, you have given her all the ammunition she needs to craft the 'truth' you want to hear. You are supplying the answers you seek. The psychic is just regurgitating them in the package you sought. The desire to believe something can override the truth for a while, but the truth always does win out, in time.

Sometimes, aside from the base price for a reading, there will be an extra charge for removing a curse (now there's a racket!) or for 'more knowledge'. It's all part of the con. As long as you supply (need) they will demand (money).

There are two ways the psychic 'knows' things about you she couldn't possibly know. Beside the above-mentioned observation and manipulation, there is a spiritual explanation. The supernatural truth is that there are spirits who have been watching you your entire life. The Bible refers to demons—fallen angels, whose aim, among other things, is to deceive mankind away from the path toward God.

There are many sources who claim they have the truth. Some of those sources mix truth with their own agenda, half-truths or lies. The only source of all truth is the Bible. This document has checked out through millennia and should be the 'go-to' source whenever anyone tells you their version of truth. You may not like what you hear from it all the time, but the Bible is designed to guide you and help you know what is best for your life. It was inspired by Someone who loves you enough to have planned you, created you, then died for you so you could live with Him forever in Heaven.

Ask yourself: has your way worked so far? More importantly: You have just handed money over to a person you don't know and who has no stake in your life, and asked her to give you answers to guide your life. Which source for truth seems more logical?

Part 1
Chapter 6

The Devolution of Courtship: Dates vs. Mates

The word *'dating'*, like almost every other word in our culture, has come to mean different things to different people. Maybe this word-relativism happened when a certain President of the United States tried to redefine the word 'is', I don't know. Word-relativism leads to moral relativism, and that's where the confusion needs to be cleared.

Up until about the early 1900s, dating meant that a man came to a woman's house, where she lived with her family, and *called* on her. Among other things, this would give the family a chance to meet the suitor and size him up. This was known as *courting*: having set times to be with the other person to get to know them in a safe environment, with the end goal of marriage. With the invention and increased use of cars and with the quickening of society in general, courtship moved away from the home and out into society. Men and women were one-on-one, leaving both parties to their own discernment and with no accountability.

The difference between courting and dating is that with courting, a man gets to know a woman with the intention of marriage. With dating, there's little promise of anything beyond the date in the way of commitment or even another date. Dating can also go on and on to the point where finding a mate can take up to twenty years.

With the trend of dating a greater number of people, your odds increase that things are not what they appear; hence the necessity for the interview.

On the other hand, courtship offers freedom and more power than a woman would think. **In a courtship:**

1- If a woman is attracted to a man, she simply goes about her business. She is friendly and is open to pursuing something with him, but that's it. She doesn't appear at places he frequents 'by chance', doesn't ask him out or call him. If he is attracted to her, he will pursue. Men need no help in this. Even the shy ones get their girl. I have seen shy men pursue and marry a woman with no help on the part of the woman. If the man is not attracted to her, she is better off. She has not manipulated circumstances that would have blown up in her face later anyway.

2- A woman isn't pawed like a bargain bin DVD at Wal-Mart. She is treated like a lady, and with value. I'll go into what this looks like further in Part III.

3- She doesn't commit herself to an indefinite amount of time spent with this man, especially alone. She knows she is a hot commodity and that there are other men who would be willing to pursue the commitment of marriage with her. She knows there must be a sacrifice on his part for him to earn the privilege of her presence with him—to be more precise, he takes her out during prime dating time (Friday and Saturday nights), not just 'hangout' time at either of their houses.

In a dating relationship (as defined presently)**:**

1- If a woman is attracted to a man, she makes her move, letting him know she likes him, calling him and otherwise chasing him. This may get him and he may stay for a while, but it will not last, given the fact that men were created to be natural pursuers. He got her easily and places no value on work he didn't do.

2- She is to be sexually intimate with a man in a short amount of time, usually after a few dates, whether there is 'exclusivity' or not. If she doesn't have sex with him, he will move on to a girl who will give him sex with no strings because he 'has needs' and one of them usually isn't marriage.

3- She can't bring up the status of the relationship or 'define' it without risking chasing off the man, so she must 'hang out' in the situation until he decides he wants to date only her. This could take years and is frustrating and stressful to her but, she reasons, at least she has someone who cares for her (even if he doesn't care enough to commit to her).

4- Having sex with her boyfriend is still no guarantee that he will stay, so she thinks she must work to keep him, which in many cases drives him away.

5- She moves in with him when he asks her to, or lets him move in with her, believing they are becoming 'serious'. This is the last nail in the coffin, in many cases, to her hope of him ever asking her to marry him. Statistics show that living together before marriage actually lowers male commitment to a spouse.[1] There is also a lower perceived value of marriage.[2]

Where is the 'girl power' in this?

The 'sexual revolution' of the sixties did little to empower women. Just the opposite: it enabled men to get free sex with no commitment, convincing women to give away all of themselves under the guise of 'having it all'.

In the next chapters we'll see how to focus on your life and what you've been given instead of what you think you lack.

Love and Other Drugs.

Here's an interesting thing about the human brain: When two people become involved sexually, the act produces a chemical named *oxytocin*, which is a natural bonding agent more powerful than the drink with the red bull on it. This was created to make it more desirable for a man and woman to stay together. This chemical is also ignited when women breastfeed their children, which is one of the reasons a child bonds to its mother. When a woman has sex with a man then separates, those

---

[1] - Rhoades, G. K., Petrella, J. N., Stanley, S. M., & Markman, H. J. 2006. *Premarital cohabitation, husbands' commitment, and wives' satisfaction with the division of household contributions.* Marriage and Family Review 40: 5–22.

[2] - Axinn, W. G. and J. S. Barber. 1997. *Living Arrangements and Family Formation Attitudes in Early Adulthood.* Journal of Marriage and the Family 59:595-611.

bonding chemicals have nothing to cling to, and it has the same effect as a drug addict who can't get a fix. A heroin or other controlled-substance withdrawal looks different, but the effect is still the same: longing, an unsettled feeling and sadness. Creating that sexual situation and breaking it up over and over again is where emotional and mental scars come from, making it more difficult to have a long and healthy marriage relationship. The more a person experiences this jolt of oxytocin and the inevitable ripping apart, as in today's disposable dating relationships, the more inoculated they become against the ability to love. They become psychologically hardened and less sensitive to feeling.

Our culture of disposable dating plays into this, given the popularity of online dating. Because people have more potential mates to choose from, they think nothing of moving through dates, sex partners, boyfriends or girlfriends when things become inconvenient or boring.

A non-Christian friend of mine tells me she has decided not to have sex anymore, because she really wants to get to know a man first and get married. This friend used to be involved in the adult entertainment industry and was very sexually active. A bad dating relationship threw her for a loop when she got pregnant. She gave the child up for adoption and then took stock of her life. She got her master's degree in education and is now a professor at a prestigious university. She is also sticking to her guns, making male friends, but getting to know them, and staying abstinent. She tells me she has more peace than she has ever had in her life.

'Relationship'

Redefinition isn't just relegated to the words 'dating' and 'courtship'. The word 'relationship' has also been redefined.

I've always thought the word 'relationship' was like 'health'. It can be good, bad, physical, mental or emotional. It is a word that needs definition because it has no qualification. When used in general, you have a relationship to everything. Your relationship to your mom is daughter or son. Your relationship to another person is as a friend. In relation to the person who hired you, you are an employee. I have a relationship to lots of people and things. I am *in* my house, *in* my car, *next to* my neighbor. If you told someone "I have a *relationship* with my dog", the present cultural meaning of 'relationship' would cause them to think you'd lost your mind, even though it is technically true: Your relationship to the dog is 'owner' (no, they are not your child, either). It is a ridiculous example, but it shows how twisted our version of truth has become, through communication. Even a doctor in the ER asks: "What is your *relationship* to the patient?" A relationship must be qualified. That's why, in this book, I call 'relationships' 'dating relationships'. The modern word for 'relationship', though, is used to describe the no man's land between singleness and marriage, is used as a new substitute for "I'm not ready for (or I don't believe in) marriage, so we'll play this out for as long as we both think it works, and as long as you don't annoy me too much."

I'm not talking about dating relationships where two people are getting to know each other with the goal of determining whether they will be married (i.e., courting). Often there is a time limit to that situation. If you've gone on for years and years and there's no ring in sight, it's time to cut bait and go to another pond. In this case, I'm referring to dating (or 'seeing' each other) for the sake of having someone indefinitely without marriage, with no promise of a future together.

'Relationships' are a state of being where a woman may be able to feel wanted and a man can assuage his loneliness or sexual desire without the complication of a commitment (the words 'committed relationship' mean the same thing as 'relationship'). If it's not marriage, it's not commitment. Being in one of these indefinite relationships puts off any chance of marriage for an indefinite time, if not forever. Both parties in the relationship are hanging in there as long as the other person satisfies them.

In marriage, both partners agree to love the other unconditionally, to forgive, and to rebuild trust when one inevitably lets the other down. They promise to work things out. They have made a commitment—legal, and in the heart, and work toward the upward motion of making the marriage successful. Both have agreed to have a stake in making it work, no matter how bad it gets.

In a 'relationship', because people can walk away with no strings (except for the inevitable bruising and scarring of heart and emotions, which are permanently changed), it teaches both people that they need to find someone who pleases them. It teaches that they can walk away if things don't work out, or if things get difficult. Because 'relationship' usually starts with physical attraction and fun (nothing wrong with that!), when the euphoria of those first weeks starts to wear off and real life drops in, one or both people make a break for it. Sometimes they will stay together until something they believe is better comes along. There is no focus on being the right person and putting in the work love requires, only in finding the right person. But with more effort put into finding, is anyone trying to *be* the right person? When that person lets us down, as we all inevitably do to each other, the hunt is on for the new ex-Miss or Mr. So and So. In a healthy marriage, when spouses let each other down, they work to fix it, thus building a stronger union. Maybe this is why arranged marriages seem to work so well. I know a few people who are in such marriages and the results are fascinating.

The notion of courtship and marriage may sound old-fashioned to some. Wheels are old-fashioned too, but they still work and they take you where you want to go.

Why Marry?

With the popularity of living together in lieu of marriage, some people ask the question: Why get married? There are more than a few reasons:

- Marriage is good for society. It creates a foundation of security, peace and productivity upon which successful societies are built. Because an involved mother and father foster higher self-esteem in a child, that child—that family, is more connected to its community; fostering a greater well-being. Commitment within a family flows into commitment to others and organizational helps that non-committal and transient relationships can't possibly do.[1]

- Married people live longer and have better mental health, are safer, and have better sex than singles.[2] If you think this isn't true, why are many singles' emphasis on finding the best sex partner instead of finding the right life partner? Why does it seem so important to

---

1 - Richard Niolon PhD
2 - 'The Case for Marriage: Why Married People Are Happier, Healthier, and Better off Financially' by Linda J. Waite and Maggie Gallagher

many people to dress 'hot' rather than to develop character? Because character doesn't sell fashion magazines.

- Unmarried cohabitations are overall less stable than marriages.[3]

- 86% of the married people who rated their marriages as unhappy but stayed together rated their marriage as improved, 5 years later.[4]

- It's not 'just a piece of paper'. Money is a piece of paper, and because of the value behind it, people die for it. A mortgage is just a piece of paper, and is even more expensive than some divorces, but people don't have a problem with that commitment. A marriage is a promise before God and man and is a legally binding document. Besides, if it was just a piece of paper, then what holds some people back from doing it? Here's the strange thing: now there is something called a 'Cohabitation Agreement' which has surfaced for couples who just want to live together...another piece of paper. Obviously, the cohabiter's problem is with more than just the 'piece of paper'.

- As far as "50% of all marriages ending in divorce", those statistics must be qualified as well. In 1980, the divorce rate was 7.9 and in 2008, was 5.2 according to the most recent government research.[5] Presently, the economy is partly responsible for increasing the divorce rate, but other factors must be considered, such as this statistic from the Centers for Disease Control: 'The probability of a first marriage ending in separation or divorce within 5 years is 20 percent, but the probability of a premarital cohabitation breaking up within 5 years is 49 percent. After 10 years, the probability of a first marriage ending is 33 percent, compared with 62 percent for cohabitations.'[6]

---

3 - Center for Disease Control: New Report Sheds Light on Trends and Patterns in Marriage, Divorce, and Cohabitation. Cohabitation, Marriage, Divorce, and Remarriage in the United States. Series Report 23, Number 22. 103pp. (Page last updated: January 13, 2010)

4 - 'The Case for Marriage: Why Married People Are Happier, Healthier, and Better off Financially' by Linda J. Waite and Maggie Gallagher

5 - per 1,000 people (aged 15-64) U.S. Census Bureau, Statistical Abstract of the United States: 2011. Table 1335. Marriage and Divorce Rates by Country: 1980 to 2008.

6 - Center for Disease Control: New Report Sheds Light on Trends and Patterns in Marriage, Divorce, and Cohabitation. Cohabitation, Marriage, Divorce, and Remarriage in the United States. Series Report 23, Number 22. 103pp. (Page last updated: January 13, 2010)

People who parrot the '50% of marriages end in divorce' phrase leave out some important considerations:

1. How many of these marriages should never have happened in the first place? Namely these people married on a whim, married because the sex was great, because they 'just clicked' (a seatbelt clicks too, but I wouldn't want to marry it), or the many other reasons people figure it's time to tie the knot.
2. How many got married knowing they would get out when things got difficult? That's a death sentence to a marriage.
3. How many married for money then left when the money did?
4. How many married before truly knowing themselves or what they wanted out of life?
5. How many got married before knowing important, decision-changing things about the person they married?
6. Green cards come in here somewhere, I'm sure.
7. How many committed adultery with someone else's spouse then married them, only to have that shaky marriage end in divorce?

I could go on, but as you see, if we balance the equation by saying: "Most marriages that probably shouldn't have happened or started on shaky ground, end in divorce," it is much more accurate.

Living Together Does Not Equal Marriage

There are more than a few guys you may date—even in the church, who think that living together is 'like marriage' or 'gets you ready for marriage'. Check this out then make your own decision:

Cohabiting couples: Do not have the same kind of commitment. They are less likely to be sexually faithful, and have more to worry about regarding sexually transmitted diseases. They are less likely to manage finances well. There is less 'teamwork' and coming together with different gifts and talents because they know the relationship could end at any time. Cohabiters tend to think more positively about divorce and less so about marriage. They don't have any stake in the outcome.

COURTING	DATING
'THE ACT, PERIOD, OR ART OF SEEKING THE LOVE OF SOMEONE WITH INTENT TO MARRY.'	'A SOCIAL APPOINTMENT, ENGAGEMENT, OR OCCASION ARRANGED BEFOREHAND WITH ANOTHER PERSON.'
• protects the woman because it is meant to include the family and other accountability who do not have an emotional stake in whether the pairing is a match. They can be objective.	• offers no protection for the woman because it is only arranged between the two participating parties. Sex is expected. Personal safety is questionable because daters are usually alone.
• has marriage as the goal. This woman knows she has friends to assuage her loneliness, and doesn't need to turn to a man or sex to do so.	• is used to try to satisfy loneliness, and can go on indefinitely because there are no promises. When a woman demands more, the man may stay and marry her, but more often than not, he wants to keep the status quo, or he simply runs.
• There is security in the relationship because both the man and woman have chosen each other and each other only.	• is built on insecurity. Both choose to be together as long as desires are met. When things get difficult or distasteful, a person moves onto the next person.
• is built on a covenantal relationship—on keeping one's promises and unconditional love, which fosters a feeling of safety.	• Serial dating prepares people for divorce because of the high 'turnover rate', especially for women. It increases anxiety and lowers self-esteem in women.
• There is trust in the marriage because there was sexual and emotional purity in the courtship. The woman knows the man wants her for her and will wait to have sex until after the vows.	• brings emotional scarring from multiple partners, comparison and distrust into a marriage, making the union more difficult. Trust is spotty because there was no self-control and there were blurred boundaries before marriage.
• is not a substitute for *not* dating. This is a great time to get to know people and live your life, doing your dreams before you meet that 'someone'. Courtship should only happen once.	• is not a cure for loneliness or for living your life and accomplishing the things you want to do.

Married couples: Are more likely to monitor each others' health, speak up about dangerous behaviors (smoking, drinking) and prepare healthy meals—in short, to look out for the other's welfare.[7,8]

In short, marriage is legally binding, and so people have more of a stake in watching out for their spouse's health, the couple's finances and have more clearly defined roles in general, which alleviates power struggle and provides for a healthier environment.

The term 'gender roles' may set many people's teeth on edge, especially those who think this definition infringes on their 'freedom' of some sort. If your goal is the culture's definition of 'freedom' (which can be translated 'license'), you can achieve that. Just don't think you can do so and live the life of a happily satisfied married woman. Sure, marriages have problems, but marriages are made of people.

Marriage is one large sailboat in the water powered by two people and God. Cohabitation is two rowboats, each powered by its owner, lashed together by a rope. Cohabitors put all their freedom and energy into rowing until storms and repeated buffeting of the wind tears them asunder.

You are not a Buick

One of the most annoying and obtuse statements I have heard from Frogs is: 'You test drive a car before you buy it, don't you? You've got to try before you buy.' Translation: "I want to have sex with you and I don't plan on sticking around afterward." It is an ignorant parroting of something someone somewhere probably tossed off at a party. Now an unknown number of men repeat it and repeat it, revealing their shallow character and even lower mental acuity.

If a guy tells you this, he has shown you his I.Q, which is usually lower than the gas mileage of the car to which he is referring. There are several reasons why this wrong statement lets you know you're dealing with a particularly slow Frog:

---

7 - 'The Case for Marriage: Why Married People Are Happier, Healthier, and Better off Financially' by Linda J. Waite and Maggie Gallagher

8 - 'Why married couples live longer and do better than singles' by Trudy S. Moore, http://findarticles.com

1. **You're not a Buick**. A guy who can't tell a woman from a car has worse problems than you probably want to know about.

2. **'Test driving' is NO guarantee that he'll marry you.** In fact, it severely lowers the chances he will marry you. Those chances exponentially decrease, the sooner you do have sex with him. How many cars have you gone through before you finally found 'the one' that made you want to sign your income away to be with it?

3. **Even car dealers don't let you keep 'test driving' the same car.** The 'test drive' excuse for a one-night stand just means he's inflamed with lust and knows he has an easy out. He wants to try you out for an unspecified amount of time, with no commitment. Either way, to him, you're easy and he can get out easily.

4. **Realtors never let you 'test drive' a house.** You sign the contract, or keep moving. It's why squatters stay and trash a house until they're forced to move on by cops, or grow bored and move on their own. Free stuff is never respected. Don't be squatter bait.

5. **He's really 'test driving' your body, not caring anything about who you are.** This is the epitome of selfishness. It's like the way some people are with rental cars. Someone I know will drive over a curb, shrug, and say: 'It's a rental'. He would never do that to the car he had bought with his own money and payments. Like anyone who disrespects a rental car, he will disrespect you, too.

I know my car's sounds and movements very well because I've been with it for years. When two people truly love each other and marry, maybe sex is great the first time, maybe not. But when you commit to a life together, you explore, which increases intimacy. There's no chance of sex getting better and better if a guy hops around from woman to woman. In fact, it trains a guy to hop around and actually decreases his sexual interest and even his erection. Now, he knows what many, many women like, but has to get to know another body (yours) all over again.

The only way you can do sex 'badly' or be 'bad in bed' (and not in the adventurous way) is to be selfish. Two people who love each other will give extra attention to, be sensitive to, and do things for their partner to please them. It is an experience which grows, evolves and builds intimacy as the years go on, which is what God intended.

Friends with benefits

I almost laughed out loud when I first heard this term because both 'friends' and 'benefits' are misleading—in a huge way. I couldn't imagine women would fall for this. But sadly, many do. I was even offered this stellar deal not long ago from a man I knew: the chance to be used as just a body, with no commitment and no respect from him while he went on to do whatever he wanted with whomever he wanted, and until he found someone apparently worthy of a dating relationship with him. I think I probably should have been more gentle in my refusal. I guess I was just annoyed that he had exact racial, bust and height requirements for a mate, none of which I matched, yet wanted to rent me just for 'benefits'.

Any man who wants the 'rental' plan of your body is neither a friend, nor out to benefit you. This set-up will not lead to marriage or even a serious dating relationship, despite what the movies say. No woman has so much sexual prowess that a man will fall to his knees with an engagement ring after she has given him his 'benefits'. If anything, this arrangement causes him to disrespect her. As mentioned before, we can't help but bond during sex as humans. When the inevitable tearing apart happens—when the man grows tired of using you for sex or finds someone else, it is the woman who is wounded emotionally, not the man. He receives his own wounds, but not ones which would cause him to want to stay with you.

Of course there may be exceptions to this rule, like there are exceptions to the lottery. Maybe a male friend will stay for more than benefits. But do you really want to spend all your dollars—and years — on a number that never hits?

A man who wants this arrangement from you is not a friend, but a Frog in every sense of the word. He has no regard for you, for sex or for marriage. A Prince will guard your feelings and will be a true friend, putting up the boundaries he needs to, being honest with you, and exercising self-control.

The next time a male 'friend' hops up to you with this request, ask him first if you can have his credit cards and car and just 'take them for a test drive' for as long as you like. See if he doesn't value his material possessions more highly than you. Then be sure to leave.

Eight reasons NOT to get married

1. **Your best girlfriend just got married.** I know it's difficult when you see that ring on her finger or buy that bridesmaid dress, not to feel the desire to be married yourself. Sheila's best friend Toni, not wanting to be left alone, when she knew Sheila was getting married, wed a man she hadn't known for very long. Sheila had advised against it after her lawyer husband found some questionable things about the guy on a background search. Toni severed her friendship with Sheila—and then disappeared with the guy. Not everyone who marries on a whim will disappear with a criminal, but it usually doesn't end well. Marry because you have peace that this is what you should do, you have received Godly counsel and because you have checked your own heart on why you are doing it.

2. **You want money or a 'secure' life.** We all want that. When you trust God, no matter what your circumstances look like, He is always there for you and will always provide for you. *'Once I was young, and now I am old. Yet I have never seen the godly abandoned or their children begging for bread.' – Psalm 37:25.*
One woman I know married for money—a lot of money. The man left his first wife and married her. This new wife's husband was laid off a few years into their marriage and has let himself go physically due to depression. Now she must work and live with a husband she never loved. If you want money, make it yourself, but never let your trust be in that money.

3. **He pays you a lot of attention and showers you with gifts.** He may, but what is his character? What are his motives? This whole book is about giving you the wisdom to see the difference between good character and a good line.

4. **This guy seems nice, and I may never find anyone else to marry.** That is settling, and you will regret it. You don't know the future. In a few years, after you marry this guy, you may be longing to be single again.

5. **Getting married will get me out of _____.** Fill in the blank: 'my home situation', 'loneliness', 'debt', whatever state you're in, some situations are better left alone than to be cured with marriage. Again, wait. Situations and circumstances always change. God may be trying to teach you something or do something in your life in these less than savory situations. Marriage is not the cure.

6. **He's hot!** Bad news: 'hot' fades. I don't even like the term 'hot'. It was associated first with porn. When I first heard it applied to regular people, I was a little uncomfortable. Now, it's commonplace to reduce someone to this physical term. Even I have used it. But, 'hot' being what it is, consider this: when physical 'hotness' fades, the character of a Prince and his ability to truly love you stays hot. A Prince's sacrifices for you are hot, and these will continue into old age. Hair plugs and new twentysomething girlfriends when a Frog is sixty are not hot.

7. **My/his/our families want us to get married.** I know the old saying about marrying his family when you marry him, but no, you don't. You marry the man. You go through things with the man, and you have to deal with the character, personality and actions of the man. Family is curiously absent at these times, unless it is to give advice. *'This explains why a man leaves his father and mother and is joined to his wife, and the two are united into one.'* – *Genesis 2:24.*

8. **You're bored.** Go find something to do. Make sure it has nothing to do with a veil or an aisle.

"YOU LOOK A LITTLE DIFFERENT FROM YOUR PROFILE PICTURE."

Part 1
Chapter 7

The Date (a.k.a. 'The Interview')

So how can you tell if a man's motives toward you are in your best interest? You have to go on the interview…I mean, the date.

Patti's story isn't as dramatic as some, but shows how you can let the Frog do all the talking and barely do any yourself:

"I went on a date with one particular guy, against my better judgment. This isn't a dramatic, serial-killer Poison Frog story, so don't get excited. It's a Bull Frog story. I don't exactly know why I had misgivings about the date—I met him at church. A friend knew him and said he was nice. I had just gotten dumped, and when I saw this guy (we'll call him Derek) notice me, I braced myself for the inevitable 'asking out'. He started talking to me, told me he wanted to take me out sometime, and asked for my number. I really wasn't interested in dating anyone at that particular time; my heart hurt from the current breakup. Always having my 'business' hat on, I gave him my card, stating the clear intention that I needed some 'down time' and didn't want to date anyone right then.

So he did the opposite of what I said: he asked me out for that afternoon. I reiterated: 'No, I'm really not ready'. I wished I hadn't given him the business card. In truth, I liked spending Sundays alone at a bookstore or out somewhere else and really needed that time this Sunday. In fact, despite my broken heart, I was looking forward to time alone.

When I was at the bookstore two hours later, he called me and kept me on the phone for a long time, despite my polite attempts at hanging up. He asked me to come over that night for dinner. Now the red flags are waving and I am mentally burning the business card I gave him. But, because of my unwarranted misgivings, I couldn't just hang up on him. After all, I thought, I'm supposed to be a Christian. Besides, it would be weird seeing him at church after that. So after the phone call finally ended, I saw him call again, and let it go to voicemail. You would think the story would have ended there, but no. The next week, he insisted we go to a diner for coffee. He had told me about a leg problem he had, and said he couldn't be there long. I reviewed my past dates with Frogs and other guys and figured I should give the guy a chance. He wasn't my type, but I thought I should keep an open mind. But I did put my 'listening' hat on. The guy spoke so fast and so much, I didn't even have to ask any questions ...not that I had the opportunity to. He continued to complain about his leg and said he needed to go home. He suggested I follow him there, and insisted I would be safe.

I didn't get that kind of bad feeling about him; just an annoying feeling. I told him no and said I needed to go do some things. I felt bad. Again I reminded myself that I should 'give him a chance', and I went. It was the first of my personal rules broken: no going to guys' houses alone with them. I'm not even sure why I did it. Maybe I needed to play this out and make sure this wasn't the guy God had for me, this little squirty, Joe Pesci, South Philly type. Derek hadn't given me any sense that he was weird or perverted, so we walked around the apartment complex where he lived, with his dog, and I don't think he took a breath once, he talked so much. I remember thinking, 'Now I know how guys feel when a girl goes on and on and won't shut up.' We visited his neighbors and all in all it was a pleasant afternoon. His parents stopped over as they did on Sundays, and that's when I got a little pearl of information.

All this time he had been talking about his daughter and his ex-wife. He brought up his leg, and his mother said, 'Well, now you've got something else to complain about.'

Yes. He was a complainer. I didn't think much about that. After all, none of us is perfect, and I've done my share of complaining too.

I left when his parents did, again, not really getting any 'danger' red flags, but just feeling like I wanted to be somewhere else. That was my answer: this guy wasn't for me. No harm, no foul.

Weeks later, after we'd somewhat lost touch (to my relief), someone who was friends with Derek was speaking with me. I mentioned how we'd gotten together once (thanks to his insufferable prodding and convincing), and she told me that he had been talking about me. "Oh, really?" I said, expecting to hear something nice. If anyone had a problem with me, they usually came directly to me. "Yes," she said. "He said you were chasing him and wouldn't leave him alone and that he didn't know if he was that interested in you." But that wasn't all. "He said you deserved what that guy who broke your heart did to you, when you were crying the first time he met you."

Really?

To say I was angry was an understatement. But the evidence had been there: incessant talking, complaining about his leg and his ex-wife. The guy was of low character. Even his own mother had revealed some of his nature. I hadn't needed to interview this guy, only to listen. I should have ignored him at the outset. But that's how I learned to leave when I'm sensing any lack of peace."

What did she learn?

1. Do not give out sensitive information about yourself too soon, if at all. He didn't need to know why Patti was crying. Say nothing. Transparency is for later, when trust has been established.

2. If you get a bad gut feeling for no reason, pay attention to that, too. A guy doesn't have to have bodies in his basement or a homicidal gleam in his eye to give you a reason not to go out with him. If you don't want to date him, don't do it. There's always a reason not to.

3. Don't break your rules or cross your boundaries. They are there for a reason. If a guy tries to push past them, leave.

4. You can still be polite and take charge of the conversation. End it when you want to end it. Never be led by anyone into anything you don't want to do.

5. People will tell you everything you want to know, if you just listen.

Sometimes, you barely need to ask any questions—the truth is there in front of you. But sometimes questions are in order. There is a difference between an interview and an interrogation. You are aiming for an interview: a non-accusatory information gathering conversation which is structured but flexible and has a time limit. Your date shouldn't feel like you are gathering information, but that you are conversing.

> *'So then, my beloved brethren, let every man be swift to hear, slow to speak, slow to wrath.'*
> *– James 1:19*

An interrogation is a list of questions. You have evidence that someone did something and guilt is reasonably certain. The result is usually the guy running away from you like you sprayed him with Raid.

This interview—this date—is nowhere near 'guilty until proven innocent', but can be classified as *fact-finding*, like anyone else would do in order to get to know someone. Have fun! Expect to just meet a nice person and, above all, do not project onto your date your dreamy imaginings such as his eternal, undying love for you while the two of you sail on his yacht. Keep your mind clear of your own storytelling and self-deceptive tendencies so you can see things as they actually are, not like Hollywood would make them.

Your Preparation

You may not have little bluebirds wrapping you in swaths of silk like Cinderella did before the ball, but you will want to be ready for your date. Preparation, however, starts long before you choose the dress you're going to wear. Your preparation begins with your heart. Here are a few things to consider:

Your Spirit

1. **Fueling up** - Each morning, instead of flipping on the t.v. to hear what the talking heads are yammering about, find a peaceful place and spend some quiet time reading the Bible. Start with the Psalms and go slowly. If you ask God to reveal himself and his will for your life, he will. This time also empowers you for your day—including your future date. This meditating on the scriptures isn't just for your date, though. It is a lifestyle choice, just like eating right and exercising. You wouldn't expect to run a marathon after having only one day of good diet and exercise. Why would you try to do your whole life without the counsel every day of the One who knows everything?

2. **Prayer** - God is waiting to hear from you. I still can't imagine that—the Creator of the universe wanting to hear from little me—but it's true. Prayer soothes you, unloads burdens from your heart and opens up your heart to hear what he has to say. Believe me when I say there's nothing like the peace you feel when you are speaking and listening to him.

Your Body

1. **Food** - Just like your spirit needs to eat, your body needs fuel, not just food. You've probably read it in many other books and know the answer for Date Day (and again, this should be a lifestyle): stick to energy foods; vegetables, protein. Stay away from heavy meals or foods that will make you gassy like pasta or bread or anything stinky. (Red onions have a half-life of, like, three years on your breath.) If you do end up with a Prince, you'll want to save your gastrointestinal secrets for after marriage...not for the first date! (I know; women don't 'do that'. I'm just sayin'...in case we did.)

2. **Exercise** - Physical activity makes you glow inside and out, and gives you energy. Again, this is something which should be a lifestyle thing, not a 'day-of' activity, but even if you haven't worked out in a while, take a walk after your Bible time to mull

over what you read and what you think God is saying. It is an amazing boost to your mood and heart! It will relieve stress and nerves, too.

3. **Rest** - A lifestyle of rest at the right times will help you stay young-looking. It is why God called one day out of the week to be a day of rest. Rest helps keep weight off (no lie!), and gives you energy for work, the gym and social events...like your date. Rest is just as important as work. I must admit, this is an area where I am hypocritical. I am writing about it, urging you to rest, but I constantly find myself on my computer, or doing art. The result: imbalance. I have gotten better with this, but sometimes I fail. What does this have to do with your date? It is the same as keeping your body and mind in a healthy lifestyle: you will be ready for your date, sensitive to deception indicators, and most importantly, you will be a peaceful, glowing you, which is very attractive. If your date is after work, try to have some kind of down time so you can rejuvenate and clear your mind beforehand.

Your Mind

1. **Influences** - I had a friend whose beliefs were diametrically opposed to mine. The fact that he referred to himself as Satan should have been a clue. I knew that when he called, even if I chose not to get drawn into his verbal sparring, there would be an argument. At the very least, I would hang up feeling like I had a caffeinated sea urchin in my stomach. If you have a 'friend' like that, hopefully you've distanced yourself long before today. If you haven't, don't take the call. The last thing you need is to have a scowl on your face tonight, or worse, relate the story of the inevitable phone battle to your date.

2. **Intake** - The day of your date, don't pop in a romance DVD. As innocent as it may be, it only sets you up to have stars in your eyes and expectations this dude isn't prepared to meet—and why should he be? It's your first date! Instead, opt for positive music or reading, or get some coffee with a friend.

Good health—spiritual and physical—should be a lifestyle. Much like muscle memory in dance or karate, your radar will have been exercised and practiced, so none of this will come as a surprise to you.

A Prince will have made the same preparations as you have in his life. While a man may not have the same walls up that women do, he will be measuring you just as you are measuring him, that is, if he is a Prince. If he is a Frog, he's been busy doing other things and, instead of sizing you up to see if you could live in his palace, he is watching you like a predator to see if you can warm his lily pad for a little while.

Another preparation you have made is talking to some of your friends ahead of time, who will be praying for you. Prayer is a powerful tool. Every time I have asked God to take someone out of my life if they weren't supposed to be there, He has. I was talking to a man on the phone for a few weeks who I had met as a result of work I did. He spoke to me as if he wanted to get to know me better. I prayed that if this man was not my husband, for God to take him out of my life' Exactly 20 minutes later, his fiancée called to ask why my number kept coming up as dialed from his phone! He hadn't told me he was engaged, yet wanted me to fly out to meet him in another state! Needless to say, I ended it right there. The woman and I did have a long, interesting talk. Apparently this had happened between them before.

Boundaries are another important preparation. Know what you will and won't do, where you will and won't go, before you go out. We'll mention this more later, but getting these boundaries set for yourself beforehand and promising yourself to keep them will help keep your safety and self-respect intact.

If we let God into our relationships and every aspect of our lives, He will protect us.

'No temptation has overtaken you except such as is common to man; but God is faithful, who will not allow you to be tempted beyond what you are able, but with the temptation will also make the way of escape, that you may be able to bear it.' – 1 Corinthians 10:13

The 'Interview'

Knowing who you are dating starts with changing your perception of what a date is. Many of us women think the first date is the beginning of the rest of our 'happily ever after', and it could be, but don't start picturing how your kids will look or trying on his last name for size over the bruschetta. This first date is a fact-finding mission—a fun one. Your job, Investigator Princess, is to find out who this man is. It is no more than anyone would do if they were, say, looking for a candidate for employment or a babysitter. In those cases, interviewers go much deeper with their investigation. Will you know his true life story over a few hours? No. Neither does an employment interviewer, and neither do cops who are interviewing witnesses or suspects. But you will know enough to pass him to the 'second interview'—or not.

So how do you find out who he is?

Well, one date is not going to give you a total biography. Even some of the more practiced sociopaths can give you the personal history you want to hear. The key to knowing whether you should have a second date is not difficult and takes virtually no work on your part, which is good, because this is supposed to be fun. There are three things involved:

1) asking questions

2) listening to the answers

3) listening to your intuition

Your Demeanor

Your behavior and demeanor have a direct affect on the behavior of the person to whom you are asking questions. When you walk into that nice restaurant, guns blazing, looking like you already know he's a Frog and want to brand him as such, he might be a little defensive. When you appear non-confrontational and politely reserved, your date will be more comfortable in opening up to you. When you sit too close, he may take a defensive posture: arms crossed and leaning back…or he may take it as an invitation. Someone's *intimate zone* is about 0-1.5 feet of distance between him and you. His *personal zone* is about 1.5 to 4 feet. His *social zone* is about 4-12 feet.

Many investigators, especially those who question child predators, find themselves more successful when they take a humble, friendly and submissive posture. Does this mean you should be someone you're not? Not at all. Just be nice. Be disarming. By exhibiting these qualities, you are putting your date at ease and he will be more apt to trust and confide in you. But, you may ask, isn't that manipulative? Not at all. You are nice to most of the people you meet, right? In this instance, you are simply watching more closely the resulting words and actions on his part after you are nice to him. You are training yourself to listen and observe. You are putting him at ease—which is something we should all do for people anyway—in a timely effort to get to know the real person inside, and to make them feel accepted and encouraged in who they are.

Asking questions

Baseline questions

It is important when interviewing your subject (making conversation on your date) to get a baseline from your guy. A baseline, in this case, is your observation of how he *usually* sits, *usually* speaks and how his hands and body *usually* move. Now, you may need more than one date to get an idea of your date's mannerisms, but you should be able to watch him long enough on that first date that when you ask your target questions to see his reactions, they will be different enough that you will see them. You will get better at this.

The other purpose of baseline questions is to relax your date. When he is relaxed, conversation—and evidence—flows. Try to keep your questions 'essay' ones; i.e., questions that warrant more than a 'yes' or 'no'. Here are some examples of baseline questions:

1. Tell me about your day. (A good icebreaker.)
2. What good movies have you seen (t.v. shows, concerts, games, good books have you read)?
3. Tell me about where you grew up.
4. What is your family like?
5. What do you like to do in your spare time?

Other questions can have 'yes' 'no' or other one-word answers, but plan to follow up on them to get more detail. For instance, "Do you like your job?" Him: "Yes". You: "What do you like best about it?"

Asking questions like these not only gives you a baseline of your date's mannerisms and speech patterns, but opens up great conversation and allows you to start to get to know him. If you take time to focus on him and listen, you will hear his take on certain issues, see his capacity for kindness and other qualities, and will be open to seeing his good character...or red flags.

Target questions

Asking these questions can be like pulling a cat's tail. Watching his reaction to the questions will give you more insight into his righteousness, or his covert agenda. Remember, you're not looking for a direct answer. You may not even get an answer. Remember the *redirect*? Very good manipulators can edge you away from your question without answering it, leaving you to wonder how in the world you got distracted enough to forget what you asked. But most people will react to a question that could reveal their true intentions with revealing expressions of their own.

1. "Are you in a relationship right now?"

At this point, you should be prepared for his reaction. Part of the 'baseline' observation you've made is about his body language. There are certain places your arms, legs, hands and feet rest naturally. This is someone's natural positioning. It may be the way he sits or stands all the time, or how he sits or stands on your date. The key is to watch what happens after you ask the question. If he is sitting in his chair, both feet on the floor, leaning back on his chair to the left with his hands pretty much on the table most of the time (except for normal 'expressive' hand gestures), what happens after the question? Does he shift to the right side? Cross his legs? Put one hand up to cover his lips? Again, this is not a 'hands down' (pardon the pun) indication that he is lying, but it is an orange light which says 'Keep probing; he is obviously uncomfortable'.

He may throw in a pause after the question to buy himself time. He may also repeat the question, for the same reason. This question demands a simple answer.

Believe it or not, some guys think it's perfectly okay to be taking you out while they have a girlfriend—or wife—somewhere else. You may feel stupid asking this, but not as stupid as you will when you find out you aren't the only one in the relationship with him. Remember; don't expect a straight answer. The reaction is what you're looking for. Do you get the 'flashbulb eyes' or that millisecond of shock shown on his face? Make a note and seal it away in your memory.

2. "Have you ever been involved with a married woman?"

This question may be better for a second date, but should not be something you just ask out of the blue. It is a shocking question, and should have some indicators leading up to it, like references he makes to cheating, talking about sympathy for one of his friends who cheated on a girlfriend. If you're having a nice time with an apparently nice guy, this question will make you look suspicious and like you have baggage. We all have baggage, but we don't want to bring it on this trip!

Adultery, is not an 'affair'. An affair is a party, a business transaction, and sometimes a ridiculous dress. Adultery is a disaster waiting to happen. Strangely, some people think of adultery in varying degrees of badness. Some guys don't think twice about it. These are our Frogs. But they know you won't go for it. Enter the lie.

An innocent man will simply answer 'no' with no physical indications of deception. If you do happen to get a 'yes', don't be shocked. You want information so you can make an informed choice. When police interview a suspect, they remain deadpan; that is, having no expression, or no change to their expression. Your expression can be one of neutral openness, not expressing any kind of judgment. When he sees he can speak freely, he will give you more information. I can't tell you how many people still open up to me and then say, 'I don't even know why I told you that...I feel like I can talk to you.'

If the adultery was a one-time thing and was a while ago (I'm talking years), you must decide if the man's character is now such that it would not happen again. Was it before he gave his life to Christ? Was it a years-long relationship with the wife of someone close to the man? Was he married and did this to his wife? If either of these last two cases, *run*. Don't even wait a second. Get out. This is a man with no regard for right and wrong, or for others' feelings or well-being. There is no future with a man who lives in this kind of situation for any length of time. Marriage is difficult enough without you wondering if he will do the same thing to you.

He should not give any excuses or cast blame on his wife, the other woman or on anyone other than himself. Refusing responsibility shows he thinks that on some level cheating is ok. On the other hand, does the man say, no, he was never involved in an adulterous relationship, and yet he reacts with 'flashbulb' eyes, or grows annoyed at the question? Does his body position change? What if he accuses you of judging or overreacts to the question? Yellow light. Proceed with caution. You want to pinpoint, either at the time or later, why he had this reaction.

Any of us can be susceptible to letting our own desires bind us and lead us into sin. The question is what do we do with it? What did he do with it? Does he believe what he did was wrong? Did he repent (to turn around and walk in the other direction) of it? Does he blame the other party involved with him? Or has he wholeheartedly accepted responsibility and God's forgiveness and now lives to serve God and others, considering others better than himself? Has considerable time passed since the event? Has he taken time to heal, grow in God's word and be alone until he knew he was ready to be a good husband (i.e., selflessly love a woman)? Does he protect the hearts of the women around him by not leading them on, not playing games and not spending inordinate amounts of time alone with them just to 'hang out', or is he on the hunt for the next female?

3. "Have you ever hit a woman?"

The answer to this will most likely always be 'no'. But that's not the end of your inquiry. It just establishes him as an abuser, if he shows signs of being a liar. If you're unsure of him, look for signs in your next date with him, of physical abuse or control: 'play' fighting, wrestling, talking about 'dominating' or 'destroying' someone, or other violent (not necessarily profane) talk, and, believe it or not, tickling. You will get a feeling of apprehension or fear around an abuser. Don't mistake it for excitement or 'butterflies'. Leave when you feel it, and don't try to give him the benefit of the doubt. You don't owe him anything.

4. Quality questions

These are open-ended questions that will allow you to actually get to know him more in two ways: First, like any conversation, if you ask him about, say, his mom, he will tell you about his mom and you will know more about his mom. Second, you will have more information to compare against other information he gives you. But you're not just getting information; you are watching and listening to how he talks about his mom. Does his face take on a warm look with smiling eyes when you bring her up? Does he tell you he never knew her or (red flag) that he jokingly hopes she meets with a tragic end? Remember, even jokes are to be taken seriously. Probe a little if you're curious about that last one, but do it in a lighthearted way (if the present tone is lighthearted).

Just as damaging as a madman shooting a deadly weapon is someone who lies to a friend and then says, "I was only joking.' – Proverbs 26:18-19

The second part of getting to know him is gathering information, making sure it all fits together and looking at the information itself to use in your discernment. Have his parents been divorced? Are they still together? Divorced parents are not a red flag, but again, you are gathering an entire picture. Each part has its place. Has he been married multiple times? Was he ever institutionalized? You don't have to ask some of the more sensitive ones outright. I have known men who have offered shocking facts up to me, and we weren't even on that subject. I say it again: People will tell you all you need to know, if you'll just listen.

One police major I knew told me about a cadet candidate he'd put on the polygraph machine. The major asked the baseline questions, then he went through the battery of test questions. He asked one in particular:

"Have you ever killed anyone?" The man's answer: "No." But the needle jiggled. The Major looked up. The guy looked thoughtful. "You mean in this country, right?" The major remained silent, letting the man sentence himself. "Because in Canada, I killed my girlfriend." The major did get his man that day—as a guest in the corrections system.

Ask about politics and religion—not in so many words. The person who invented the concept of 'not discussing politics or religion' was probably talking about interacting in light social situations. For determining who will be your future spouse, these are pretty important. Your questions may sound more like this: "So do you have a motto or saying you live by?" or "what do you think of (certain current event)?" That second question always leads to both political and spiritual or 'religious' discussion. He may go off on a certain issue or political party. Listen to the passion he uses when he speaks—or the lack of passion. It won't be very long before you know where he stands...and if you could stand with him on those things. (Side note: you may think it's crazy to ask this in a church setting or of a Christian man, but many people in church do not share the same beliefs. Some don't even believe in God. Anyone can walk into a church. Make sure you are on the same page first. Ask God to guide you. 100% of the time, He will.)

Ask about the future. You don't have to throw the "Where do you see yourself in five years?" out there, but asking him what kinds of dreams he has for the future and what he's doing to get there can yield interesting results. If you get an "I dunno," and he has no goals, that's ok—if you are in the same place. But if you hear your date say he has dreams of living in India indefinitely as a missionary while you plan on being in the States for the next few fashion seasons so you don't miss Fashion Week in New York City, you may want to reconsider your future with this man.

Listen

Being quiet is another tactic which tends to let your date reveal more information. In one of my FBI Academy classes, each of us was paired up with a classmate (the 'witness') who was shown a photograph of a suspect for 60 seconds. The other classmate (the 'interviewer') was told to get a description of the man in the photo from the witness. During the interview, we interviewers were encouraged to stay silent for as long as possible, asking few questions and not interrupting. Because of the natural inclination of people to want to fill uncomfortable and empty airspace, the witness classmates kept talking when there was quiet,

"ME ME ME ME ME ME ME ME ME ME ME ME!"

even though they knew the drill. On a date, you don't want to leave an uncomfortable silence because that may backfire into the guy thinking you are strange. Pregnant pauses, however, and not interrupting when he is speaking will cause your date to open up more to you, not to mention making him feel honored that you want to know so much about him and are a great listener!

The *Linguistics* section goes into more detail about what to listen for. Listening is your most powerful ally and works in tandem with the last point:

Listen to your gut

Otherwise known as your intuition or discernment, this is your 'knower'. For Christians, we have the Holy Spirit to tell us when something is not right. I don't know if it's the same for everyone, but for me, I get a sharp physical warning in my gut when I need to flee. God endowed all people with a survival instinct which is made up of things we have seen and heard in a certain situation that we might not be able to put a finger on at the moment, but which come to us in the form of an 'interior warning'. We do retain everything we see and hear, we just have a problem consciously recalling it sometimes. I believe God uses this to warn us when something isn't right.

Asking yourself questions

There are some questions you can ask yourself about a man who has already shown you red flags, which may get your mind to kick in when you may have let your heart go unguarded. At the first red flag, you should have run. But maybe some clarity will help. Any of these questions to yourself is good reason to withdraw from this man:

- 'Why do I feel like I'm crazy or less of a person around him?'
- 'Am I really as bad a person as he says/makes me feel?'
- 'Why do we always seem to get into arguments? I never argue this much with anyone!'
- 'Why do I feel like I'm walking on eggshells around him?'
- 'Why does everyone seem to be against him?'
- 'Why do I feel angry around him?'
- 'Why do I feel like I'm giving him more than he gives me?'
- 'Why does he call me 10-20 times a day?'
- 'Why do I feel guilty when I can't do something he asks me to do?'
- 'Why do I feel an uneasy clench in my gut when he calls or when I'm around him?'

One question you can ask yourself is: 'Who does he hang out with?' There is a saying: "Tell me who you hang out with, and I'll tell you what you are." Now be careful with this question, not to judge by appearances. If your potential mate is hanging out with bikers, are they really bad guys? Or are they Christian motorcyclists who feed the poor and do Toy Runs for kids? Does he hang out with guys in suits? Don't just assume they're respectable because of how they are dressed. What are their actions? What comes out of their mouths?

Sometimes the man will let things slip about his friends; things that bug him about them, or things they do. Listen. Are the things he mentions about them irritating him because his friends do moral things that make this man's own actions look bad? Or are his friends involved in less than exemplary activities? If so, why does he hang out with them? If at all possible, given any opportunities, try to watch how he is around them. Does he change significantly? Is he nervous with you and them in the room together? If so, there may be more than meets the eye, and more of a reason to investigate further.

Alibis can come easily to a liar. The trick here is to look for inconsistencies. An honest man will tell you exactly where he was last night. As we just learned, the guilty will also tell you without missing a beat where they were but will lack detail. If you dig further in a friendly way and meet with resistance of any kind, file that fact away. Some Frogs will even offer up an alibi before you ask-—a preemptive strike of sorts, so you won't get suspicious.

Whatever technique he uses, ask yourself questions—especially if something doesn't feel right. If necessary, write it down or journal it; you may be surprised at what you read when you go back on it even a short time later or down the road. When other events have happened or words have been said, and your memory has fuzzed a little, you may see that those black and white words you wrote are giving you clues about what's really going on.

Clues That Demand More Investigation

The following traits and actions may seem trivial or even paranoid to point out. Often times, though, smaller tells are exactly what you need to see that either growth needs to take place in the man, or that there is a bigger problem—one that you should have a part in solving. You may recognize some of these from our earlier Frog Lineup:

1. He treats servers and wait staff as 'below' him, while still treating you well.

'For there is no partiality with God.' – Romans 2:11

2. He makes more than a few comments about cars, clothes, the cost of houses, cars, watches, etc.

'A man with an evil eye hastens after riches, And does not consider that poverty will come upon him.' – Proverbs 28:22

3. He insults you, but passes it off as humor, saying something like: "It's a good thing you're so pretty; you're not much of a mathematician."

'Like a madman who throws firebrands, arrows, and death, is the man who deceives his neighbor, And says, "I was only joking!"'
– Proverbs 26:19

4. He comes clean about a lie he told you. There was a man who told my friend he was divorced, with two kids. The truth he told her the next day was that he was separated from his fourth wife and had four kids; one from each marriage. The fact is he showed he had no problem with lying, even for a day.

'A lying tongue hates those it hurts, and a flattering mouth works ruin.'
– Proverbs 26:28

5. He puts others down, especially men who may be stronger or more attractive than he is. He is competitive with other men, either in their presence or behind their backs. This shows insecurity, which means that in your relationship he will sell you out for the price of being recognized, admired or even being attractive to another woman.

'We do not dare to classify or compare ourselves with some who commend themselves. When they measure themselves by themselves and compare themselves with themselves, they are not wise.' – 2 Corinthians 10:12

6. He talks about 'crushing' or 'destroying' people, and likes to flex his muscles in front of you. No kidding. There are guys who do this. This guy is an abuser.

'A fool gives full vent to his anger, but a wise man keeps himself under control' – Proverbs 29:11

7. He talks against certain things repeatedly, such as using steroids or how he hates when women 'come on' to him. You might not be able to see this on a first date, but the frequency of his protestations should tell you he is probably indulging in that very thing.

'It's no good, it's no good!" says the buyer; then off he goes and boasts about his purchase.' – Proverbs 20:14

8. He's got big dreams, but what has he done about them? Does he talk about being a screenwriter, but hasn't written anything? Owning his own restaurant but has never been to culinary school?

'The one who works his land will have plenty of food, but whoever chases fantasies lacks sense.' – Proverbs 12:11

9. He has dreams, and looks like he is working toward them, but can only do them 'when he gets the money'. He may not include you in this request right away, but beware. This could be the earmark of a con. He won't directly ask you, but may make his dreams so appealing or talk so big that you're drawn into his web.

'Dishonest money dwindles away, but he who gathers money little by little makes it grow.' – Proverbs 13:11

10. He wants to make sure you 'trust' him, so, a short time into your relationship, he offers you his bank account information. Later, be prepared to be asked for your bank account info by him, 'just to show you trust him'.

Patience is the weapon...

It may seem like the date went well, and this man is in the running for the office of Prince in your life. That's good! But that's where you need to maintain your spiritual vigilance and continue to observe. Observation is not as difficult as you may think, and it is essential, coupled with prayer, to be able to see and hear the things you need to in order to avoid deception. Some people may think all of this 'observation' and 'detecting' is paranoid, but, unless you live in a bubble you will, at some point in your life, encounter deception. It may be by a business partner, a boyfriend, a date, a friend, coworker or any number of other people who, had you been observing, asking the right questions and listening, you would have marked as dangerous to you. Don't push your own agenda of being married or 'getting' a man. Be patient. As someone once said: "Patience is the weapon that forces deception to reveal itself."

A word about 'judging'.

Many people misinterpret the word 'judge':

"Judge[2919] not, that you be not judged[2919]. For with what judgment[2917] you judge[2919], you will be judged[2919]; and with the measure you use, it will be measured back to you." — Matthew 7:1-2

The numbers in the scripture above are from the *Strong's Concordance*; a reference book which defines each word in the Bible in its original Hebrew (Old Testament) or Greek (New Testament) translation. Because these languages—especially Hebrew, are so much more rich and definitive in meaning, we get a more detailed and extensive meaning of a word. Notice the difference with 'judgment'. When people make the blanket statement not to 'judge' people, they usually mean not to 'condemn', and they are correct. But with this statement some people even condemn healthy discernment which could save you heartache. There are two Greek words in this paragraph with the root 'judge':

- 2917. 'krima': 'Condemnation of the wrong, the decision which one passes on the faults of others; the sentence of a judge, the punishment with which one is sentenced'.[1]
- 2919: 'krino': 'to select, choose, approve, esteem; to pronounce an opinion concerning right or wrong.'[2]

To *judge/discern* comes from the desire for the best for another person, with all the information you have available, and with grace, as you would want someone to judge you. Without discernment, we would go through traffic lights and crash, would sign contracts with anyone who happened across our path and, yes, would marry the first cute guy who happened along. Actually, that last one does happen often in this world. Then the nightmare begins.

1 - Strong's Concordance, G2917
2 - Strong's Concordance, G2919

Many Frogs are famous for this misinterpretation of the word 'judge', especially because of their goal of getting what they want from you. They will say you are 'judging' (or condemning) them if you call them out on something they say or do that you don't like. You are discerning what is good for you. Don't get sucked in by someone who is trying to guilt you into avoiding discernment by trying to shame you. In your discerning, make the decision about who you think this guy is from the information he has shared and shown, and politely exit, leaving the Frog and his condemnations behind. We are not in Jr. High anymore, and his lame attempts at peer pressure and forcing you to fit into his bizarre idea of how to treat you, or pushing you to sleep with him should make you run. You don't need him.

How to Attract a Frog

'Most men decide within 10 minutes of meeting a woman if she's appropriate for marriage, or just for a casual affair.'[3]

So you're on a date with a guy who you think could be the future father of your children. (But, you're not thinking that way because of the 'preparation' section you just read a few pages ago, right?) Here are a few things you should NOT do if you want a Prince...or if you DO want a Frog:

1. Act desperate. You may not even think you're doing it, but this includes being too accommodating, overlooking red flags, being too friendly and otherwise letting a man treat you in a way that is not respectful of you. To a manipulative man, you are like a deer in bear country. Your high tolerance for jerkiness sends a Frog a message: 'Treat me however you want to, because I don't have the confidence to walk away.'

2. Dress to 'advertise'.
If your neckline and your hemline are mere inches from each other and you're expecting to find a quality guy, think again. You are advertising, and your market—whether you like it or not, are Frogs. Tuna lures attract tuna. Swordfish lures attract swordfish. Frog lures will not net you a Prince. Whoever you do attract will expect consistency. When you turn the tables and tell him you want the commitment of marriage, he will

either laugh you off and bolt or marry you and then look for a younger lure when previously perky parts of your body start to sag.

You may also tempt a Prince. You will definitely tempt other womens' husbands, boyfriends, sons, and who knows what else. You may think flaunting your wares like a summer tent sale is 'freedom', but it just shows self-doubt. Men are visual—all of them, not just the ones you are interested in. It is difficult for them to keep their minds away from what lies barely under your scant clothes. Our culture laughs at this belief and calls it 'prudish'. But when men are led to value only women's bodies, and seek out pornography for satisfaction, the result is anything but normal, and it comes right back on a woman's head. Ask yourself: if you found the love of your life, would you feel comfortable having a woman standing right in front of him dressed in little more than a handkerchief? Hey, I'm talking about myself too; I used to do it. I thought that was all I had to offer—and it got me nowhere.

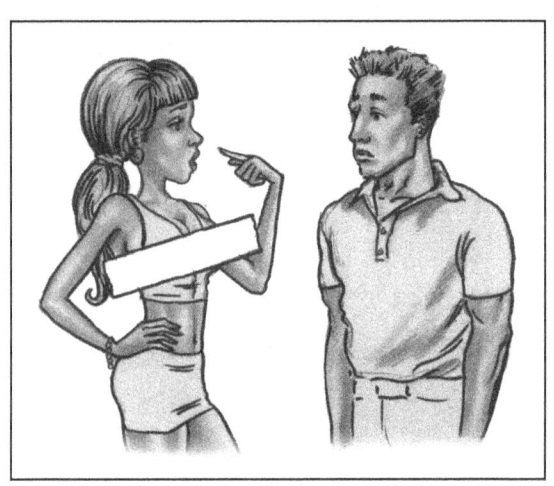

CLINT WANTED TO HAVE JUST ONE WEEK WHERE SOME ATTENTION-STARVED GIRL WASN'T TELLING HIM WHERE HER EYES WERE.

3. Choose scary and self-seeking friends. By surrounding yourself with people who tell you what you want to hear, who are out for their own best interests instead of yours, who talk about others behind their backs, and who talk about others to you (not that they would ever talk about you behind your back) and friends who enjoy drama (not the kind that takes place onstage) you will have no guard against a Frog. Your friends won't tell you of red flags they see, or they may just let you march on in a relationship with a Frog, just to see what happens, because they're bored with the Friday night lineup on t.v.

4. Stay away from your Bible. Why would you read a book of wisdom when you are trying just find 'Mr. Right Now'? While you're at it, don't pray. Prayer will open your eyes, move mountains, and help you keep Frogs away. You can still go to church and act like you know what it's all about, but to a Frog, biblical wisdom and intimacy with God are like a cross to a vampire. Don't mind all those scriptures in Proverbs about the characteristics of a wicked man or the fool. With the Frog flying under the radar, he'll play the part of a Prince, but you'll find out his true identity soon enough.

5. Set your sights low. Don't believe God has the best for you, even when you see your girlfriends getting married. No, in order to attract a Frog, you must tell yourself the next good-looking, smooth talking guy is a Prince, and when he starts sprouting warts through his disguise, just believe that's all you deserve anyway…or that he'll change if you wait long enough.

How To Attract A Prince:

1. You do NOT have to be desperate. The God of the universe has the very best for you and all you have to do is wait! Believe me, it will pay off. On that honeymoon night, you will be thanking Him for instilling the strength and wisdom in you that allowed you to let the Frogs pass on down the stream.

2. There are some exciting and creative ways to dress without showing your stomach through your cleavage. Honestly? Guys do notice that this way of dressing is cheesy. Only SEVEN out of 2,000 men interviewed actually said they married women who were dressed in a very sexy outfit when they met, according to John T. Malloy's 'Dress for Success'. That's pretty telling. Check out some of the style shows and see how you can dress for your figure and skin tone. You may be surprised at how much positive attention you get for being a walking masterpiece, decorated with clothing suited for you—and that's very attractive.

3. I will talk about friends in the next section, and what makes a good friend who will hold you accountable. Proverbs is valuable for telling wise people from fools and wicked.

4. Your Bible? I think we cover that in this entire book. It is like gold. Like food. Don't believe me? Commit to read—and really digest its words—for some time every day for two weeks and see the difference in your life.

When it comes to the Prince you may marry, you DO deserve the very best! We have a gracious, creative and loving God who created not only you (you stellar, gorgeous Princess), but the not-so-perfect man who will be perfect for *you*. Do not settle! What you settle for today will be with you for the rest of your days, or until the divorce hearing! Wait for the Prince. He is out there.

Part II
Why Women Ignore Their Red Flags

Part II
Chapter 8

Red Flags

Animals have it right.

If you watch any of those nature shows long enough, you'll come across a scene like this:

A herd of gazelle is feasting on some tall grass on an African plain. Cut to a shot of a barely visible cheetah, its spotted coat moving with the cat as it settles into a crouch behind the long, tawny blades of grass. As the cat sneaks closer, there is a wide shot of the herd grazing and the predator edging closer. In a millisecond several gazelle heads shoot up and a moment later the herd is off as one body, barely escaping the unfortunate cat, who made his presence known too soon.

If there was audio and the gazelles could speak English, it may sound something like this:

GAZELLE: "Danger! GO!"

NARRATOR: "At the warning of one gazelle, the herd takes off, avoiding certain death and living to graze another day."

It should never sound like this:

GAZELLE: *(thinking to herself)* "Hmm...there may be danger, but I can't be sure. Maybe we should hang out here a while. I'd look like a fool if I got the whole herd running for nothing, and besides, I don't want to seem like I'm lacking compassion toward the predator, if there is one. Oh, look! It's a cheetah! He's so handsome! He looks hungry, but maybe I can change him. He'd make a great addition to our family...I wonder what he drives."

Animals know what to do. So why do some women ignore red flags when they feel the alarms going off inside them?

At my sheriff's office job, I had to go on ride-alongs sometimes with the deputies. One sheriff's deputy told me about a time he was sitting in his car, after writing a ticket.

"I was sitting under the highway overpass, writing my daily report, and all of a sudden I felt like something was coming. I couldn't explain it. Something told me I should put my seatbelt back on, but didn't have time to look and see why, so I put it on. I tensed up just as a vehicle slammed into the back of my patrol car. I walked away with minor injuries, but if I hadn't put on that seatbelt, I would most likely be dead."

Because my deputy friend obeyed without hesitating, he is alive today.

I know God protects His people, but I have seen a strange thing while working with the police: even cops who don't believe in God seem to have a supernatural sense about events before they happen. I have also been there when crimes seem to happen right in front of them. The cops are in the right place at the right time. I don't believe any of this is happenstance, given the fact that God rules the universe. Sometimes He lets circumstances go against their favor, for no reason we can know or understand. It still stands that when He warns and our innate 'knower' goes off, we need to obey immediately and take action.

How red flags show themselves

An early use of the 'red flag' was in the 1700s when French National Guard leader Lafayette raised it to order enemy riders to disperse.[1] In the 1800s, it evolved into a term used to indicate danger.

Paul says: *'No temptation has overtaken you except which as is common to man; but God is faithful, who will not allow you to be tempted beyond what you are able, but with the temptation will also make the way of escape, that you may be able to bear it.'* – 1 Corinthians 10:13

I wish I hadn't had to learn this scripture personally, but I have. I'm sure if you look back on the bad relationships you've had, you would remember the point at which you saw red flags. Maybe it was a twisting in your gut, or invisible spiders up your neck, or a general feeling of spiritual or emotional malaise. And I'll bet you can remember what happened after you ignored the red flag. I know I can.

1 - Thomas Carlyle, French Revolution, p. 408

On one occasion, after I had already lived through months of red flags (at the time I mistook them for 'love butterflies'), I stumbled onto a phone message from a female, on the phone of the man I had been involved with. I'll call my male friend Nate. I won't go into details here; I wasn't doing anything wrong, just helping him with an issue he was having with his phone. When I heard the syrupy female voice dancing around on the voicemail, a suspicious twisting seized my gut. Something wasn't right. This man had led me to believe he cared about me and, in addition, was around me almost every day for hours on end. Now, it appeared, he had a girlfriend somewhere. When he called my cell from a friend's phone, I told him I had fixed his phone issue. Wanting to be honest, I told him I had stumbled onto a message from a woman. I wanted an answer, but didn't voice a question.

When I tell you he was two miles away, but appeared at my door 5 minutes later, it may be generous. He flew low in the little V4 beater he had. Later, the reason for his speed in arriving at my house would become

clear. At the time, he told me it had been his boss's wife on the voicemail, arranging a gift for her husband behind his back with their family friend: Nate. The lie was so convincing that the coil in my stomach released in an instant. If MatureMe had paused to pick apart his story, I would have seen the holes, but MiniMe was at the helm, and she heard what she wanted to hear. The fantasy world was intact again, the cracks so minor no one would see them…until the relationship hit an iceberg.

Later in the book, I will tell you about the entire experience, but for now, know that I assisted my male acquaintance in deceiving myself. I cut up those red flags and burned them, hoping never to see them again. The annoying thing about red flags is, they don't stay down. They rear their heads again and again. It is not their nature to disappear. They may leave for a time, but their warnings will keep nagging at you, no matter how small they are. And they will be back until you heed them — or until you hit an iceberg. Don't cut them up, burn them, attach them to a passing bike or otherwise try to make them leave. They are your friends. Listen to them. They may be ugly—the truth sometimes is, but they will protect you, if you let them.

Part II
Chapter 9

Why Women Miss Red Flags

Red flags show up for a reason. They are like the rack of lights on top of a police car. If you don't stop when they start announcing their presence, you're in for much more of a penalty. Their purpose is to help, but if you don't know what to look for, it is just as bad as ignoring them.

The following is a list of reasons—not excuses—as to why you may have overlooked your scarlet sentinels:

1. Family Conditioning – Raised by Wolves

You can't choose your family. But you can become aware of and change those unhealthy learned behaviors and beliefs you grew up with, to avoid the effects of unhealthy patterns in your life.

I know of a little baby named Sarah years ago who is probably a teenager by now. I had a summer job babysitting her and the two creatures who shared her DNA. Her brothers weren't horrible, just terrible. They were seven and five and Sarah was about 5 months old at the time. My teenage dreams of being able to hang in front of the tube sipping soda and eating everything in sight evaporated when I caught a glimpse of these two little werewolves tearing through the house. They were like wild dogs that had caught the scent of blood, only their prey was their baby sister. They slapped her—not hard enough to hurt her, but enough to make her cry. I knew nothing about 'parenting styles' or psychology or what inner demons these two had as a result of having a new baby sister, and I probably wouldn't have cared. I tried incarcerating them, but they made sounds in their rooms like contractors making renovations. Letting these two out into general population was out of the question, and yet they had everything a little inmate could desire right inside of their rooms. They were impossible to punish. I knew somewhere there had to be two wanted posters, each one featuring one of their pinched little faces.

Little Sarah was going to have her work cut out for her trying to grow up with these two around. I find it hard to believe they're not jail right now. (In jail, or in office…) Like all of us, she didn't pick her family. I like to believe she grew up strong because of the brothers, and was able to dish it right back out at them.

Truth: Parents, siblings and other family have a great deal of influence on your core beliefs and reactions to situations in life and on how you value yourself.

Sarah could have grown up strong, with her own identity and a good grasp on which behaviors are acceptable and which are unacceptable from a man. Or she could have bowed under the weight of her brothers' abuse, if it had continued, and may now put up with way more than she should from men. I lost touch with the family long ago, but have seen both outcomes to the same scenario in others' lives. The good news is, even if you come from an abusive family, there is hope for you to overcome your past and put aside the lies you were told about your value. No one tells you how valuable you are. You are valuable because your Creator has already determined it.

It was a similar situation thousands of years ago when God used Moses to free the Israelites from slavery in Egypt.

God allowed them on their way out to plunder the Egyptians—or, to commit the shopping spree of all shopping sprees in Egypt. It was like running through Neiman Marcus to grab as much as you could for free…$800 jeans, designer shoes and even the little chocolates they had at the cash registers.

God provided food and water in miraculous ways for the Israelites' trip to the Promised Land. He gave them everything they needed; even making sure their shoes did not wear out. In addition and best of all, He provided His guidance and constant attention. His eye was not off of them for a moment.

So how did the Israelites react to God's goodness while trudging through the wilderness toward their prized goal of their own land?

'The entire Israelite community grumbled against Moses and Aaron in the wilderness. The Israelites said to them, "If only we had died by the Lord's hand in the land of Egypt, when we sat by pots of meat and ate all the bread we wanted. Instead, you brought us into this wilderness to make this whole assembly die of hunger!"' – Exodus 16:2-3

They whined like three year-olds in an ice-cream shop.

Their minds were still captive, which made many of them miss the blessing God had for them. They had suffered verbal and physical abuse at the hands of the Egyptians. Somewhere along the line they had learned to live with their captors' berating words and the slave conditions, but the 'good old days' were anything but good. When freedom came—with it a promise of a land of riches, abundant food and joy—it scared them. A path had been worn into their minds that, while abuse and bondage were not ideal, this was their lot in life. It was familiar. It was safer than the unknown. They had adapted. Freedom and the possibility of having their dream of a Promised Land come true at the hand of a loving God did not compute.

Many women are still living in this captivity, having grown used to the bad behavior they experience from men who see these great women don't value themselves.

Someone once said it takes twenty one days to form a habit. A habit, a lifestyle, a bonding with another human, even repeated verbal, emotional or physical abuse gets worn like a track into a person's brain.

Vera was one woman who thought that way.

"When Peter wanted to be intimate with me, I didn't want to. I wanted to save myself for marriage. While he was kissing me, I remember thinking, 'He doesn't want me as a wife, but I may as well give in…this is probably the best I'm going to get.'"

It's heartbreaking to see a Princess giving herself to a Frog because she doesn't believe she deserves or will experience anything better. The root of this belief is one that says God is holding back or doesn't have anything for her. That is a lie. To take a moment in time and think that's all there is, is to deny yourself a future; worse, it is to think you know the future.

God's will is good, pleasing and perfect. He does not have a man for you who will lie to you, use you, or put you down. He doesn't give garbage to His children. The man He would give you would be a lot like Him: kind, patient, good, joyful, peaceful, and faithful.

Your past may not have been strewn with roses, but the future always holds the promise of better things. A caterpillar sees only her earthbound condition and thinks about all the shoes she must buy. But once the pain of change comes and goes, the future yields brilliant, buoyant wings that will take her on adventures.

So how do you unlearn a past that has schooled you in the art of people-pleasing, 'peace at all costs' or taking abuse in varying degrees? Maybe your past didn't include severe abuse, but simply busy parents. Or maybe it wasn't a home issue at all, but verbal slurs you received every day at school or from some other place? Your past is just that: passed. You can dwell on what Egypt did to you, and crawl in the dust of the familiar, or fly through the wilderness, letting God hold your hand and trusting Him to provide your every need.

꙳

Chloe's Frog-pleasing stole much of her time and energy:

"I had known Greg years ago, before I moved out of the area. He had also moved out to California. We reconnected about 15 years later, and he called me. We had a conversation that turned to politics. Greg, it turns out, is very politically motivated. I also learned he believed the opposite of what I did. That conversation ended with him in a rage when I brought up my beliefs, and I politely ended the call. Two years after, we connected again. This time, I listened to him and, when he raged, I pointedly told him he was being very mean and it made me not want to talk to him. I told him I had listened to his point of view, but he didn't want to hear mine. He called me an idiot and a fool for believing as I did. I am a Christian. Time went on, and as long as we weren't talking about politics or religion, things were fine. I remember the

Greg from years ago: someone charismatic, gorgeous, talented, and intelligent. I pictured him in my head that way. He charmed me just enough to keep me talking, but we would inevitably get into arguments about beliefs. I thought that by keeping him in my life, I was his chance at getting to know God. I knew I let myself down when I argued with him, but much of the time I kept silent.

Greg started telling me of his dire financial condition, saying he was not eating and was going to lose his apartment. I sent him a little money—after all, we'd already known each other. I was in between jobs myself, but certainly had enough to help out a starving man! With all the phone calls, I started liking him, then on the day I was to make the most difficult move of my life over a thousand miles away from my friends of 12 years because of my layoff from my job, Greg emailed me, telling me 'there was nothing between us, and to stop thinking of him as though anything could happen between us'. I was so hurt. I was exhausted from packing and was missing my last get-together with my friends there. I already missed them. I cried all night.

I cooled off our phone conversations for quite a while. The move was exhausting, driving across the country, and I didn't really want anything to do with him. When I started taking his calls again a couple of months later, we got into one last fight. He said things about God I could never repeat. My first regret is not cutting things off a year earlier. My second regret was only having a cell phone to hang up, and not one of those heavy old phones I could slam down. Still, I hung up on him. It was New Year's Eve and I felt more peace than I had in a while. Four months later, he left a message to apologize. I called back to thank him, but nothing had changed. He was still a Moocher who had nothing going on in his life, and who was looking for the government to support him while he sought someone to tell his bitter tirades to. It wasn't going to be me. I haven't spoken to him since."

2. The Princess In The Pot: Cultural Conditioning

Have you ever been sitting, watching t.v., and noticed after a time that your jaw was slack and you were almost hypnotized? There's something mesmerizing about t.v. And that was just at the commercials.

Advertisers know how to get our attention, and how to program us, and so do film directors. That's why some people can recite entire scenes from Star Wars.

Entertainment media aren't the only ones who know the power of mass communication. A more devious use of the media was in WWII Germany, where the Ministry of Propaganda Office was responsible for dictating what went out in the media, to make sure it was Nazi-friendly. The U.S. Office of Strategic Service described Adolf Hitler in a profile: 'His primary rules were: never allow the public to cool off; never admit a fault or wrong; never concede that there may be some good in your enemy; never leave room for alternatives; never accept blame; concentrate on one enemy at a time and blame him for everything that goes wrong; people will believe a big lie sooner than a little one; and if you repeat it frequently enough people will sooner or later believe it.'[1]

What does all of this have to do with dating a Frog? We cannot control the influence of our surroundings, only our reaction to them.

Susan was smitten with Jim the first time she saw him. He seemed to say what she had dreamed of hearing. He obviously spent a lot of time at the gym. He was tall, his skin was a beautiful, smooth tone; a mix of olive and Dresden. His eyes were so brown they were almost black like onyx stones. When he smiled at her, her heart melted. With all the romance novel visuals and cinema-worthy lines Susan was getting from him, it's no wonder she missed the red flags. After a year of overlooking these warnings—a feat which became more difficult to do as Jim's beauty faded under his anger and strange behavior, Susan finally saw past his candy coating to his deceptive, creamy center. Susan had bitten into a morsel of chocolate that had looked so good. She winced as she realized he was filled with worms. She learned he was seeing two other women. The increasing stress of his lifestyle was increasing his anger. Fortunately she left before he hit her again.

Verbal advertising isn't the only effective influence on the human mind. Visuals can be just as powerfully stunning—and alluring.

---

1 - Hitler as His Associates Know Him (Office of Strategic Services report, p.51)

So next time you see that magazine with that perfect model in that perfect bikini talking to that perfect man, remember one word: photo editing software. I know…that's three. Actually four: soft-focus filter. That's five. Oh, and the other filters. And make-up artists. No offense to models or actresses, but even they would be the first to admit they need some work when they get up in the morning like all of us. Hair in all directions and eye boogers? Mmm…attractive. But even I am swayed by the work of graphic designers, stylists and animators when I watch t.v. I forget about the smoke and mirrors—and filters—for a moment and wonder: why don't my thighs look all smooth and buttercream like that? (Never mind that as I'm editing this, I'm eating a marshmallow treat.) I know I can't afford to pay union fees for make-up artists and lighting guys to follow me around all day. The expectations we have for our bodies as women because of our cultural influences can discourage even the strongest soul.

"And do not be conformed to this world, but be transformed by the renewing of your mind, that you may prove what is that good and acceptable and perfect will of God." – Romans 12:2

Our grandparents came from a generation where they were pretty satisfied playing with a stick and a ball in the street. They read the classics and actually went outside and talked to their neighbors. We isolate ourselves with audio, video and sensory input from every direction. In some cases this input takes our emotions on a roller coaster of highs and lows. In other cases, such as with t.v., it throws our brains into a passive 'beta-wave' state, stealing time and energy by anesthetizing us. Now, I like movies, maybe more than t.v., but I still feel the need to quiet my mind sometimes in order to have peace.

I noticed when I didn't turn off the world that I was scattered, tense and grouchy. I wondered if it was caffeine, but no, I hadn't had coffee for a while, in this one particular time period. I realized what it was: I never had quiet time. My life was filled with media. I watched television in the morning before work, radio on the way to work, during and on the way home from work. But other things contributed to the noise in my head. I was, essentially, training myself. Media was not the only input.

The opinions of my coworkers gossiping about the latest celebrity scandal, tirades about the current administration or other meaningless noise knocked around in my head. On lunch break, I would go to a bookstore where newspapers and magazines preached their gospel of beauty, world terror, climbing and dropping stocks. Even at the mall or in a restaurant, someone was singing their opinion at me. Everyone I came in contact with, whether in person or through the airwaves or print, had an agenda. Many of them reinforced what the culture put out there, as it is in our nature to 'fit in'. I didn't see it that way then. I simply reaped the effects: noise, lack of peace and my soul set on edge. It was only when I took a little vacation from media and input as far as I could, and spent some time each day reading my Bible did I get my peace back.

Media is used so effectively to sway opinion, especially in an election year. That's why I like to call it the Ministry of Propaganda. After all of this input into the human mind, there is an effect. Unlimited input of certain media into an 'open mind' without the guarding influence of God's word is an open door for belief systems of varying degrees of sanity to tromp through your mind with no accountability like a Hollywood starlet down a red carpet. Dressed flashy enough, anyone else's version of 'truth' seems attractive and tasty. You can't escape the world and its influences, but you can dull its effects. Be *in* the world, not *of* it.

A woman is not of the world when she cleanses her mind daily with the washing of the Word—God's agenda. This will help you when you need to tell the difference between a Frog and a Prince because:

1- You will have peace and will be able to sense an interruption of that peace in the presence of a Frog.

2- You will not have to bow to the pressure of doing what the culture says a woman should do to 'snag' a man: manipulating or giving up your body and heart before you know him. You have set standards.

3- You will know God's truth of who you are and how precious you are so that when you stick to your guns and the Frog stalks off, you let him go and feel fine about it.

So how do you achieve this peace?

1- Morning devotions.

Starting out the day quietly, talking to God, sitting still to hear Him and reading your Bible will allow you to hear from Him. There are some good devotional books and plans which can guide you. Check online or your local Christian or church bookstore.

2- Do a 'media fast' for a week.

Don't worry; it's not forever. But you'll be amazed at the difference it makes. You will slow down, see things, notice things. I was forced to do this once when a hurricane knocked out the power for several days. At first, it was depressing and jarring (especially when my Bunsen burner didn't work and I had to eat cold soup). But, while I was glad when the power came on four days later, I missed the quiet peace I was forced to have during that time. Just try it for a week: no t.v., no radio, CDs, DVDs. You may need to be on the Internet at work, but try to stay away from music, social networking, games and movies. You will see a difference by the end of the week.

3- Being still.

It doesn't mean you have to sit motionless for a day, but try it for a few minutes. It helps to be in a place that doesn't distract you, like a park or backyard, studio, den or bedroom...wherever you don't notice things that need to be done or cleaned. If those things pop into your mind, write them on a piece of paper and put them aside. You'll do them later. Being still makes you go against the flow. The things that matter will wait for you. Those that won't are just as well gone.

4- Go to a place filled with creation.

A park, arboretum, marina, field, beach, anywhere there is not the hustle and bustle of humanity. I used to sit on Ft. Lauderdale Beach at dusk, on one of the lifeguard stand ramps. I figured some things out, other things I just told to God. I always had peace by the time I left.

5- Journal.

Your 'media fast' week is a good time to write down your thoughts: what you're experiencing presently, your dreams and plans, even prayers to God. Writing them does count...God can read! Journaling is a great and free way to get things out and even see things differently, without a therapist or counselor. You may even come up with the next great idea for a book or invention.

6- Hear and see.

When you're in that quiet place filled with creation, pick out the sounds you hear. Pick out things you see that you wouldn't have seen, rushing around. You might find cash on the ground! I was lagging behind a group of friends in college who were in a rush to get somewhere and found money wadded up at the roots of a tree. (Your blessings will be more valuable and eternal, but it was kinda cool. We ended up spending it on pizza anyway.)

The battlefield is in the mind, not in the fleshly world. The battle is not human against human. It is waged in the spiritual realm. Do not believe the propaganda that tries to say you are not a princess because you don't have the media-worthy body or face. Do you notice some of those perfectly-styled people have multiple marriages and relationships? The evidence says the outside of a person may be fun at first, but in the long run it is insufficient for making a truly lasting relationship. Do not believe you have to manipulate and grasp for a man because that is how you see the world do it. Do not believe that in giving a man your treasure—your sexuality and heart—before marriage will endear you to him and seal your destiny as the love of his life, as it appears in the romance novels and movies. Think for yourself. Go against what the ministry of propaganda is preaching.

'Bodice Rippers' and other forms of brainwashing

Long ago, I used to read romance novels. I mean, I devoured them; not the inspirational ones (read: rated G) where characters actually get to know each other and are engaged or married by the end without having had sex beforehand. No, I read the ones the industry calls 'bodice rippers'. They are the female equivalent of men's pornography magazines. Pornography engages men using the visual 'gate'. Bodice ripper novels engage a woman through sensual description, engaging her imagination through words. In these formulaic novels, the female is captured by the rugged male (or is otherwise at odds with him, in the modern romances). They play cat-and-mouse for a while and, inevitably, have sex because she can't resist his brute maleness. Things would be great for a while, and then there would be a fight between them. However it happened, they would separate. The story would come to a climactic point and the lovers would be together again, the male usually proposing marriage to the female because, apparently, she was so good in bed he couldn't live without her; or was it her personality? I never did understand that.

I'm ashamed to say, I actually believed these novels, to a point. I saw my friends having sexual relationships with their boyfriends. I thought that was the way I should get a man to love me. Television and movies reinforced that belief. Don't get me wrong; I was always responsible for my own actions. However, I was making decisions from 'faulty intel': the shifting tides of the culture and their varied definitions of love caused me to walk down those paths and, as a result, become more confused and hurt as the rules changed and the tides shifted…and the guy would inevitably leave anyway. I remember thinking: 'If me having sex with a guy is the only thing keeping him here, what makes me different or more special than any other woman who would have sex with him?' I remember feeling an unhealthy sense of competition when faced with the reality that other women could sway my boyfriend into bed, and that I had to be some boudoir gymnast or have snappy comebacks to keep him.

A word about pornography—another offering from the Ministry of Propaganda that many think is perfectly normal. Porn is like school. It teaches a man that:

a) a normal body is not enough for him

b) one body is not enough, and

c) his wife's (or future wife's) body is not enough

Like any other drug, pornography has claimed its casualties.

Here are the facts:
- Some types of pornography are directly involved in sex trafficking. Teen boys, girls, and women are coerced into work promising high pay, and then they are trapped as slaves into the industry by traffickers.
- Some pornographic films are homemade, of men abusing women and children, and filming it. It doesn't all take place on a Hollywood soundstage.
- Pornography is used as training in the sex trafficking industry to teach women and children what to do for their customers.
- Pornography gives exploiters of women rationale as to why it is ok to sexually exploit women
- The performers themselves are subjected to dangerous conditions like sexually transmitted disease, long work hours, physical and emotional abuse. Don't believe me? Check out www.shelleylubben.com, where a former porn star details the not-so-glamorous life of an adult film performer. The site is clean photographically, but the descriptions of what former performers lived are graphic and heartbreaking.[1]

Thank God for the word of a loving Creator who knows everything and is the true definition of love.

I read different books now—what the industry calls 'inspirational romance'. These are uplifting stories about true, sacrificial and committed love, written by authors who spend time reading and meditating on the ancient scriptures that reveal what love is. I have also started liking Bollywood films, from the Indian film industry. In most of them, there is no sex—not even kissing, and their effect is even more potent as a storytelling vehicle. Like a dating relationship, the Indian film director and writers are forced to develop their characters and rely on story to attract and enthrall the audience, without the use of sex. It is truly fascinating and I am uplifted whenever I watch one of these examples of pure and sacrificial love. They are still movies and are fiction, but they are great alternatives to the cheap offerings out there now. One film in particular I would recommend is *Rab Ne Bana Di Jodi*, starring Shahrukh Khan. Without giving too much away, the story shows love as an action between the two characters; heartbroken Tanni and simple, buttoned-up Surinder. Its portrayal of sacrifice and the blessing of being yourself and standing your ground is equally charming and inspiring.

The Christian marriages I see also show me how a man who truly loves a woman acts, and how a woman, who has respect for herself and her man, shows it.

I made the decision to change my thinking, climb out of the boiling pot of the culture, and bathe in the refreshing water of truth. Oh, I still watch movies and t.v.: I love a good story. Only now, I am aware of when I am being sold something, and I take more time away from media. It is during that time that I get ideas, and I get restored.

'Now it's time to change your ways! Turn to face God so he can wipe away your sins, pour out showers of blessing to refresh you, and send you the Messiah he prepared for you, namely, Jesus.' – Acts 3:19

When I changed my viewing and reading habits, I noticed a distinct change in my life and in my mind. Everything was lighter and I had joy. There was nothing that could compare with that.

'For we do not wrestle against flesh and blood, but against principalities, against powers, against the rulers of the darkness of this age, against spiritual hosts of wickedness in the heavenly places'. – Ephesians 6:12

3. Miss Fix-It

Imagine you are shopping at a furniture store and you see a big, beautiful leather chair in the back. Well, it would be beautiful if not for the claw marks in it from some bored child. The right front leg was broken, but someone replaced it with a chunk of pine, crudely constructed to try to be like the other three legs, which are cherry. The arm is stained with coffee, which you're convinced that the clawing child drank, because he's still bouncing up and down on the chair like a jackhammer. Once he leaves to look for more pristine and untouched

upholstered lands to destroy, you look over the chair. The color is exquisite—it's your favorite. If it weren't for the broken leg, coffee stain, claw marks and now, you see, a family of mice living in its ripped back seam, it would be perfect. It's got a lot wrong with it, but that color is so charming! Certainly you could do something with this chair…you could FIX IT! You take it home and hundreds of dollars, lots of sweat and a few trips to the upholsterer later, you sit on your beloved chair only to find the wood frame had no integrity. You end up on the floor, frustrated and hurt. You had seen the chair in a pretty reputable store, so you have no idea what the problem was. Sure, you ignored the signs that this chair wasn't up to standard, but the vision you had in your mind was so perfect!

This kind of self-deception regarding an unworthy mate is crafted out of a woman's tendency toward compassion, nurturing and projecting. A wise woman knows that compassion is a Godly trait, and nurturing is a character of God. Projecting—imagination—is a creative gift. But the problem comes when a woman, seeking a relationship with a man outside of God's plan for her, ignores the red flags she sees in his character, figuring she can either change him, or stick around and wait while he grows. This is pride. God will not bring you someone you need to fix. It is God's job to fix someone, and if He uses you, that is a blessing. But half the time you don't know it. And most of the time, we as humans are in no position to know what someone needs spiritually or how to provide it. Sticking with a dating relationship with the intent of playing 'interior designer' to an immature or dangerous man's 'Extreme Home Makeover' life only leads to frustration, heartbreak and wasted time. It is not God's plan to give you a half-built house with a rotten foundation.

'But each one is tempted when he is drawn away by his own desires and enticed. Then, when desire has conceived, it gives birth to sin; and sin, when it is full-grown, brings forth death. Do not be deceived, my beloved brethren. Every good gift and every perfect gift is from above, and comes down from the Father of lights, with whom there is no variation or shadow of turning.' – James 1:14-17

Another word for perfect is **complete**.

'If you then, being evil, know how to give good gifts to your children, how much more will your Father who is in heaven give good things to those who ask Him!' – Matthew 7:11

God is in the business of giving good and perfect gifts to his children. We as humans wouldn't even think of giving an unfinished cake to a loved one. Imagine not only what the receiver would think of such an offering, but how it would reflect on you! People would know you had the means to finish baking and icing a cake, but when you hand your loved one a bowl of eggs and powder, they would think they needed to commit you. Another take on the situation would be that you lacked the interest in taking the time to make the cake right. In effect, you obviously don't care anything about the one to whom you are giving the cake.

Do you sometimes think of God that way? Maybe not consciously, but if you are planning on ignoring the God-given warnings about a man's character and relationship with God and insist on fixing him, you are proving your distrust of a perfect and loving Savior who wants more than anything to bless you not with a bowl of eggs and flour, but with a beautiful scrumptious cake frosted with the very icing that makes your mouth water. Wait for the banquet, not the scraps. Don't settle and don't give up.

Marnie thought John's treatment of her was all she deserved:

He never took me on dates. We sometimes went to restaurants in the beginning, but it was dutch. Once he made me go into a restaurant to get the food so we could eat it out of the back hatch of my car. He said we both looked 'tossed' and people may think we had just slept together (we never did! why would he say that?) if we actually went into the restaurant to eat together. I found out later all his paranoia was because he was sleeping with an acquaintance of mine.

Many times a Frog will show his lack of character by what he accuses others of. Don't try to fix him, or prove him wrong. He is telling you who he is. Move on.

4. Compassion

Compassion is a great gift, but some can use a person's compassion for their evil gain. In the Korean War, the enemy would wire explosives to a child in hopes that a compassionate warrior on the other side would approach the child to help her. When the enemy touched the child or tried to help, the bomb would go off, killing the compassionate soldier along with the child. It was a brutal but effective way the enemy used compassion to kill its foe.

Compassion is one of God's most amazing traits, and He has passed the ability to have compassion on to His creation—us. But some who lack in that area use the compassion of others to get their way.

Paige's story:

"When you move 1600 miles away from your family and friends, being without a support system and people you can trust is one of the drawbacks. You don't know anyone," Paige says, "And you are more susceptible to accepting kindness from people, even if it is not in your best interest.

I wanted to get out of Greensboro, where I had lived, so I went to Las Vegas to start a new job as a teacher. When I started the job, I noticed people were really nice to me and I thought that I had lots of instant friends on the faculty. I should have used caution and realized there are all kinds of agendas people have that you can't possibly know about.

Alone in a new city, I did what one did to ward off loneliness: I went out. I met a man there who offered to pay to put my coat in coat-check. His name was Tom. I had never seen such gentility or kindness, so I gave him my coat. I couldn't even believe I did that; it had my wallet, ID, everything in it. Not my best judgment, but I did it. I was very attracted to him, even though he was a little younger than me, and at the end of the night we left the club and I ended up going to breakfast with him. He was a grad student and an aspiring artist. My friend let me crash at her house and he followed me there, where I showed him my art online. When the night was over, he went to leave and asked for a kiss. I ended up going home with him; something which I had never done in my whole life.

The time I spent with him was so amazing I figured it had to be from God. I was so deceived. In hindsight, I know this wasn't from the Christian God. I wasn't even obeying what the Bible said. I wanted to know about this guy, and chose to pray over him for an answer. I had what would only be described as a 'major disturbance'. He had told me about his past; that he had a mother who had died of cancer and had left him money. He told me his father neglected to supervise or care for him, and then finally abandoned him. He became a bad kid in his teens, got arrested and was put in jail. He'd spent his early twenties in jail and then was paroled. I reasoned that all of that was over now. I had compassion for him because I'd done lots of the same things he had; written bad checks and done petty crimes, but hadn't been caught. I didn't judge him. Other female teachers knew about him, and said to be careful—that it shouldn't be an issue, but to keep it quiet, since teachers couldn't date students. Lots of guys were after me because they thought I was cute, and I was older.

The 'disturbance' I had felt didn't seem to be any of those things, though. He told me had a bike injury at 19 and had been in a coma. I didn't think he would lie to me. I had lived all over the world and had done extraordinary things, and as a result I assumed anyone else had lived a life as exciting as mine. He had a storytelling element when he related his past to me, but I didn't consider it over-the-top. Soon we moved in together.

Things changed immediately…or maybe they just came to light. He started losing the articulateness that I had first noticed. He got mad that I wasn't doing dishes, blaming the need for perfect order in his house on the brain injury he had from the bike accident. He couldn't handle the mess I made while I was working on a project.

I soon noticed he was living beyond his means. He had said he owned his house, and that the money he had received from his mother's death had allowed him to own the house. He said that his grandparents had put stock in his name. He hadn't told me he worked at a grocery store. The fact didn't bother me—I had worked at places which were probably below me, but you have to do what you have to do to make a living sometimes. What bothered me was the fact that he hadn't told me about his job. And, it didn't make sense that he had worked there, if he had all this money.

Another event rang strange for me. One day he rear-ended someone. Rather than having a normal response, like trading insurance information and paying for the guy's bumper, he decided to blow up the car of the person he had hit. He started talking about people he who could get him C-4. When I became alarmed and told him that his car accident was not that big a deal and just to pay for the bumper, he got violent. He didn't hit me, but he flew into a rage.

After the accident, I learned later, he had gone drinking. He told me that was the reason he had reacted to the accident the way he had. I had believed up until that point that he was the kind of guy who held the door for a woman, and paid the check. But the reaction he showed, told a different story. It didn't fit. But, I figured I should stick it out.

I knew he was lying to me, but when I questioned him, he would redirect the subject. He would focus on his coma and head injury, feigning forgetfulness and misspeaking. Because I knew people who had head injuries, I had seen this type of behavior from them—gaps in memory and misstating facts. Every time I started asking questions he would say he had arrhythmia *and needed to go to the doctor. I have great intuition, but I neglected to see that he put up these 'redirects' in the form of his brain injury.*

Something else I noticed was that, while he would tell me his life story, including all details, he wouldn't let me talk about him to anyone else. It was his desire not to have the world intrude upon his personal life, he said.

Well, I had met him at a certain club, and it ended at that same club. I had business out in Las Vegas for four or five days. That was when I decided to end our relationship—after eight months. I decided I would try to go back to school. I had caught him making out with some girl earlier in our relationship. Then, he had explained he had drunk too much. When I couldn't find him on this night, I went to the men's bathroom, where I had originally found him with another girl before. No one was there.

He was up at the bar getting another drink. I picked him up by the back of the shirt, and dragged him out to the street. The bar's bouncer was ready for a fight as I demanded the guy unlock my bicycle I had ridden there in lieu of taking the car, in case we drank too much. I rode the bike home and packed the car, planning to talk things out if he had come back before I was done packing, but he didn't.

I went to my parents' house and decided to crawl into bed. Someone would have to put me in a sanitarium because I wasn't coming out. After a time of crying, I thought about him. I realized he could be dead in a ditch somewhere. I was concerned. I'd met his family, so I went and talked to his grandmother. His grandmother said he'd had a difficult life. I agreed, mentioning his learning disability and coma. His grandmother said, 'What coma?'

I learned his mother is NOT dead, but alive and well in Greensboro. He had told me he'd traveled to Australia. In truth, I learned even now he was still on probation (i.e., not allowed to leave the country). Earlier in our relationship, before the accident, cops had come to the house and poured out the alcohol we had. At the time, I was perplexed. Now it made sense: parolees aren't allowed to have alcohol.

Grandma alluded that he did do something wrong: that he broke out of juvenile hall and didn't follow through with what the court ordered him to do, but that was it. To me, he had told big stories of big crimes. Now I know they weren't true.

Now I see he was intimidated by me. I had lived an extraordinary life and he wanted to have a life that matched it."

Compassion coupled with loneliness prompts bad decisions…and lots of drama. Like all of us, Paige knows now that she needs to temper misplaced compassion, ask questions and leave when things don't add up.

5. Girl's Gotta Have It

You've met the man of your dreams. He's charming, smooth and compliments you, but something is not right. You can't put your finger on it, but there's an alarm going off inside you. Because you are careening toward another birthday with no prospects in sight, your girlfriends are married, and this man is attractive and he bears all the outward markings of a nice man, you push aside the red flags flapping in the breeze and proceed. You think about him, letting your mind run rampant with scenes of which a romance writer would be envious. You spend much of your time talking on the phone and being with him. He calls almost ten times a day, which interrupts your work and life, but that must mean he's interested! The red flags are still waving. You hear the Sunday sermon about Godly relationships where the pastor highlights the earmarks of a healthy relationship and a Godly man. Well, that's not exactly who you're dating, but your charmer talks a lot about his tithing, how *you* can be a better Christian, and all the wonderful things he does at work and church. You don't really see him do these things, but love 'believes all things', right? The Bible wasn't written on rubber, but you twist the scripture to suit your desires and you proceed anyway.

As the days go by, your heart bonds more and more with this man, which is impossible not to do, considering the amount of time you spend with him. You project onto him what you want him to be; your dream man, so that soon you have fooled even yourself. You are past guarding your mind and heart, and soon, you sense yourself sliding away from doing what's right. You don't know why you feel that way; he hasn't even touched you. But the way he talks about others and the way he seems so fixated on material things makes you uncomfortable. But maybe you need to stop being so legalistic. God is a good God and He wants to bless us, right? And there are so many people in the church who need to mature; he's just pointing them out. *I should listen so I know what he likes and doesn't like, then he'll be even more attracted to me*, you reason.

Some of your friends notice a difference in you and gently say so, but you shake your head in defense, disputing with them. You're starting to sound a lot like your boyfriend, they say, but you don't see it. You don't see the red flags waving as vigorously now. This relationship has to be from God! After all, it's like this man is reading your mind! You haven't been able to clean your house for a while and, out of the blue, he cleans it without being asked (not that you would ask him).

Because he is isolating you, you are not around friends who can see the two of you interacting anymore. And because he wants to keep your relationship on the 'down low' until you both 'see where things are going', you aren't seen together at events or in public. The hiding is exciting and dramatic and makes your heart race. There are things that don't feel right, but you're on the roller coaster now. There's no getting off until the end of the ride and, at this point, you don't want to. You start doing things for him; cleaning his house, doing his laundry, running errands for him. This is how it will be when you're married! It's so good to have an intimate friend; a man who really cares about you. But if he cares about you so much, why does he hide you? Why does it feel so strange when you hear him on the phone 'bending the truth'? Why do all of his conversation center around ___(you fill in the blank: sex, money, material things, insulting other people and their reputations…)?

At this point, you find yourself exhausted and stressed, when your life has begun to revolve around him, partly because of you and partly by his design. It begins to cost you your time, where you have all but neglected household responsibilities, money management, work, time with girlfriends, etc. Soon, when God knows it is time to release you from a relationship that was not His will, and from which you cannot release yourself, He allows the crash. Whether this man has become bored and must chase another woman, or a lie he has hidden is uncovered, whether you just can't keep up with the 'him-focused' relationship anymore or you have given him your body, which you swore you wouldn't do before marriage and everything has changed, it is over.

You go through tears and the excruciating pain of a broken heart, and you may blame God. But God is the one who is saving you from your own destruction. This all started because you wanted your own way and did not listen to Him. Now you know not only what a red flag looks and feels like, you know how to see deception, lack of character and you know the sting of the chastening of a loving God; something you will hopefully carry with you to protect you from making this mistake again. You knew you were right when you felt those warnings—you just didn't listen.

But, again, the choice is up to you. You know the cost of disobedience. You are living it. And you know firsthand where certain choices will lead. If this has happened to you, take heart. What man meant for evil, God uses for good. In Chapter 11, we will talk about healing 'post-Frog'. For now, know that it is so much easier to stop sin at the 'thought' stage than it is to heal after the 'action' stage.

6. Everyone else likes him.

This guy may come off as a nice guy, but who is leading your decisions? And who are the people who say he is a Prince? This isn't to say you don't give a guy the benefit of the doubt in simply meeting him, but again, if you get your red flags rising and your gut is telling you to run, don't set those aside just because others—who may or may not know him—give him rave reviews. The rave-reviewers may be upstanding people, but may not know him very well. There is no rush. Get to know the guy. Not only does patience reveal deception, but in this case, it would have revealed to Charmaine that she didn't know this man well enough:

꿈

I had just moved from my crazy life in Los Angeles to Pennsylvania for a change. It had been one bad relationship after another in L.A. and I was tired of it. I lived with my brother, Vince, in Pennsylvania and rededicated my life to Lord and started going to church again.

Some friends invited me and Vince and (unbeknownst to me) a guy named Colin. Vince couldn't make it that night, but I showed up anyway. Colin and I didn't hit it off at first. I thought he was arrogant. I sensed his attitude the moment I walked through the door, thanks to my time in L.A.—I was used to it there. Colin and I were total opposites. He was raised a strict Muslim, wasn't allowed to date, didn't drink, and was straight as straight could be. I learned that when he'd gotten to Miami, he partied and let loose. I seemed to have switched roles with him: I was now the straight one. I didn't like this guy; he had worldliness all over him. When I left dinner that night, I was annoyed at my friends for trying to fix me up.

Over the next couple of weeks, I saw him at church and we'd say "hi". I was sitting with Vince one day and Colin joined us. The conversation moved to him wanting to get his life back on track, how he had been partying, doing drugs and sleeping with different girls. He and I talked over the next few weeks. One night I joined some friends at a restaurant. When I got there, Colin was already there. Later I learned that when I had walked through the door (in a baseball cap and sweats), it was then, he said, that he had fallen in love with me.

He told me later he knew he had to straighten out his life for me. We continued going to church together, and more than a few times he mentioned how he was straightening out his life.

One night I was lying in bed listening to praise and worship music, thinking about how lonely I was, and about my life in L.A., and wondering if I was going to be with anyone ever again. Colin called at that moment, and I sensed some sort of feeling that I couldn't identify come over me as we spoke. I wondered if he was the one God had for me.

I saw him at church the next day and felt an instant attraction for him. We got very serious very fast, went to premarital classes, spent every second together and logged lots of time on the phone. We didn't want to do anything sexually before marriage, so it was hard to be alone together. This was a motivation to be married. The pastor confirmed our decision and said he didn't see any reason why we shouldn't be married. We'd known each other for six months.

On my wedding day, I was uneasy and started to panic right there in the church. I almost didn't go through with it, but I just shrugged my feelings off as nervousness.

The first six months of the marriage were great. After that, we got to know each other. There were things we didn't like about each other. I still had had residue from living and dating in L.A. He was very needy and overbearing and smothering. We did not get along. We went to a Christian counselor. Both of us worked on ourselves and the marriage. We both felt stuck, but tried to make things work.

There came a point a couple of years into it where I wasn't sure he was a Christian. He was philosophical and always questioned the Bible, faith, and Christianity without searching out answers. He pulled back from going to church, while I still wanted to go. Little by little, though, I stopped going to church too. We would go out and drink and weren't connected to God anymore. He started to put doubt in my mind about heaven, hell and God. I could definitely see Satan opening the door and wedging a foot in.

Colin started his import business and had to travel a lot—weeks at a time. I wasn't happy in the marriage anyway, so this suited me fine. I kind of liked my new married 'single' life, being able to go anywhere I wanted whenever I wanted while he traveled to other countries. I started to really like him not being there and wanted to be alone and single. I would go to New York City for three months and love it, and settled for just being away from him. Both of us acted like everything was ok.

A couple of times in New York I reconnected on a social networking site with some old boyfriends. I have to say, the conversations were inappropriate for a married woman to be having. Colin would call and tell me about going out with business associates to bikini contests. When he returned, there was nothing there in his eyes or actions related to love or attraction, and we took it out on each other. He felt rejected, so he threw himself into his business and I got back into acting, moving to Austin to film a movie. I came home from shooting the film and wanted to start a fight with him to sabotage everything. I wanted everything to end, but didn't want to be the bad guy. We got into a huge fight and everything was over.

I went back to Austin and finished shooting the movie, then came back to Pennsylvania and found out my other brother, Dominic, was sick. Colin was not supportive. He admitted he was sleeping with other women and partying, and I made the decision that this was unhealthy and not something I could even work on anymore. Colin didn't want anything to do with God. We decided to get a divorce.

༄

Charmaine admits that when she leaned on a man, he let her down, as anyone would. Counting on a man to be a Christian role model and leader is no substitute for stepping up to the plate and keeping one's own relationship with the Lord close. She admits she allowed him to take her with him down the road she was traveling.

What post-Colin Charmaine would have said to pre-Colin Charmaine: "There should be a minimum two year period of getting to know someone…NOT six months. Never jump in too fast."

Also, the red flags were all there. Obey that gut instinct, she says. She got that the day she met him…the feeling she didn't like him. She let everyone talk her into it, and she did not marry for the right reasons. She married him for security; he promised her the world. Men should have to prove their words, Charmaine says. Don't just go on his words alone! Look at actions. It is a matter of time before the mask slips. After about one and a half years, Colin's mask did slip.

Part II
Chapter 10

Breaking the Pattern

If you have been sucked in by a Frog, fear not. There is hope. You don't have to keep thinking the same way you always have and doing the same things you've always done. The two are interlinked, but the chain can be broken at the source by doing a few things:

1. Change your thinking

The contents of the minds of every woman in the world could fill books and, since I am not a psychologist or other kind of 'dome doctor', I will address one thought pattern common to all women which compromises her ability to wait for God's best in a mate. That mindset is the fear that God is holding out on her.

Adam and Eve thought the same thing: that their Creator was withholding the knowledge of good and evil from them. When they rebelled (sinned) against him and ate the fruit, they had severed the

relationship between themselves and him. They did it because they believed they could satisfy their own desires their own way, despite the fact that God had told them exactly what not to do.

I don't know exactly what kind of relationship Adam and Eve had with the Lord, but I know they were with him every day and that the relationship was as close to perfection as a human could get. They knew him. They walked with him and bonded with him. So what went wrong?

It was that stinkin' snake, right? Not necessarily. The serpent is alive and well today, although not in his original form. But his words are the same, and they are all lies. Satan, the enemy of human souls, doesn't change his tricks. He still tries to convince people that God is holding out on them. He knows that if he can persuade mankind to disobey God's *wait* command and race forward to grab what he says is theirs, it will bring the destruction the scaly one desires.

Adam and Eve had chosen to trust in themselves rather than in God because they believed they knew better. Satan told them 'You shall be as gods' if they ate the fruit of the Tree of the Knowledge of Good and Evil. We do the same every day. Broken trust comes from a broken relationship. Broken relationship comes from lack of intimacy and lack of time spent between you and the one with whom you are in the relationship. That allows the enemy to tell you, 'You got this'…'It's your life' and 'You're free to do what you want.'

I have noticed now that when I sense a certain guy is bad for me, I put distance between us. That breaking of relationship, the interrupting of time spent together, gets my mind straight and helps me to see clearly. It weakens any hold he has on me. I don't have contact with him and the feelings wane, emptying my heart of him so that I can get my strength back. But I would never want to have that kind of breaking between God and I.

Here's the thing I've learned, time after bruised and bloody time: God knows what he is doing. I don't need to race ahead and help him find me a mate, or with any other opportunity. By owning that thought—that God is in control—and relying on it as if it were a life saver in a tossed sea, I can be assured that Mr. Tall, Dark and Warty can pass through my life and be gone and I haven't missed a thing—no matter what things look like on the outside.

2. Know your weaknesses

We all have our weaknesses. Superman had Kryptonite. Samson had Delilah. My weaknesses range from cocoa-roasted almonds and chips and salsa to certain men who could charm the stripes off a wasp. It doesn't matter how tall or pretty these men are. I have encountered little buggy-eyed guys with three hairs sprouting on their heads whose kindness made my heart race. I have also met one or two gorgeous male-model types whose garden-spider charm made them look ugly to me. But at first, they were charming.

Before I knew what my weaknesses were, and before I realized my value, I would fall for the attention of any man who expressed any interest in me. Fortunately, I held on to myself and did not let the man take what he wanted. Still, it was an empty existence of a person who, wanting to be married, lived in the cage of doing the same thing over and over again, crouching at the table of lust for scraps of toasted frogs' legs, while the full banquet of love waited for me somewhere…if I would just trust God and let him bring a man who truly respected me enough to give me himself and not try to take from me.

As of the writing of this, I am still not married but I enjoy my single life. While I wait for Mr. Wonderful to show up, single friends around me are dropping like flies, giving up their free-soaring ways for married life. While their love stories are all different—some met at church by sitting in a different place in the sanctuary, some met at work, some online; one thing seems to be the same: they knew but avoided places and situations where their weaknesses could overcome them, they avoided men who treated them below what they deserved, and got on with the business of living their lives and serving God.

And that's when their Mr. Right showed up.

3. Change your habits

Knowing your weaknesses is not enough. I have a weakness for lime-flavored nacho chips and salsa. Lucky Charms, however, is my kryptonite. Just because I know in my mind that I go all quivery when I see a box of the stuff from ten paces doesn't mean I should go test myself by walking down the cereal aisle just out of curiosity to see if there's a two-for-one sale.

Your Lucky Charms may have a dashing smile and that one piece of hair that flops over his forehead just so. Run, Forrest, run! You don't get points for testing yourself with temptation.

I was amazed when my pastor read Romans 12:2 to us and I learned what it really meant to change—or renew your mind:

'Do not be conformed to this world, but be transformed by the renewing of your mind, that you may prove what is that good and acceptable and perfect will of God.'

Now here's the cool part: When we think thoughts and do the actions that follow, it wears a physiological path in the brain—a habit. This is a proven scientific fact: Focused learning of new information, or exposure to new situations causes the *dendrites* in your brain to release a chemical targeted to new neurons in your brain, which then link differently, essentially making a new *neural path*.[1] It's like the grooves in the ice when skaters glide across it time and time again. The big skating rink machine comes by to smooth them out. God says to go further: create new, healthier grooves that are in line with His will.

'87% to 95% of the illnesses that plague us today are a direct result of our thought life. What we think about affects us physically and emotionally. It's an epidemic of toxic emotions.'[2] . You can have control over your mental and physical health, and you can change your own mind.

And you thought God and science lived on different planets. Nope. God created science.

4. Boundaries

Chickens have them. Football players have them. Prisoners have them: Coops...sidelines...cages. Whatever you want to call them, they

---

1 - whatisneuroplasticity.com
2 - Dr. Carolyn Leaf. http://drleaf.com/thought_life.php

are boundaries. They are designed as a stop. In dating relationships, boundaries give a woman respect for herself and others.

Boundaries can take different forms: Boundaries for safety; those for a date; those for friends. Boundaries are not something you want to make up as you go along. God gave commands in his word, but you must make them real for yourself.

The important thing, especially in a dating relationship (whether it's the first date or further into a courtship) is to have those boundaries marked in your mind. If necessary, write them down. So where do you start?

It helps first to know what you want. If you want to be married, don't pursue a relationship with a serial-dater. If you want to have children, don't be with a man whose desire is not to have any. Those are more goal-oriented boundaries. You cannot (and should not try to) change a man, no matter how cute he is or how charmingly he speaks to you.

The other boundaries are moral; what you will and won't do with a man. This should be a lifestyle. If you're a Christian, this should be obvious, but it is interesting how, when Mr. Tall, Dark and Gruesome takes the stage, some women want to shift their morals to do what he wants. Don't. Instead, before you meet someone, right now, while you're clear-headed, think about your boundaries, then write them out. Live with them; see how they work and how well you adhere to them. You may need a girlfriend who is out for your best interests to help you along with her accountability.

Looking to God's word, we can form boundaries which keep us safe and keep our goals in mind. Here are a few of mine:

God says: *'Run from sexual sin! No other sin so clearly affects the body as this one does. For sexual immorality is a sin against your own body.'*
– 1 Corinthians 6:18

You say: 'I'm not going to hang out with a man at his house for long periods of time' or 'I'm not going to be alone kissing a guy and doing 'everything but' sex,' or fill in the blanks wherever your temptation lies.

If sexual temptation is a weakness (and it is for a lot of us!), make a boundary: no men alone in your house with you unless they're fixing your cable or your kitchen sink. You may think sexual boundaries are excessive, seeing people in the world—especially on t.v., laugh at these boundaries. I have heard purity referred to as 'prudish'. Sex is a gift from God, but people who mock those who are trying to be pure neglect the value, power and beauty of sex. They are like kids who take a Fabergé egg and bang it with a hammer again and again, saying they have the freedom to do so, ignoring the destruction and looking down on those who don't join in. Those people will not be there when you are pregnant or struggling with an incurable STD. And t.v. never shows the repercussions of sleeping with numerous and strange people. It is never good.

God says: *'The LORD has appeared of old to me, saying: "Yes, I have loved you with an everlasting love; Therefore with loving kindness I have drawn you.'* – Jeremiah 31:3

You say: 'Because I am loved and valued by God, I will leave the presence of a man who doesn't treat me with respect, who puts me down or who otherwise hurts me.'

If a man disrespects you with his speech, tell him so politely: "I'm not used to people speaking that way to me. I would prefer you didn't do that again." He will either respect you and not do it again, or will continue to do so, at which time you need to get rid of him and don't look back. As with children, boundaries that are not reinforced are not boundaries at all. If you say you're going to take the toy away in response to bad behavior, take it away. Keep your promise, or you will have no respect from the man.

God says: *'You say, "I am allowed to do anything"—but not everything is good for you. You say, "I am allowed to do anything"—but not everything is beneficial.'* – 1 Corinthians 10:23

You say: 'I have freedom to do whatever I want, except what God has specifically said I shouldn't do. I can have a beer right now, but is that a good idea in this situation? I can spend long amounts of time on the phone with a guy, but is that good for me? Does it get me to my goal? I can fly Down Under to look for a tall Australian husband, but is that what I should do with my money? Is this wise?'

Again, these are personal and to be customized to your particular weakness. Maybe you just got a job in Australia, so that particular last boundary may be a different one to you. Think of the times when you start coasting downhill in relation to temptation, and mark that. Learn from it, then write down exactly what you will do next time. You may be amazed at how these little guideposts help you when you really need them. These are just a couple of examples, but it's important to think beforehand how you'll react and what you will put up with, before you are in the situation.

If this sounds constricting, it's not. You'll do what you want to do anyway. If you do what you always do, you'll get what you've always gotten. When you finally get tired of eating slop, you'll do things differently. You have the God-given freedom to choose, but no one will do it for you.

The most important thing is to realize when you're bored or lonely and just want someone. All of these boundary suggestions are worth nothing if you plunge ahead to find a temporary appeasement for a deep-down longing. It is the problem everyone who struggles with letting a Frog into her life encounters. And in the next section, you will see how to build up your boundaries not because someone said you should, but because you want to—because you are worth it.

Part III
Your Identity

Part III
Chapter 11

```
Identity Theft: Reestablishing Your Value
                One of a Kind
```

When I worked at a local sheriff's office as a graphic designer, I met a detective named Laurie Bryce*. Laurie was investigating a child kidnapping case. Deputies had just found the missing child alive in a closet, bound with gray duct tape. The child was shaken and otherwise okay, but a major part of the case was still unsolved: who had taken this child? With the presence of mind that would later earn her an award for this case, Detective Bryce dusted the inside of the duct tape for prints, reasoning that the abductor would have had to touch the sticky inside surface to rip off the tape.

> 'For You formed my inward parts; You covered me in my mother's womb. I will praise You, for I am fearfully and wonderfully made; Marvelous are Your works, and that my soul knows very well. My frame was not hidden from You, when I was made in secret, and skillfully wrought in the lowest parts of the earth. Your eyes saw my substance, being yet unformed. And in Your book they all were written, The days fashioned for me, When as yet there were none of them.'
>
> – Psalm 139: 13-16

She was right. The adhesive surface revealed a good, clear print and the perpetrator was apprehended. The case was used on an episode of *CSI: Crime Scene Investigation*.

They say no two fingerprints are alike in the world. It is the same with DNA. To believe that these individual details on and inside all of us are happenstance is ridiculous. So, given that these aspects of us are individual, how much more are we, as people, designed individually, each with a purpose?

This has set me at ease more than once, given my own strange 'fearful wonderfulness'.

*Names changed

I realize there is no one like me, who can do what I do. No one who looks like me. Even identical twins have differences and separate purposes.

I was always tall. I had hit the six-foot mark by the 8th grade. By then, I had grown used to kids teasing me about my height. I made myself believe it was good-natured even though the little delinquents in school encircled me like pirhanas to point it out.

But I'm not bitter.

Eighth grade was the year I got braces. I was constantly getting my lip snagged in the brackets that held the wire, so it looked like I was snarling. I actually had to pull my lip back down over my braces with my fingers. Try that when you're in front of the class giving a report on amoeba. I won't even mention the sores inside my mouth from where the brackets rubbed. The same week I got braces—as my gums were beating painfully from the wire wrenched tighter by the sadistic doctor—I got glasses. For some reason, maybe trying to fix things, I decided to dye my hair honey blonde because I saw that's what all the boys seemed to like. The box said 'strawberry blonde'.

Honey. Strawberry. Close enough.

It turned out closer to the washed-out orange-red of a bleached Irish setter. Always positive, I made the best of it and insisted it would look okay the next day at school. It didn't. I looked like a psychedelic tabby cat, sans stripes. My perfectly good light, soft brown hair was now the color of that pinky-orange magic shell stuff Dairy Queen used to put on their soft serve ice cream. I couldn't imagine someone would have bought that box of color voluntarily intending to look that way, even if they toured with a band.

So let's review. As a mathematical equation it would have looked like this:

Six foot tall + tabby cat pink orange hair + snarly-faced braces + glasses = my junior high class chasing me down the hall with lit torches and sickles like angry villagers.

Alright, it wasn't that bad, but it was torturous.

It went on that way until the hair grew out. The soft brown/shocking orange half-line of demarcation a few months later was particularly interesting. I looked like an illustration of the 38th Parallel. The braces came off two years later. By then, the little delinquents had found other prey to toy with. To say that I had some identity issues after that was an understatement.

But it gets better.

What made me feel more different than the other kids was the fact that I grew up in a rural area across the street from a mental hospital. The hospital had a stockade for criminally insane teenagers behind its main building, just a few hundred feet from our front door. The neighbors next to us ran a goat farm with 56 goats, some horses, dogs, cats and a bull who liked to escape their fence and stand in front of our sliding glass door to admire his reflection. My mom would cower in the car on those days, just home from work, waiting for the neighbors to come over and lead the hulking black thing by the ring in his nose back onto their side of the fence. The husband and wife who owned the goat farm were ivy-league university graduates, each of whom had a doctorate. I always thought the wife resembled Larry from The Three Stooges. She also had a high-pitched way of screeching at any one of the goats, who would climb atop one of the many truck bed covers laying on the lawn to get a better view of things. The only other thing I remember about her is when we all went out for dinner, dressed up, her in some sort of Aztec muumuu. When the waitress asked how she liked her steak, her eyes protruded as she said, "BLOOD rare!"

Seriously. You can't make this stuff up. But I digress.

You may not be a goat farm/mental-hospital-dwelling six-footer with orange hair and braces, but you, like everyone, have the trials and situations from this life that have imprinted on your identity. Pair that with our natural tendency to find our meaning and purpose outside of a relationship with God and the purpose He has for us, and you get a skewed identity. We're all broken in some way until we realize Who our source is and connect with Him.

Sorely Insecure

Jr. High School was particularly difficult for me. I hated it. I believed it was the closest thing to jail that one could come, even though there were no bars on the windows or yellow uniforms, though gym suits came close. It was all there: the nasty food, the prison guards, the exercise yard and, of course, the pecking order: the geeks, the brains, the stoners, the jocks… you get the picture. There was even the occasional beating. (The girl fights were way more entertaining than the guys' fights, in my opinion.)

I fit into the geek category, I'm sure, and I seemed to have a target on my back. One of the cheerleaders liked holding court with her female hangers-on, hissing little insults at passers-by, including me. From the first day of first grade when the class bully pushed me down in the hallway so my front tooth went through my lip, to grade school when the wall-eyed girl and her friends trapped me in the soccer goal cage and made me sing songs, to when a gang of city kids tripped me in the hallway every day, to every day in between when, it seemed, the jocks pointed out my lack of physical endowments that their cheerleader counterparts had, it was like living in the jungle. It was classic school years. I escaped major physical harm, but the emotional wounds left their marks.

If I were the person I am now, I would have handled things differently. I wouldn't have been so serious, for one thing. I would have realized that, in 20 years, some of these people would have grown out of their imbecility, some wouldn't have, but would have forgotten about me, and some would be pumping gas at the local Stop-and-Rob. I would have convinced myself that there was no reason for me to hold on to those wounds even a minute after they had been made. But being the person I was then, I did hold on, for a while. I didn't know my value. These classmates were my world. I technically spent more time with them—seven hours a day at school—more than with my parents: a measly three or four hours each night. It was the equivalent of brainwashing: repetitive statements about me over years. No wonder I walked slumped through most of my teenage years. I definitely should have learned the art of the smack-down during those bully years.

I and the rest of the students were also defined as 'evolved'; a term which lowered my individual worth to that of pond scum and excused any need for a moral compass. In Sunday school, they taught us about Adam and Eve, so I figured Adam and Eve were cave people who evolved from paramecia. I didn't think past what I was told by school, by my church or by the media.

When I went to college, life changed for me. I was no longer 'Skinny Sticks' or 'Tree' or some names I can't repeat here. No one knew me at the college I attended, which was an hour away from home. Better than that, men were attracted to me. I started playing up what was, in high school, my bony and non-existent curves. Now I had a perfect body; purely because of youth and good genes. I noticed I got male attention when I did so, and that was good, right? I didn't realize that the currency I would use to bargain with was the value I would get back. If I used physical wiles, I got physical attention back. The lure I was using would never get me the loving husband (or at the time, great boyfriend) I wanted. The only problem was I wanted more than that. I wanted the handsome Prince who would give me his heart. But, at Dirty Frank's Bar near our college on Broad Street, men weren't really looking to give their hearts away, and they certainly weren't looking for a woman's heart either.

> *I didn't realize that the currency I would use to bargain with was the value I would get back.*

I only flirted. I never got physically intimate with the men I met at parties or college bars. I certainly never went home with anyone, thinking even then that would have been a crazy and stupid decision. At that time in our city the local murderer, Gary Heidnik was a Philadelphia celebrity.

They had found the bodies of two women in his basement and four female captives still alive. I knew that going home with someone was dangerous and that I wouldn't get marriage out of it. But the attention for a while was nice. The problem with deceiving others is that soon you start to believe your own disguise. My first Frog was my boss at the time.

We worked in the music industry, and I was enraptured with the fact that he was well-traveled and had run with the biggest rock acts in the industry. I must have been like a tiny white mouse to him, it had been so easy for him to bat me around like a cat, flatter me, manipulate me and get what he had wanted. The whole time I had thought I'd had control over the situation. After all, I had my newfound ability to flirt, and some new clothes. All I'd ended up getting for my troubles was lost virginity (sex had been a far less-than-stellar experience… that was it?), and the new knowledge that this Frog still had a girlfriend on another continent he'd neglected to tell me about, who was coming over to the States to live with him in a week.

> A woman trying to be what she thinks a man wants her to be cheats the man and the woman.

I had given away my most valuable treasure to someone about whom I'd had no information, and from whom I had no commitment, and I'd walked away with deep wounds.

My mom had always told me to save myself for my future husband. Now that that wasn't a possibility, I continued living the romance novel life, and getting the same result: no husband and more wounds. Evan, the last boyfriend I had in what I like to call my 'old life' was the worst experience, although the man himself was decent. He was more of a Bullfrog than a Poison Frog. He had issues, but tried to love me. Evan told me at the beginning of the relationship that he was moving to the other side of the country at the end of the summer, but I dated him anyway, recklessly throwing myself again into the vortex of an impossible relationship. When he did leave, as he said he would, I went into a depression so deep I wanted to die just out of sheer will. In the days following his departure, I stayed up extremely late at night in an attempt to sleep through as much of the next day as possible. It never worked. I would wake up at 6 a.m. and start crying; trying to stay in bed and go back to sleep, but it didn't work.

I didn't bother drinking or doing drugs because somewhere deep down I knew it would prolong whatever pain I had to get out of me. It would also waste a great deal of time and cost too much money. I hated wasting time and money. Even in my severe depression, I was always maddeningly pragmatic.

A friend of Evan's, Blake, always invited Evan and me to his church. We were quick to decline every invitation, hiding our mocking smiles adequately, we thought. I had stopped going to church before college, having seen all the hypocrisy it had to offer. I didn't see the point of it anyway, all that standing up and sitting down, reciting verses and singing old songs. The last thing I needed was church.

But now, I was desperate. It was summer. Everyone was on vacation, or had moved away. I was utterly alone in my tortured state. Maybe I would go to his church just for something to do. It was better than sitting at home.

'Church' turned out to be a group of twenty- and thirty-something people milling around in the bright early sunshine, talking. We got there in the morning and, technically, it wasn't church, but more of a Bible study. The church service was somewhere else, in the evening. Mercifully, Blake led us to the back of the atrium room where everyone was gathered. I was a sniveling, snotty, red-eyed mess. I didn't want anyone to see me, and I sat there and looked at everyone, hunched in my corner like a threatened cat. I finally looked up and around the room, terrified I would catch someone's eye and have to converse, but I was curious about my new surroundings. I was struck by the joy I saw on their faces. It wasn't a weird, put-on expression or fake smile, but a light which emanated from within. Every single one of their faces shined.

Blake introduced me to his group of friends. We went for lunch at a local pizzeria afterwards. None of them pried about my red eyes, but just accepted me and included me in their banter and fun. As the afternoon progressed, my heart melted. I know now God was working on me, but then, I had never known God that way. After lunch we all sat in Blake's car and he asked me if I wanted to pray, and I did. I had no idea what I was doing, but as I prayed I began crying, hard. Again, I don't even know why. I was told I had given my life to God. I didn't even try to figure out what that meant at the time. We went to Blake's house, the four of us, and talked a while, the conversation dwindling into all of us taking a nap on the floor in the living room, thanks to the pizza. It was the first time in weeks I had slept a solid sleep. It would be the first time in life I had ever experienced such deep peace.

God's Girl

I would love to say I have not experienced a broken heart ever since that last one with Evan, but it wouldn't be true. We still live in a fallen world where we all make our own choices. I am still waiting for my wedding night, and have been since that day in the parking lot when I gave my heart to God. But I have, over those years, allowed a couple of men access into my heart that they never should have had. And it still hurt just as badly as those old days when I had given everything to Evan. Today, I value the lessons about not giving any of my heart away to someone who isn't my husband. And that strength comes from the Person whom I now know is watching me, loving me and who has the best for me.

One of the world's favorite mantras is 'We're all God's children'. But no, we're not. A child acknowledges that her father has authority over her. She resembles her father, in appearance and deed. She adheres to the rules of the house. When she disobeys, he chastises her, but only because he loves her and wants her to grow into a strong, healthy adult. She spends time with him and loves his presence.

For the longest time, I had walked through church doors as a kid and into adulthood, up until college, but I didn't know God. I did the religious things and had my own rules. With that, I tried to find my own value—to be a 'self-made woman', but it didn't work. Every achievement I did, every outfit I wore, or witty remark I said or bit of money I made served to give me a sense of value only for a short time. None of it lasted.

When I had begun to learn that I was delicately knitted together in my mother's womb, that I was assigned DNA specific only to me, that I was given gifts—humor, artistic ability, intelligence, and various other things, I began valuing myself. I was thought-out. Planned. I was created for a reason. I am loved.

And so are you.

When I got to know more about the sacrifice God made so I could live forever with Him, the thought of giving my body to a man for a few minutes in exchange for some perceived value in myself falls dreadfully flat. I do still get tempted, but I weigh my options and decide against doing the wrong thing.

Other women know this, but I don't believe enough women do. If every woman truly knew her value, the supply of her time, heart and body to unworthy men would be cut off. Could that happen? Anything is possible. I don't believe it will happen in this world, but if women could know how valuable they are and wait for God's best for them, their worlds and the world at large would change. I have seen it happen individually.

Fitting in or standing out

As an artist, I am always interested in visiting art galleries for inspiration and to see what's out there. In the Philadelphia area, there is quite a mix of incredible artwork. Closer to the city, the work tends to be less conservative and more daring and inventive. Further from the city, landscapes and the rustic, stony and wood architecture of Chester County are more popular. I have my own style, as many artists do. I like characters—faces, collage, detail and lots of color. I describe my work as surreal…kind of like my life. People like my work, but it doesn't fit in all galleries or in all markets.

Recently, while visiting a gallery specializing in realistic rural watercolor landscapes and buildings, I thought to myself: *I could do that.*

I knew I could paint the way these artists painted. I believe part of the reason I had that thought was because I saw the price tags on the art. I figured I could get quick sales by doing what someone had already done. As I continued to look at the detail in the pictures and calculate the work and energy it would take, still knowing I could do it, my spirit started to dry up inside me. While this art was well-executed and brilliant in quality, it wasn't my taste. It wouldn't challenge my imagination. I would be bored halfway through painting it. Not only that, I would have to do twelve or more pieces for any gallery to even want to look at me. I also knew that the pieces probably would not be successful because they would lack the spark of interest and passion it took to make them truly sing. Someone had already worked through the artistic processes that had taken years to arrive at these paintings. I would just be mimicking them.

Sighing, I walked out of the gallery and took a breath. I knew God had created me to be more than just a copy machine creating an income stream on someone else's path. I might need to change the location where I looked for galleries. I might need to change the way I marketed my work. I might need to keep persisting in putting my work out there so I could find my market. One thing I knew I shouldn't change, though, was my art. I may evolve in style or technique or medium, but that is growth, and it comes from my own will, experiences and affinities as an artist. I couldn't change my work to fit a perceived mold—it would never say the things I want it to say, which is the reason I am an artist. I need to be able to communicate my way to say what I want in my style. I made that decision, but how many years did I try to change who I was as a woman, to fit into what I thought a man wanted?

I see that often in the world of art: unknown artists copying established ones. I showed in a gallery in Florida once where local artists hung their work. One piece caught my eye because it looked exactly like the work of an established artist whose show I had seen about an hour north, a few weeks earlier. The unknown artist—we'll call him Tim—was so convincing in his execution that I thought the famous artist—we'll call him Erik—was showing at our gallery, but no. As I thought about it, I knew Erik owned his own galleries across the country and showed at those. He didn't need to inhabit ours. Tim had used Erik's technique, color palette and style. He had even used the characters Erik had created himself. It annoyed me to no end. Tim's work cost about one-eighth the price of Erik's, but it looked it, too. There was a shimmering depth Erik achieved in his work that came from hours of experimentation, discovery, layering and observation. Tim's work showed none of this. Tim was a 'budget' Erik. I wondered how long Tim would pursue this style, before he found something else that he thought would work for him. In identity-hopping, I wondered how many times Tim would miss success and true fulfillment as an artist because he wasn't being himself.

A woman trying to be what she thinks a man wants her to be cheats the man as well as herself. Guys can smell this a mile away, too. My friend, Luke, was talking to me on the phone one day about our friend, Kayla. Luke and Kayla have known each other a long time. They used to date, but are now friends. It looks like they may have been moving toward a dating situation again, but Luke told me he noticed how Kayla tries to be something she's not around him. "If I tell her the sky is green, she'll agree with me."

It's a shame, because I wonder if something great couldn't happen between Luke and Kayla if only she would be herself. I know Luke loves being around her, but she won't give him the chance to know her because she is too busy trying to change to be what the 'market' wants.

The maddening part of all of this mask-wearing is that, while you think you're being what a man wants, he could be wearing his own mask, being what he thinks you want. Now you've got two plastic mannequins staring at each other while two flesh-and-blood human beings sit inside them, stock-still, fearing that one wrong word, action or taste in movies or restaurants will send the other running.

Consequences of insecurity

I learned the illustration of not being yourself firsthand years ago, after I got out of college. I submitted some art to a famous magazine. Many illustrators featured in this magazine became successful after even short stints within its pages. To my amazement, the art director wrote back to me expressing his interest in my work. He wanted to see more samples. I began looking for more pieces I had done along the lines of the ones I had sent, but all of a sudden something popped into my head: if he liked my work, maybe I should do some pieces a little more in keeping with an artist who had already had a successful run in the magazine.

I know. It wasn't exactly brilliant thinking. Most art directors are interested in finding something new and dynamic, which my original samples had been. But I created a few pieces that resembled one of their most famous featured illustrators. The models and setting and compositions were mine, but the style was that of the other illustrator.

You know what happened. I got the nice 'thanks but no thanks' letter. I had blown it with one of the biggest magazines ever. It taught me a lesson with my art, but as a woman, I continued to try to be something else. I got the same result.

Losing a potentially lucrative art job is one thing, but marrying someone and finding out one or both of you is not who he or she appears to be is far worse.

I'm glad I never married the wrong guy, but I have to wonder how many nice guys I missed out on because I wasn't being myself. I know God is a God of second chances, so I look forward to what He has for me, which I know will be pleasing and a perfect gift for me.

Olivia's story:

I was in a bad marriage with an emotionally abusive husband whom I was already contemplating leaving. My husband said I needed to get a job and that's where I met Peter. Peter was very attentive—even to the point of listening in on my phone conversations after I was hired. I felt, naïve, gullible and insecure so when Peter started talking to me, it was comforting. We started going to lunch together with a group from work. After that, we got together on weekends. He would always say 'Don't leave your husband for me'. He didn't want the blame of ending my marriage.

Well, I did leave my husband. A year after meeting Peter, I moved with him into his parents' rental house. I felt I couldn't go home because I knew my husband would want to know where I was and where my kids were. I felt endangered. I got a restraining order against my husband. Peter and I kept the relationship out of the workplace—kept it camouflaged. Peter left that job and got another, where they gave him a cell phone and pager and he worked night hours.

In time, I began to notice certain things in the house were out of place. For instance, multiple damp towels were left on the floor from a shower. He was tired all the time. Someone would call him on his cell (we didn't have a house phone) and he hid the caller's identity from me. He wouldn't tell me about his job. When I asked, he always found a way to blow it off. Soon I placed things throughout the house so that, when they were moved, it would tell me someone had been there when he was supposed to be gone. I noticed a change in the amount of laundry, towels and linens (and men don't change bedsheets!). The wet towels were on the floor only on certain days. There was lipstick on one of them. Since I didn't wear makeup at the time (my ex-husband had been controlling and was insecure, not letting me wear make-up), this was a big clue. I purposely drove over to the house once and I saw him asleep, but felt another presence in the house. I surmised the woman was either dropped off or had walked over—there was no other car in the drive. I brought up the laundry issue; the towels on the floor and frequent loads of wash. He assured me nothing was going on and he wasn't cheating on me.

One day he got new cells from work and brought them home in a box. There were no bills for the cell phones. There were never statements for bills or any register for his checks. I was very suspicious about how the bills were getting paid. I didn't want the cell he gave me and told him to take it back. Mail would come and he ripped up the envelopes without reading them. It was difficult for me to get mail because he got home before me.

Later, I went for an annual exam and found I had an STD. When I confronted Peter, he blamed it on my ex-husband.

Peter's parents said they were putting the house on the market and asked him for rent which hadn't been paid. I had been giving him rent, but it turns out he hadn't paid them. He took advantage of my divorce situation and I discovered that was why he had been listening into conversations, figuring out how much money my estranged husband and I had. To this day, I don't know why I had conversations with him at work. He had just seemed to pull me in.

HAIR SALON: $225
DESIGNER OUTFIT: $150
JIMMY CHOO SHOES: $655
MAKE-UP: $75
TEETH WHITENING: $125
PERSONAL TRAINER: $300
CELEBRITY EYEBROWS: $75
MANI/PEDI: $50

BEING YOURSELF: *PRICELESS*

I re-carpeted and fixed up the house once, but Peter never told his parents I had done this. He would never take it off the rent. He would do things to better himself, like classes and the gym, and was materialistic, but never had any money. His car was falling apart, but he always had to have it washed. Once he got a letter from court saying his car would be repossessed. Somehow he took care of it. I was used to this, having had to 'fix' my husband's financial difficulties before the divorce, so I thought this was normal with Peter. He sugar coated everything, saying the money and bills were 'nothing'.

Peter asked me to marry him one day, saying he was at that 'stage' in life. We had moved out of his parents' rental house in May; his parents saying we owed rent. I found an apartment. Because my credit was still good, we were able to move in. We were engaged at the time. Since I felt uncomfortable with him financially, I told him to give me his money and I would pay the bills. He gave me cash.

We would go out on the patio and talk. I was always suspicious of his mood, tiredness...of his personality in general. He would start to open up then shut down, candy coating things. I noticed things about his personality that I would call red flags now. He would sit there without speaking and ignore me—I thought. But he was listening to what I had to say so he could find out what I knew about him. After that he would say he had to go to bed because he didn't have anything to say about the conversation we were having. At times, he would comfort me enough to make me feel better about any misgivings I had—just enough to keep me thinking my doubts were unfounded. He said my suspicions were remnants of my ex-husband and that I was stressed about the divorce.

He went with me to the doctor's office during the freezing of my cervix because of the STD. The cells on my cervix had multiplied and become cancerous to a .5, or, in other words, Stage 1. The doctor said he could determine if Peter had it too and that Peter could test himself at home—to pour vinegar on the affected area and if it bubbled, he had it. He learned how to do the vinegar test and went home and did it, but he refused to show me the results. He never told me if he had anything, but knew he did.

A while later, I found a different job. Peter was a job-hopper and got another customer service job with copy machines. I started working for the same company. He worked with women and was constantly charming them and flirting with them. He was always around the girls. I wasn't bothered by this, and wasn't jealous. I just wanted to know what he was hiding. I always had my detective hat on but, because I was busy and working and with my kids, I let every red flag fly by, unheeded. Peter didn't want the child seat in the back of his car, so he never helped me with the kids.

One of his favorite lines to me was, "without me what would you do?" He used this when he helped me get the job, too. He accused me of wanting more money, when all I wanted to do was feed my kids. Peter knew about my terrible insecurity and played on it.

This job where we worked ended up going into bankruptcy, but I found another one the same week. Around that time we were busy trying to plan the wedding. Red flags were going up, but I wasn't paying attention to what was going on. Peter would always smooth things out, saying nothing out of the ordinary was happening, even though he would flip his computer screen down whenever I approached him in his den. He told me he was looking for a job.

We were married in March. On our honeymoon in Cozumel, he wouldn't come off the ship onto land, which I thought was strange. Again, I shrugged it off. When we got back, by father told me he needed help at his cabinetry shop and said Peter knew the computer. I figured I would reciprocate for the job Peter had helped me get, so I got him a job there. He started embezzling from my family's company immediately, forging names on checks, paying bills in my name. He was there from January to May and had embezzled over $20,000. He went through my things, taking my car payment stubs and paying them before they were due, all through my dad's company, using my dad's money. He was 'making' lots of money—in one year made over $2.5M! Being the office manager, he saw all the numbers, so it was easy for him to steal from all of us, even forging my now-husband, Sam's signature, who was a partner in the company at the time. He also never wanted to use his car to go grocery shopping, and would get 'shipments' delivered to the shop.

My kids were at their dad's for the first half of the summer and I usually saw them on weekends. One day Peter walked me out to the car for one of those trips—which was very out of the ordinary for him, and gave me a big hug and kiss. I got into my car and took off for work that Friday. I got to work, called him on his cell and he didn't answer. He wasn't at the shop either, and the company said they really needed him. I kept trying his cell. Nothing. I was concerned for his safety. My boss's partner sensed something was wrong and told me to go home to see if he was hurt. My boss agreed, saying my mind wasn't on work today because of this. Later, my boss shared that he sensed something around me he didn't like. I drove back home and saw that nothing was out of place. His clothes and toiletries were still there. I went to our home computer to try to find an answer as to where he was and I did. He had been chatting with a woman in Canada.

I saw the woman online, started talking to her, and asked where she was. She confessed to me that Peter was flying up to her that day, from Miami, connecting in New York, then to Toronto. I called Air Canada, gave his name and said that there was an emergency from his wife—that he needed to come right back home. The airline attendant gave him the message in his seat and his jaw dropped.

I learned when he came back that the Canadian woman wasn't what he had expected. As will happen online, both were lying to each other, he saying I was just a roommate helping him out with bills. The woman had a 15-year old daughter and was not his type, nor anything he thought she would be. He had lied and had told her he had a yacht and house in the islands. I also learned that this was why he didn't come off the ship in Cozumel that day on our honeymoon—he had been on the internet talking to her.

He blamed his activities on mental illness and being bipolar. He cried and my dad called him a "crybaby". I told my dad he needed to check his books. My stepmother investigated and saw the embezzlement and forged names.

The police came and took him away to a state mental hospital. I moved out of the apartment complex and rented a townhouse from my dad. When Peter got out of the hospital, he moved in with me. He was on medication and had no insurance. He'd gained weight from the medication. He slept *and ate all day. I told him he needed to find a job. He whined that he couldn't and I booted him—something I know I should have done long ago. I'd had enough and didn't have the money to support my children AND him. I told him I regretted marrying him. He had hurt me and my family and destroyed my trust. I ordered him to leave and would see that the marriage was annulled.*

My dad was on the phone to Peter's parents telling them how I had put so much money into their house. They blamed Peter's problems on my kids and how they stressed him out. My dad defended me and said they needed to pay him something to reimburse his company or their son would go to prison. I gave my dad the money from our wedding as well. The divorce was final before our first year anniversary.

Olivia urges other women to know who they are before they get married, and to obey red flags and not rush. "You are two imperfect people," she says, "but you should be complete and happy in your life before you get married, not expect a man to rescue you out of your situation." Olivia is happily married today.

Part III
Chapter 12

The Mirror Lies

Every woman loves the mirror on some days and wants to cover it with a black cloth on others. Mirrors don't lie. But there are other mirrors in which everyone sees themselves reflected.

They are filters through which we see ourselves. The only problem with most of these mirrors is that they distort the truth. Culture, opinion, the desire for achievement, relationships, and even our own views, beliefs and experiences color what we think of ourselves as women. Such filters need to be adjusted before the fresh new growth of truth can take root.

The Mirror of Achievement

How many corporate ladders do I have to climb before I feel good about myself? How many triathlons do I have to race? contests do I have to win? degrees do I have to earn? paintings, movies or books do I have to produce? dollars do I have to make? pounds do I have to lose? children do I have to raise right? companies do I have to own?

Just writing the list is tiring. If you are relying on achievement in order to be something, you will always be running, earning, producing, but not for the joy of doing it. When it is lost, so will be your value—in your eyes. There will always be someone to outdo you, and there is nothing you can do to change that.

'What profit has a man from all his labor in which he toils under the sun?' – Ecclesiastes 1:3

This mirror works in tandem with the *Mirror of Opinion*. For some, working and achieving gives them a sense of worth for themselves. For others, it gives them a good opinion among their neighbors and coworkers. Jesus rewards hard work and wants us to be and do the best we can. Work is a blessing and when you're doing what you were wired to do, it is a joy. But it is only a part of life. When work is the foundation upon which your 'house' or life, is build, be assured, it will come crashing down. Know your purpose and do it with all your heart, but play to the audience of One so that when the time comes, you will have praise from the same.

The Mirror of Self

'For we dare not class ourselves or compare ourselves with those who commend themselves. But they, measuring themselves by themselves, and comparing themselves among themselves, are not wise.' – 2 Corinthians 10:12

It wouldn't be so bad to judge yourself using your own opinion if you didn't have moods, emotions, influences like T.v., movies and magazines or other people around, and if you were perfect. Our natural inclination to compare ourselves with others either puts us proudly above someone who we misjudge as lesser than us (do we really know a person enough to lower them in our eyes?) or we misjudge someone as above us, which is usually from judging on appearance alone; looks and material possessions. But do we really know if that person is happy or kind? In either case, the result is a constantly changing opinion of ourselves which most commonly ends in an insecure view through a tiny mirror.

I've been amazed (and embarrassed!) with myself constantly when I thought this way, and many times I was put in my place. I still get tempted to compare or measure myself against someone else. It's hard not to do, but it is not good to do. God has a way of showing us our own ugly insides and, with kindness, helping us to change. The people I saw as 'having it all together' and being financially blessed, needed my mercy instead of my judgment. And the people I saw as strange or irritating usually showed me they were creative, had the gifts of encouragement or mercy, or gave wise advice. They were also much more patient and kind than I was.

The Mirror of a Man

At the beginning of most dating relationships, you can do no wrong. Your boyfriend calls you beautiful, pretty, smart, or just casts those longing glances at you. The result? You're on top of the world. Until something changes. He has a bad day at work or is grouchy. Or you say or do something wrong. Or the relationship ends. And with that inevitable downward slide goes your self-worth...if you have anchored it onto a man. But a broken heart is not the worst thing that could happen, should you have a need to be built up by the presence, words or actions of a man.

If you have a 'price'—that is, if you are willing to trade yourself in order to be liked for a while, it opens you up to be used and manipulated. A manipulator will test you first, to see if you will put up with certain behaviors or suggestions from him. If he finds that you will put up with his behavior, such as criminal acts, verbal or physical abuse, being controlled, being used for sex or anything else, the longer you stay with him, the more you will find yourself explaining away what is wrong with his—and possibly your—behavior. Your paradigm of right and wrong will shift and you will find yourself wondering what actually is right and what is wrong. As a man gets bored because he knows he has you, he will withdraw. This makes you try harder to keep him. In the process, lose your peace and increase your stress. But let's rewind...

Let's say he tests your limits with his behaviors and you tell him—politely—to change those unacceptable behaviors or take a hike. You won't put up with his behavior, or his treatment of you. He leaves. He was good looking and your heart may sink a little, but you've just drawn the line between letting someone take advantage of you and choosing to be alone and wait for God's best. The best part is that your Prince will see the line you have drawn and he'll stand behind it, admiring your self-respect, and wanting to win you!

When your self-worth is anchored in who God says you are; that is, if it is anchored outside your relationship with a man, then you are free to love that man the right way. You will not try to be what he wants or put the burden of your own identity on him.

The Mirror of Popular Culture

I have a picture of myself in first grade wearing a purple sweater vest my mom made. It had an orange ladybug on it which was kind of embossed...it stuck out from the sweater all puffy-like, about an inch. I had one of those pixie haircuts, short and chopped. I topped the whole disaster off with purple corduroys.

I looked good.

I know what you're thinking. But that was in a different time. That's my point. In that day, the culture said corduroy, acrylic and candy box colors were in. For women, those drawn-on Twiggy eyebrows were in. Then thick brows were in during the next decade. Skirts were short, then they were long. I don't think it was the drugs that had people's heads spinning, but the constant changes in body architecture and decoration. But what an ingenious way of keeping the money flowing. Bravo, Madison Avenue.

And it continues today. It is someone's job to tell you what to like. What music is hot. What movies to see. What looks are in. What food and drinks are in. What words are in! That last one I never could figure out. Words are words, but I guess nothing is safe from the Ministry of Propaganda. It is an ever changing sea of shifting sands that would make even the most sane girl forget who she is if she isn't anchored in who she is.

'Charm is deceitful and beauty is passing, but a woman who fears the LORD, she shall be praised.' – Proverbs 31:30

There's nothing wrong with looking like the beautiful Princess you were made to be, and doing it in style. But how much time is spent trying to keep up with everyone else? Why not set the trends? Why not swim against the tide and be beautiful in your own way? There is nothing more beautiful than a woman who dresses to flatter her figure and coloring, especially if it is clothing that is a little different than what every other person in the world is wearing because it suits her.

There is a show on t.v. about bridal dresses (reality t.v.—another trend). Every time I see a preview for a different episode with a different bride, I see each bride wearing the same dress: a strapless number with nothing else remarkable about it. Worse, the horizontal neckline (or chestline?) is not the most flattering for any of these women and is better suited for the stick insect-sized women with smaller chests. But never on one of these shows have I seen any other style than the 'tube top' dress (I call it). I don't know if this is a rule of the show, to have a dress that's always the same, or if these are the only bridal gowns made presently, but according to some of the bridal magazines I've flipped through, there are a great number of different and creative styles to choose from. My guess: these girls are too afraid to go against what everyone else is doing.

Because there will always be someone more beautiful or charming, or a new look or fad, a woman's identity can waver, especially when age begins leaving its footprint on her face. Swim against the tide and be who God made YOU to be! In Part III, I'll explain the practical ways of doing that. Read God's word and study how important you are to Him, the One who owns everything; your Handsome Prince. Take the trends and think forward and do your own thing! Maybe not a knitted ladybug vest, but something that is decidedly you!

When you are being yourself and are confident in who God made you to be, you exude confidence that will attract people who want what you have; people searching for an answer to the meaning of life, other women struggling with their identities, and maybe even a Prince.

The Mirror of Opinion

Everyone has an opinion and many people have no problem letting you know theirs. Opinions don't even have to come in a verbal form; they can be as simple as a look or an attitude toward you. If you rely on pleasing people, on asking everyone's opinion before you make a move, you will be forever tossed around like a ship on the ocean, never resting and always under stress.

'But when he asks, he must believe and not doubt, because he who doubts is like a wave of the sea, blown and tossed by the wind. That man should not think he will receive anything from the Lord; he is a double-minded man, unstable in all he does.' – James 1:6-7

The Bible encourages counsel when making decisions.

'Without counsel, plans go awry, but in the multitude of counselors they are established.' – Proverbs 15:22

But be wary of who you ask. Are you asking financial advice from a shopaholic? Advice about marriage from a woman on her third husband?

'Confidence in an unfaithful man in time of trouble is like a broken tooth, and a foot out of joint.' – Proverbs 25:19

The most important opinion is Jesus Christ's. If the opinions of others are too valuable to you, it means you have a price, and that those opinions are more important than the truth. Don't worry; many of us still struggle with this, but just recognize it and go against it. It is only when either we choose to make God most important, or when he, in his mercy, puts us through a hard time when everyone around us leaves us, rejects us, slanders us or is unavailable to support us, that we will hear Him. For that season of time, it is then that God draws us close and severs the cord between us and the importance of public opinion.

People may judge you by your exterior or by wrong information. Let them. You can't control others' thoughts or words, only your reaction to them. By clinging to the truth that you are priceless in the eyes of your Creator, you will know that your own low view of yourself is wrong and that what others think of you is unimportant. The God who loves you also tells you you're the apple of His eye. You may just show someone else that it's ok for *them* to be who they are.

'For thus says the LORD of hosts: "He sent Me after glory, to the nations which plunder you; for he who touches you touches the apple of His eye.'
– Zechariah 2:8

The Mirror of God's Word

There is only one mirror that gives an accurate view of our value: the word of God.

God's word says it well: the only way to make your life stable is to anchor it into something solid and immovable. Putting His commands and statutes into action is not only freeing, but gives a woman confidence to be who she was created to be:

"Therefore everyone who hears these words of mine and puts them into practice is like a wise man who built his house on the rock. The rain came down, the streams rose, and the winds blew and beat against that house; yet it did not fall, because it had its foundation on the rock. But everyone who hears these words of mine and does not put them into practice is like a foolish man who built his house on sand. The rain came down, the streams rose, and the winds blew and beat against that house, and it fell with a great crash."
– Matthew 7:24-27

When you read about who you were created to be in the Bible, you may see things that challenge you to let go of yourself more so God can live more through you. Notice I didn't say you will see things that will help you 'be a better person'. Only paying attention to his commands and putting them into practice frees you to be who he created you to be. In that is not only freedom, but confidence.

Unlike the other mirrors, which distort the truth, God's Word is the only mirror that will show you the truth about yourself: that the heart is deceitful and wicked and can't be trusted (Jeremiah 17:6); that you are so priceless to God He sent His Son to die for you (John 3:16); that He is your husband (Isaiah 54:5); that you can do nothing without Him (John 15:5); that you are beautiful and He wants to be with you (Song of Songs 2:10); that you are His masterpiece and have a purpose (Ephesians 2:10); that if you give your life to Him you will live with Him in heaven forever in a place He has prepared for you (John 14:3); that He will come back soon to judge the earth (Revelation 22:7, 12). He is truth, and by aligning your life with His, you will experience the joy of knowing you are truly loved.

Your Situation

You may not have a problem with any of the mirrors that lie to you about yourself. But what do you believe about the circumstances you are in, or the events happening in your life? Maybe you're secure in your identity, but you are believing a lie about your past, about an event or about a circumstance. Here are some lies the enemy of our souls likes to push at us through our culture:

1. **Life ends at 40.** Really? What about John F. Kennedy, who ran for president at 43 and won? Grandma Moses who, at 90, was still painting and entering art shows? People who think life ends at 40 are

usually people selling fashion magazines, writing for t.v. or are terrified of their own impending fossilization and are trapped in their own insecurity. Same with life ending at 50 or 60. I suppose if the 'young' media propagandites had wisdom, they would see the marketing value of life in general, not just tolerance for a certain age group.

2. **Being a mother isn't as important as having a career.** And who raised you? If you had a mom who stayed with you and raised you, you know the security of having such a gift. If you didn't, you know the pain of insecurity and trying to make your own way in life, although you probably grew up developing a different kind of strength. The blessing of having a mother take time out of her life for decades to wipe your butt and bandage your knees and try to help you in all your troubles cannot be underestimated. Careers don't grow up and love people. There aren't many people on their deathbeds who wish they had worked more at their jobs. Moms are the only exception.

3. **'Stay-at-home-mom' isn't a real job.** That's true. It's several jobs, none of them paying cash; only future and eternal dividends. The next time you think being a 'stay at home mom' isn't a job, try not doing any of your chores as a single person for one month. Watch the laundry pile up and the food in your fridge die. Same thing would happen to kids if their moms decided to take a 'sabbatical' and go on a cruise down in Mexico.

4. **Unless you are a size 2 with perfect teeth and the right measurements, you'll never get married.** Just go look at the couples and families visiting a theme park or mall and that theory makes about as much sense as a fur-lined teacup. Looking at the miniscule number of tragically pretty couples in Hollywood whose marriages have lasted, the numbers fall in favor of you ignoring this lie.

5. **You need a man to be happy and validate you.** The only thing a man should validate for you is a parking stub. Other than that, look for your security from above. An earthly man just won't do it.

6. **You need a man to 'rescue' you from your boring life.** Aside from the fact that Jesus, the God-Man, rescued humankind 2,000 years ago, this is not going to happen. Unless the man is a fireman and your house is ablaze, or a genius accountant who shows up at audit time, there is no rescuing you should be waiting for. You are still a Princess, but your Savior waits for you to ask Him to rescue you and help you in your life. In the next part, I'll help you with suggestions for getting a life.

7. **You need a man to provide for you.** True, a man should be able to provide. I don't know of any woman who gets sheer joy out of taking care of a man while he sits in Monday Night Football pose on her new Pottery Barn sofa, but they do exist. A man should be able and willing to provide for his wife and family, but this is not a reason to marry someone. God does provide for His single Princesses, whether you're working or out of work. We all need to make a living, but marrying a man just for provision is a recipe for disaster. Marrying a man who has a good work ethic, though, is a wise thing.

Part III
Chapter 13

Self Esteem

It's a pretty well-known fact that we are always on our minds. Male or female, as individuals, we tend to think of ourselves before others. Does that mean we automatically love ourselves? Maybe. I know I can be pretty selfish at times. But that kind of consideration of ourselves doesn't always equate to esteeming ourselves highly. I'm sure people with many more letters after their names could break down this psychological behavior/consideration of self-love, but I'm going to give it to you as I know and have experienced it, and as I have seen and heard it in other people's lives.

It amazes me that some of my friends—even some celebrities, struggle with low self-esteem. Actress Halle Berry says, regarding her being voted 'Sexiest Woman' numerous times by various sources: "Although such things do wonders for my confidence, I'm never able to take them seriously. If they really knew me, they'd realize that I'm far from secure about my looks."[1]

Halle Berry said this! No matter what your idea of beautiful, you have to admit that Halle Berry is beautiful! Yet she struggles with her looks like many of us do.

Why do we, as beautiful, intelligent, unique creatures of God, struggle with such a low opinions of ourselves? It is because we don't know who we really are. Consider these truths:

1. There was not, is not and will never be anyone on this earth exactly like you; even if you are a twin.
2. You were God's idea. Whether you were an unplanned pregnancy, or even a result of rape, God knew you were going to exist and is ecstatic that you do! He has a plan for your *now* and your *later*.

1- AskMen.com, December 29, 2004, "Insecure Halle"

Every day is a chance for a change and hope. I know I felt at my worst when I was rejected by a guy. At some point I had attached my self-worth to what men thought of me. That's like attaching your rowboat to a piece of wood floating in the ocean. There's no stability and that chunk of wood moves around with the tide. The same way, a guy's moods, tastes and actions ebb and flow, as happens with all of us. Doesn't inspire a whole lot of security, does it?

There are some things we tend to do to control our situations or minimize the pain when we have low self-esteem:

1. Chameleon - A chameleon changes its color to match those of its surroundings in order to evade predators. When a woman does this, it isn't to evade attackers, but to fit into her surroundings...to belong. This happens a lot in grade- and high school, but many people grow out of it in adulthood. Some women have a tendency to want to create an 'instant relationship' with a man in a dating situation by aligning themselves with a man's likes and dislikes, totally subverting themselves and their own personalities in the process. And he can smell this a mile away. Does he like football? What a coincidence! You like football too (you don't even know what a football is). Did he have a deaf chinchilla who died in the bathtub when he tried to wash it? So did you! Not only do you have similar backgrounds and tastes, you assure him, but you 'one-up' him all night on the date until there is practically nothing he doesn't know about you—real or not.

The answer: Be yourself. Sounds easy, yet so many women find it difficult. To be yourself means you risk losing that man who, you think, will run if you tell him of your fascination with Persian postage stamps, or your desire to work with inner city autistic children through music. If he runs, good. Let him go. Do you really want to be playing the role of chameleon throughout a marriage, changing to be what you think he wants you to be? Not only will you be exhausted, but it won't last. You will become resentful because you're not allowing yourself to be all you are, and he will be resentful when he realizes you pulled a 'bait and switch'. Instead, practice feeling good in your own skin. When you realize that everyone else is either fitting into their own skin, or has already done so and is living their lives, and that both groups are focused more on themselves than you, maybe dipping your foot into the sea of your own purpose won't seem so scary. I guarantee it will be freeing and alive with possibility.

2. People-pleasing - This is a by-product of "chameleonism". It is something else men can sense from a distance and something for which they have little respect. This means you are a 'yes' girl, even at the expense of your own morals or beliefs. It's constantly saying 'yes' to a man in those first few dating weeks, accommodating him, going the extra mile, coming to where he is instead of making him drive, making him dinner, doing work for him, smoothing over his feelings, anything that you think will ingratiate you to him. This has the opposite effect. Men love the chase. I cannot emphasize that enough. Your job is not to wave a feather fan over his head, feed him grapes or acquiesce to him at every turn. Your job is to be the best you that you can be and, if he wants to be a part of that, great. If not, great. Either way, you win, keeping your self-worth intact.

Leslie learned this:

"I did everything for this man. I did my part of the work (designing the product and all the footwork that goes with that) for the company we'd formed, and he was supposed to sell it. He liked surfing the Internet and I realized I would have to 'sell' if we were to get anywhere. Because of my attraction to him, I thought I was getting closer to him by doing all this and, in addition, cleaning his house (he was so busy at work, he needed help!) and letting him nap at my house during the afternoon (when he should have been at his day job). I soon realized I was being used. Looking back, I can't believe how accommodating I was, and how gullible. I will never do that again for a man until I'm married, and even then, I know a good man will do his share, appreciate what I do and not take advantage".

୭

My own experience with people-pleasing was because I was a 'peace at all costs' kind of girl. Don't get me wrong; my parents were the best parents in the world. I have good manners, love, and a curious knowledge of how to build a radio as a result of my parents' influence. But the accommodating nature of my personality back then invited disrespect at school, which took the form of the gang of kids who regularly teased me. They knew they could do whatever they wanted to me—that I would let them. The bullying usually culminated in me getting my butt kicked by the female jocks in the locker room. I used to have stomach aches (fake and real) whenever I had to go to school. I regularly stayed home from school or got sent home. I knew the nurse on a first-name basis. After a while, I just learned how to disappear, wearing long-sleeved shirts and long pants in hot weather, just so the class criminals wouldn't make fun of my skinny arms and legs. I covered my mouth when I smiled so they would forget I had braces. I stayed quiet and hunched down in my seat so they would ignore me altogether. As a classmate said recently at a reunion, "Junior high was my Vietnam."

People-pleasing is exhausting and steals your self respect. It also invites the man to disrespect you. A good man—a Prince, will simply walk away. A Frog will take full advantage of you, mooching, manipulating and using you until you are spent, you displease him or until you summon your courage and boot his green hind out of your life.

The answer: Check your own heart first. Why are you about to do this nice thing for this person? There's nothing wrong with kindness, but do it for kindness' sake—or are you expecting anything in return? If you are doing something for a man you are attracted to, just don't. Again, it's not about the fact that you're helping him, it's about the fact that you are telling him he's got you, doesn't have to chase you, and that you don't need respect.

If you find yourself sacrificing, serving or doing for people in general, again, you shouldn't be expecting anything in return. If you are volunteering, you should also be getting the physical, emotional and spiritual filling you need first. This is not selfish, but necessary. If you are depleted, you can't give. Churches are full of well-meaning servants who work until their families, health, emotional well-being and other parts of their lives are jeopardized. God doesn't want us to work to exhaustion, but to work out of the energy and resources he gives us.

A people-pleaser serves, gives and does, in order to get something in return: acceptance, validation and other appeasements. A person acting from a healthy foundation gives, expecting nothing in return, which is the true meaning of love.

3. Beating yourself up - I am queen of this. Just thought I'd let you know, in case you tried to say you were. I never realized I was doing it, or that it was a bad thing, until I started working at a famous coffee company once. In learning the expensive latte-cappuccino-mochaccino, etc. coffee menu and how to make it correctly, I made lots of mistakes. Add to that the customers (to be fair, not all of them were this way), who had to have their beloved 'decaf - triple - grande - nonfat -one pump - hazelnut - one pump - mocha - no whip - two snaps up in a 'z' formation' - coffee NOW, there was a little more stress involved. Add to that, me messing up a drink and throwing off the timing of everyone else's drink orders, I had the perfect recipe for a self-beat-down. The evil little voice behind me—which sounded suspiciously like my own—loved putting me down: 'Totally stupid move.'; 'They said decaf. It's a button on the espresso machine. How hard is that to get wrong?'; or my favorite, 'Everyone else is doing it right. Why can't you?' Tears would form in my eyes and my throat would tighten and I got even more upset because... really? Crying over coffee?

That's when a kind coworker reminded me: 'It's only coffee.' What a simple yet profound statement. I let it sink in: It's only coffee. No one died. Even if they had, it wasn't my fault and it was probably their time to go anyway. I'm away from the coffee company now, but the old voices die hard. They still want to berate and discourage me about other things, like when I fail at a project, make a bad decision or don't look my best. I see them for what they are now: either my own old tapes, or the enemy of my soul, who wants to discourage me. But I let the other voice rise to defend me: "It's okay," it says when I mess up. "Now you know how not to do it. Besides, it's only life."

The answer: Seriously. When you spend your life berating yourself for not being the best, the fastest, the most beautiful, smartest, wittiest, or for just messing up someone's caffeine fix, you realize you have to start evaluating things as they are instead of how you think they should be. The great thing about knowing God is that He is the King of fixing mistakes and loving you through them. There's nothing you can do that can't be turned into something beautiful, if you trust him. Let the fear go and just live.

4. Tolerating - Some women will do things they never thought they would when their self worth is low and they fear rejection by a Frog. Verbal and physical abuse by a Frog, intermittent, rare phone calls from him when he wants something, cheating, and other unacceptable behaviors suddenly become acceptable, if only to keep him in the picture. Many women stick around for the table scraps of a man's attention. The Frog may try for dates with you at the last minute, or schedule dates and cancel them, send text messages to keep you in the periphery of his life for when he wants to play with you, or demand any other attention from you, short of a commitment. The more you put up with, the more you show your disrespect for yourself and encourage him to do the same. At some point, he will leave anyway because he will be bored.

Liz tolerated things she now wishes she hadn't:

It was the strangest thing. A guy I'd dated over a decade ago invited me to his house 45 minutes away when we reconnected after I'd moved back to the area. He said he didn't really like driving anywhere, so I drove to his house. He didn't have the groceries for dinner, so he drove us out to get them, and then made the meal. He acted like he was so into me. He kissed me, and wondered to me why no one had snatched me up. He called me beautiful, and we kissed and talked into the night. Another night I drove up again and we had dinner again, though his guy friend came over and then my date had to go pick up his daughter, so I went with him. We stayed up way too late, so he insisted I stayed over. Nothing happened…we had talked earlier in the night about how I wanted to wait until I was married to have sex so we just cuddled. He sent me an email a couple of days later about how things 'got out of hand' and that he just wanted to be friends. It broke my heart and I told him I couldn't just be friends. He texted and emailed me madly the next few days and I responded right back, then the messages tapered off. Once, he texted to tell me he knew I was busy and missed my company. I don't hear from him often now and assume he found someone who could give him the sex he wanted without the commitment. One day, out of the blue, he emailed me that he'd found 'the one'...his former ex-wife #2. He still text messages me to try to 'get something'. Though I'm glad I didn't give him what he wanted back then, he still hurt me. I wish I had insisted on meeting out, or cut things off after the first date when I saw how lazy and self-absorbed he was. I guess now I remember why we'd quit dating over a decade ago.

The answer: Meeting the man often where it is most convenient for him is a people-pleasing action in response to his bad behavior: selfishness. A man should be so excited to see you that he will drive to wherever you are, or wherever you want to meet, within reason. The best thing to do is nip this situation in the bud. Kill the beginnings of bad behavior before they have the chance to flower into full-grown disrespect of you. A man will test his boundaries with you to see what he can get away with, whether he knows he's doing it or not. Being brave enough to stand by those boundaries will either engender respect from him (if he is a Prince), or send him leaping away on his webbed feet. Either way, you win.

5. Codependence - The actual definition is: 'of or pertaining to a relationship in which one person is physically or psychologically addicted, as to alcohol or gambling, and the other person is psychologically dependent on the first in an unhealthy way.' [dictionary.com]. A woman lives in a situation like this because it is comfortable and, strangely, she doesn't believe there is anything else out there, or that there is nothing better out there for her. Being with someone who abuses substances and, in turn, abuses you, is never better than being alone. In fact, because you are in someone's presence you may think it solves the loneliness problem, but that actually makes it worse.

The answer: The woman of high esteem says: 'I have kept myself in unhealthy situations in the past, but I realize it is hindering my growth and keeping me back from true happiness. It's scary, but I'm going to jump out beyond the bounds of depending on someone for even crumbs of attention and either: a) let God direct my life and not control someone else or b) rely on God for my needs and know He has already accepted me, so I don't need to seek approval from others.

6. Giving yourself away - When your self-esteem is compromised, you are like the owner of the Golden Jubilee who believes she owns only a cubic zirconium. The largest faceted diamond in the world, the Golden Jubilee (previously a raw 755 carats) weighs 545.67 carats and has an estimated value of $4-12M. You may get a buyer who wants to negotiate the purchase of the big diamond, but you cut to the chase: for $150, he can have it because you just want him to like you. Well, the buyer saw the diamond and has yet to get it appraised, but with the way you're waving it around and asking such a small price for it, he's not so sure now. Maybe it's not the real Jubilee. Or maybe all he's heard about it isn't true. Maybe it's flawed somehow. He was going to offer $7M for it, but there must be something wrong with it if you're showing such obvious disregard for it and practically giving it away. You may have killed the deal, or he may just take it—a steal, for your pitiful price.

This is not just about sex, but about your heart. By nature, if a man isn't allowed to see the value of something he thinks he wants, and if it is simply handed to him, there is little perceived value. A famous marketing company dissuades its sales force from giving samples of their product, saying 'People don't value what they don't pay for.' When you spill the treasures of your heart: your dreams, secret desires and needs, to a man you've just met, not only is there no mystery, but these gems have fallen at a man's feet with no effort on his part, and he moves on. (Remember: you're supposed to be learning about and interviewing him so you will know whether or not he's worthy of those gems.) A Frog will take all he can get and still move on, after much pain and wasted time on your part. Worse, a Poison Frog will hang around and use that information—and the fact that you gave it so freely—to manipulate and use you until you put a stop to it.

The answer: A lady of high esteem doesn't give anything away. She lets a Prince mine for gems, all the while determining whether or not he is a worthy partner. This filters the Frogs out of the pool because they get bored or frustrated at the thought of seeking anything in the diamond mine, resenting the fact that the mine won't open for just any passer-by.

When a man asks you about yourself, don't give him a novel. Set your ego aside. Give him just enough information to draw out another question. This also creates conversation, opens up space for you to ask your own questions, and puts you back in 'interview' mode where you can get to know him better.

Part III
Chapter 14

A Masterpiece

You are a piece of work.

If you've lived even a few minutes on this earth, you know it can be a great place, and a cruel place. Because I was raised with loving, pretty normal parents, I grew up thinking the world revolved around me and that everyone was nice and was out for my best interest. It was my first day of school, when I was six years old, that I got my wake-up slap.

The day started out badly. I wore a red plaid dress, white stockings and black patent leather buckle-shoes. I liked the outfit, and figured everyone would want to know where I got it, including Jimmy Marberger*. Not understanding little boys' indifference to all things fashion, I told him anyway where I had scored my special Scotch dress. His answer to my excited fashion news was an uneventful 'So?' Nearby onlookers snickered and my face reddened deeply, to match the color of my dress. Duly humbled, I stayed quiet the rest of the day, wondering why he didn't care about what I had to say.

My experience with rejection (i.e., character-building experiences) continued with the choosing of teams in grade school. You would have thought tall, skinny me would have been chosen first for the kickball team, but all that physical yardage in my elbows and knees did nothing for me as I tripped and fell, like a spider in a windstorm, all over the playground during any game of anything. I was always left standing in front of two crowds of kids, trying to hide my bony legs as they made fun of me. But I was not alone. It was me with the smelly girl who picked her nose and ate her boogers and seemed not to be phased by her status standing with me as 'last choice'. We were inevitably foisted off on whichever team captain gave in and waved us over. I felt worse for her

*names changed

than I did for me, though I heard she works for NASA now. Gym class wasn't my life's ambition, and I just wanted it to be over. So after all the stocky mean girls were chosen first and the lottery was over, we would play.

As each team captain already knew would happen, I would mess something up. It didn't matter if it was volleyball (I'd miss the ball), kickball (I would kick and land my butt on the ground), soccer (I ducked when the ball came to me, avoiding any potential Marsha Brady incidents) or basketball (I would jam my fingers on the lay-ups). If there was a way to be bad at sports, I always found it. Couple this with the fact that we had to wear teal one-piece stretch gym uniforms with stripes, which made all of us (except some maddeningly curvaceous girls who could actually pull it off) look like mental patients, gym was torture. If I had any self-esteem before the class (and I didn't), it was buried six feet under by the time the bell rang. But there was one respite: I always missed the post-gym shower.

I have always believed in God, but if I hadn't, one thing would have convinced me for sure: being allowed to miss the humiliating post-gym shower for six years. All that time, from seventh to twelfth grades we were supposed to shower after gym class. My skinny naked self would have had to stand there among fifteen other more well-developed girls, who would have had no problem pointing and teasing me about two more of my shortcomings. I can't remember exactly how it happened that I missed the shower each time—sometimes class ran over and we needed to change and get to the next class; sometimes the gym teacher simply said we didn't need to shower—but the final coup de grace of soapy humiliation never came for me.

School is long over, but life is still a lot like high school. There are still the jocks, stoners, nerds and everyone in between, only the lines are a little more blurred. In some ways it's more difficult and in some ways easier. The difficulty comes from not measuring up to someone's standards or in having to work extra hard to continue to live up to someone's standards. Marriage takes work. A good body takes work. Children take work. Work takes work. Keeping your temper in traffic takes work. Failure after failure can ruin your day or, left unchecked, snowball into depression. The easy part is knowing I'm not locked in a concrete building anymore, being forced to shower with strangers (though I've never been to jail). I have the time and wisdom behind me to know that people's opinions just don't matter, especially if they're trying to bring me down.

God knows that we are dust. Literally. We are made of the same 13 minerals as dirt. He breathed life into us and gave us personhood. He gave us value. No matter who rejects me, no matter what I failed to do or be, I know my value hasn't changed. My Savior says in the Bible that He knows the number of hairs on my head. He is closer than my breath. He will never leave me nor forsake me. He is my friend. He dances for joy over the fact that I exist. He knew me before He created me. He has plans for me.

'For You formed my inward parts; You covered me in my mother's womb. I will praise You, for I am fearfully and wonderfully made; Marvelous are Your works, And that my soul knows very well. My frame was not hidden from You, When I was made in secret, And skillfully wrought in the lowest parts of the earth. Your eyes saw my substance, being yet unformed. And in Your book they all were written, The days fashioned for me, When as yet there were none of them.' – Psalm 139:13-16 (New King James Version)

The great thing about knowing that God tells the truth is that I know my value cannot change with the trends, people's moods or my actions. God can't love me any more than He does already, and there's nothing I can do to make Him stop loving me. That's security. When I anchor myself to the rock of that truth, nothing can shake me.

What is Confidence?

You know my story about rejection in school, stomach aches and Magic Shell hair. I can only write about this because I have been there. In my own life, whenever I have dumped, been dumped, or been treated badly by a man I was involved with, or whenever that big hulking cloud of dark doubt about me and my life descended on me for no reason, I took note of what brought me out of it, and of things I learned on the path:

1. **Comparing leads to complaining.** Whenever I was busy looking at what other women have (marriages, boyfriends, children, great jobs, etc.), I got depressed. 'Where's mine?' I wondered aloud. It was a dissatisfaction, a jealousy, which worked its way down into me and made me want what I don't have. The solution? I thank God for what I do have and I get busy living my own life. I'll tell you what that looks like for me, then I urge you to make the same kind of list and take similar action.

- I am thankful for (me: my family, friends, church, artistic talent, the chance to write this book, the adventures coming up, my health, my height, being able to go where I want when I want because I'm single...there are many more things): What are you thankful for? Write them down: _____
  _____
  _____
  _____

RACHEL REALIZED THAT THE ONLY THING SHE COULD CHANGE SITTING ON THE SOFA WAS THE CHANNEL.

- What can I do now to live life to its fullest? (me: I can work on art and other books I'm writing, look into classes to meet new people and do new things, go work out, plan a trip, take a 'thinking' day and make some plans, help someone out, spend time with friends). What can you do? Write it down:
  _____
  _____
  _____

2. **Men love confidence.** I could never explain why some days men looked through me as if I was a ghost and some days they were attracted to me (and usually those 'attraction' days I had no makeup and was in workout clothes). Then I realized that it was when I was just doing my own life—arranging art shows, doing art, going on adventures and traveling by myself, I was most attractive to them. I wasn't trying for that…I simply got the most joy from living life and finding joy there. The joy radiated out because it was true joy, which is very attractive. I didn't have that look of a wall-eyed fish looking for her next date. I reminded myself who I was in God's eyes, and did what I loved most: writing and art. What do you like to do? Write it down: _____
   _____
   _____

3. **Nothing ever lasts.** Bad times don't last, and neither do good times. It is inevitable that change happens. It is the only constant in life. If you are in a slump, doubting yourself and hating your life, know that it will change…unless you are clinging to your situation for attention. I've known people like that. Don't do it. Your friends will grow tired of it and move on or suddenly get busier, and you'll be alone in your sucking vortex of depression. Let go and go out and do something, even if—especially if you don't feel like it. You might be surprised at who you'll meet and the doors that will open.

   Good times don't last either, so don't get so attached to them that you sink down in sadness when things change, because they will change. That is why it is so important to grasp every situation and event now and experience it. I'm not talking about 'living like there's no tomorrow'; we are all accountable for what we do. I am talking about appreciating each thing that crosses your path and not trying to cling to it for your future. Life is a highway, not a parking lot.

4. **Don't use a man as a depression rebound.** Getting into a dating relationship or being sexually active with someone as a cure for depression or as a boost to your self-esteem is a temporary fix. Just like drinking, the high will wear off and you'll be in the same situation you were in…maybe worse.

   Get out of your comfort zone. Maybe weekend CSI marathons and un-reality t.v. are not what the doctor ordered. Do something that challenges you. Go indoor rock climbing. Go on a cruise. Go on a day trip to somewhere you've never been. Run for office. But don't be hard on yourself if some things don't work out. The very act of getting out and doing something will boost your energy, confidence and, again, can lead to other things.

Part III
Chapter 15

R-E-S-P-E-C-T

I went to dinner once with a guy I really liked. We were friends, though I had hoped for more. If I had been honest with myself then, I would have seen and acted upon the red flags, which were waving like those at the front entrance of the United Nations. The red flags came in the form of insults and demeaning statements he made at my expense, but I continued to spend time with him. After all, I reasoned at the time: he was just joking. In his own words, he was just trying to 'toughen me up'. To this day, I still cannot explain the thinking behind that. I only wish Part II of my book had been in existence at that time so I could have read it, although I don't know if I would have obeyed it.

He chose a sushi place. We got out of the car and, as always, he left me in the dust to run and get a seat in the restaurant while I lagged behind to grab my purse and lock the car. I arrived at the door just as it was closing in my face. Growing a spine I hadn't had in the few months

THE DATE TOOK A TURN FOR THE WORSE
WHEN ELLEN NOTICED THAT MARVIN WAS ALL HANDS.

we had gotten to know each other, I mentioned his rudeness at the table, pulling my foot out of my shoe to rub it with the other one. The door had nailed my toe, too.

"I didn't hold the door because I didn't want you to think anything," he said, scanning the menu as if this insane excuse was perfectly acceptable.

"Think anything?"

"Yeah," he put the menu down, knowing he wasn't getting away with his lame answer. "When I hold the door for a girl, she automatically thinks I like her."

"Really?" Even then, I saw this guy's head enlarge to a point where it was in danger of a buzz cut from the ceiling fan. "Well, how about if we clear that up right now and you just hold the door for me out of politeness like any stranger would do? Trust me, I won't think anything."

I shrugged off the events of the night, believing I had made my point and thinking nothing of what they meant. However, hindsight, with its crystal clarity, showed me a few things about this guy:

1- He was selfish. This guy showed his true colors, not only by neglecting to hold the door for me, but by admitting his colossal involvement with himself in saying that the act of holding a door made girls think he liked them.

2- Walking ahead of me and leaving me in the dust showed me the words he didn't say: 'I'm not with her'.

3- He was narcissistic. As I just stated, he was very sure of his ability, real or imagined, to attract the opposite sex.

4- He treated me badly because I let him. The way you treat yourself shows a guy how he is allowed to treat you. There are words and actions which, if you let them slide, show a man that he can get away with bad behavior with you. Silence is not always golden.

Rude Boy was good at laying down ground rules for me too, assuring himself the freedom to do whatever he wanted without having me call him on it. He told me that when someone texted him, he didn't want me acting like we were married and getting nosy by asking who it was. His preemptive strike in laying down this rule did work on me. I was silent when the late night texts, which inevitably came in, caused him to leave my presence abruptly. I felt a wrenching in my gut every time he looked at his phone, but, thinking I would please him, I didn't ask him anything about the texts. Little did I know I was playing right into his double life, letting him go wherever his little werewolf errands took him, and reinforcing the lack of respect toward me. By the time I found out he was sleeping with someone, it just confirmed the answer I already had. I had allowed him to sap my time and emotions while he went and got sex. His Double Agent con had worked…for a little while.

You can't reward bad behavior.

Just like with children (sorry, guys), it teaches a guy nothing about how to treat you if you gloss over bad behavior and think it's going to get better. It won't. You're not 'cool' for not addressing it and you're not pleasing him by keeping the peace. Do you really want to spend your life with someone who disrespects you and just think 'well, this is just part of love'? No.

1 Corinthians 13:4-7 says, *'Love is patient, love is kind. It does not envy, it does not boast, it is not proud. It is not rude, it is not self-seeking, it is not easily angered, it keeps no record of wrongs. Love does not delight in evil but rejoices with the truth. It always protects, always trusts, always hopes, always perseveres.'*

Does your man match up with that? You will have disagreements here and there, but arguments, put-downs, covert activities and other bad behavior are part of a lifestyle which drains you, disrespects you and makes you feel inferior, taken advantage of, cheated or otherwise bad. It's time to ask yourself why you are with this man in the first place.

Get it out on the table. Ask him why he treated you the way he did. Don't get emotional or argumentative, just state the facts. Listen to him, then tell him that his behavior is not acceptable to you. At that point, it is up to him to be willing to change (but not because you say he should) or for you to leave. But you have to follow your words with action. If you don't, he will see not only that you don't stick with your word and that he can still get away with his bad behavior, but that you don't respect and value yourself enough to be willing to leave.

Signs that you're losing yourself in a dating relationship

A healthy courtship is two imperfect people coming together, not to complete each other *Jerry McGuire*-style, but to glorify God through their union by loving each other despite their differences, flaws and sins. When you start losing yourself in order to please (or keep) a man, it is an unhealthy union that will not get any better and is no good for your mental and emotional health.

Signs that you may need a break to think, or to break if off:

1- You cancel dates with family and friends to be with him, because he doesn't want to do things with them.

2- You censor yourself when answering him or giving an opinion, not wanting to start an argument or 'turn him off' by having a differing opinion.

3- You are overly concerned about your appearance around him, to the point where it has become more important than just being with him. You feel that if you have a bad hair day or don't look good at some point, it could jeopardize your relationship.

4- You start taking on his negative mannerisms, speech and behavior.

5- You feel pushed into things you never thought you would do.

6- You feel that if he dumped you, you would be lost, depressed, possibly suicidal. You wouldn't know how to go on without him.

7- You find yourself doing things for him more out of desperation to keep him, rather than out of love.

8- You have stopped doing the things you enjoy because you are sad he's not with you and you want him to be around doing them with you.

9- You have put off your life (buying a house, starting classes, starting a new career) because you are waiting to see what he wants out of life.

10- His friends are now your friends because you don't see your friends anymore. His friends are creepy but, hey, they're his friends, so they're in your life now.

11- You put up with bad behavior. He yells at you; verbally abuses you; constantly cancels plans at the last minute to go do stuff with the guys or someone else, leaving you alone, but you don't say anything to him, just accepting this.

12- You make excuses for him to your friends when they express doubts about him, even though you know they are right and make a good case as to why you should leave him.

13- You have argued with or lost a friend after she has told you what she thinks of him.

14- You have lost the peace and joy you had in life

If you see any of these behaviors in yourself, step back, ask a trusted girlfriend or family member to sit and talk with you. Be open to ending the relationship with this Frog, which, quite obviously, is not healthy for you.

What about girlfriends?

After my last Frog encounter, I began researching deception, manipulation, and all the things I mention in this book, and something unexpected happened: I saw a few of my female acquaintances who had these qualities. These women, two in particular, were friends who sort of came and went and who were not really consistent in my life. As with the men, I thought the problem was with me—that I was overly sensitive and needed too much attention, or that I was nitpicking about my friends, but nothing could be further from what was really going on. I didn't dump these friends, but now I know how to speak with them, how to give them choices in how to treat me, and I know how not to be mowed over by their manipulation.

Frogettes:
A Not-So-Princess Lineup

This is a section for men, or for women who may want to check their friendships. Again, these are not necessarily qualities all found in one woman, but one or more qualities an immature woman may possess. As with the Frog lineup, these qualities may exist to some degree in a woman who is still maturing. The important thing is, are these qualities disappearing day by day, or are they being nurtured as a lifestyle, to the hurt of you and everyone around you? Choose whether you can manage this friendship, or whether you need to leave. Manipulative women can be just as frustrating and dangerous to other women as men can.

1. The Golddigger: Just like her male counterpart, she is out to make some money, but doesn't want to work for it. If dating were a career—and she may consider it just that—she is climbing the corporate ladder. She may look up the value of a man's house or open a conversation with wanting to know what her date pulls in annually. She may make comments on what things cost, on name brands or on how a friend of hers just bought this or that expensive new item. She is rarely caught in the same outfit twice.

The description of The Golddigger oozes into the next Frogette:

2. The Queen Bee: She is high maintenance. Her perfectly-coiffed hair and otherworldly facial paint job may cause you to look twice. If you are a man, you may look twice because of attraction, but most likely it is because you wonder how many coats it took to cover whatever she is hiding. Her clothing is usually tailored, but even if she wears jeans, she jingles when she walks because jewelry is a non-negotiable staple. It is not her appearance, however, which earns her the title of Queen Bee. It is her attitude. Her security rests in how she appears to others, and this may manifest in automatic defensiveness, especially toward other women she considers threats. Men, if you decide to court her, do so at your own risk. Be aware that she is into appearances and you will need to keep her in the manner to which she is accustomed, part of which is looking the part. Unfortunately, your looks and material things she so loves are a small part of that. She will need constant affirmation and will expect you to be at her beck and call. Because she is concerned with herself, she has little time for others and will only cater to you because you somehow satisfy her needs.

3. The Manhunter: This woman comes in two calibers: 'Boy Crazy' and 'I Want Your Man'. The Boy Crazy Manhunter is either a serial dater or just wants to be in love. She may think that when a man looks at her he is interested, or when he asks how she is, that he is thinking up names for their children. Men should be aware of this woman's agenda and not feed into it. Her counterpart, the 'I Want Your Man' Manhunter, has her agenda rooted either in poor self esteem or a mental problem. Whether it is the chase to see if she can lasso an already-spoken-for man, the lack of boundaries in her life, or just the validation of accomplishment, this unhinged huntress should be avoided at all costs: she wants someone else's man. While a woman's fiancé or husband may be strong, there is nothing to be gained by allowing this woman close proximity to you as a couple or, especially, alone with your boyfriend or husband, even to 'help' her. Counseling her is best left to a wise counselor who knows what this woman is about and who can wisely lead her out of this snare in her life, if she is willing.

4. The Bitter Babe: You will want to stay away from this woman so you don't get any on you. You can probably pick up some clues as to her prickly personality on a first date, but if there are any doubts, listen to how this woman talks. She may bring up the past often, or speak negatively about men and/or relationships. She has sworn off relationships, but is 'giving it another try' with you after having her heart broken multiple times, but, inevitably, you will be guilty until proven innocent. It may be an inciting event or something you say, but when you unwittingly bring up something that reminds her of a former boyfriend, when she feels insecure in the relationship, or when she feels jealous of blessings in another woman's life, she will turn ugly. Her bitterness may come out obviously, as in an argument or a fight she picks, or it may show itself in a passive-aggressive way, so that you think you are going crazy. Either way, when your life with her starts to become a burden and the drama rises like the music in a western, see it for what it is and ride off into the sunset...alone!

5. Drama Queen: She can also be known as 'histrionic'. A histrionic woman—and this is more common in women than men—is one who likes the spotlight and demands attention. She can be amusing

at parties, but during the not-so-exciting times, she will create her own drama, accusing friends of gossiping about her, her boss being unreasonable and a bear, or any other number of slams against someone else which put her in the spotlight. She may even create situations where she is the 'gatekeeper' or the 'go-between' in the middle of two arguing factions. women's network t.v. writers could make a mint off of this girl. Usually, the nearby man will get dragged into it, and so will any friends who happen to be around. Because of her desire for the high of drama and constantly being onstage, it is all about her, and you will be on a roller coaster. Men, set aside any considerations of how pretty she may be, because those looks will wear thin when she demands your applause for the thousandth time. Get off of the coaster and come back to earth where the nice girls are.

6. **The Manipulator:** Yes, these come in the female variety, too. She knows how to get what she wants, and sometimes you may not know you are getting played. Anything listed as manipulative earlier in this book can be used to describe this feminipulator. There are a few differences in her tactics, but the act is the same. She may use a little girl voice, sweetness, histrionics, feminine wiles or even threats to try to

force you to do her bidding or give her what she wants. She could have grown up getting her way, or she may be confused because of a lack of discipline growing up, and not know what behavior is expected of her. She also may have learned how to manipulate along the way in life, but either way, she knows how to push your buttons.

Whether it is a Frog or Not-So-Princess quality, there is a common thread in all of these characteristics: insecurity stemming from not knowing one's purpose or value. From knowing who you were created to be and the great plans God has for you individually, you become stronger and more secure in who you are as a person, and will be able to love others fully. This will be covered more in the 'Identity' section.

"I WANT TO RETURN THIS PHONE.
IT DOESN'T RING ANYMORE!"

Part III
Chapter 16

Your Seven Pillars

'"Therefore whoever hears these sayings of Mine, and does them, I will liken him to a wise man who built his house on the rock: and the rain descended, the floods came, and the winds blew and beat on that house; and it did not fall, for it was founded on the rock.' – Matthew 7:24-25

I can tell you how important it is to rely on God for all your hopes, but having your legs kicked out from under you is the best way to really see God come through. I'm not talking about religion. Lots of people confuse the two. Religion is 'an ordered set of rituals designed to worship a deity or deities'. Ugh. Sounds like work to me. God is the ultimate

Prince and He is in love with you. Other 'gods' make you jump through hoops to please them with rituals, church attendance and forking out money. Jesus is the only God who reached down to save us and let us know Him. And He is the only one there when everyone leaves.

∽

"I had reached the last stop on my train to Frogville: my Frog informed me that he not only was involved in adultery with his friend's wife, but that now he had his eye on a new girl. Because I hadn't guarded my heart, I was crushed. He also threatened me: that if I told anyone, he would make things 'ugly'. I spent the rest of that day curled up on the sofa, wondering, who was this man I'd been involved with for over a year?"

∽

This woman knew God and His word, but had chosen to hitch her wagon to a burned out Frog-shaped star…one which let her down further than she could have ever imagined. When she got involved with this man, her routines, classes, friends and personal projects had fallen by the wayside. She had allowed this Narcissist to dictate to her how he thought her life should be. She is embarrassed, but glad to be on the other side of it, and stronger today. She guards her House, but is constantly renovating—and she has fun doing it!

Your House, also known as your life, can be split into seven main parts, or 'pillars', which I have done to make things easier to address: Spiritual, Physical, Financial, Vocational, Recreational, Relational and Rest. Each is pretty self-explanatory, but we can add detail here to give a better idea of what each pillar entails.

1. Spiritual: This pillar would be located in the center of your house; it is the 'bearing column' which holds up everything. Without this pillar, you may as well be living in a cardboard box on the beach. And if a Frog is taking up this space and holding your House up, it is temporary. Things will come crashing down.

Your spiritual pillar should consist of time reading God's word every morning. While most people consider breakfast the most important meal of the day, time with the Lord is as important to the spirit. Prayer connects you to your Heavenly Father. It prepares your heart for the day; to hear from the Lord, to encourage, share the gospel, to comfort people. It increases your wisdom, as does reading and memorizing His word. But the makeup of your spiritual pillar doesn't stop there.

'And they continued steadfastly in the apostles' doctrine and fellowship, in the breaking of bread, and in prayers.' – Acts 2:42

There is no substitute for time spent with other believers. For one, it gets you out of your own little world and teaches you to care for others. It also provides encouragement and strength for you. We weren't meant to do life alone, and God loves us and builds us up through His Body, the Church, which is made up of other believers.

'Blessed be the God and Father of our Lord Jesus Christ, the Father of mercies and God of all comfort, who comforts us in all our tribulation, that we may be able to comfort those who are in any trouble, with the comfort with which we ourselves are comforted by God.' – 2 Corinthians 1:3

Sometimes the Lord will even use other believers to help and comfort us, who have been through the same things we are going through now. You can't deny someone's testimony and life experience, so when you hear of a hardship they have been through it not only gives you encouragement that someone has been there and come through, but it also gives you different 'eyes' or a different point of view on the situation. And who knows? You may be that person through which God speaks to encourage someone else.

2. Physical: *'Or do you not know that your body is the temple of the Holy Spirit who is in you, whom you have from God, and you are not your own? For you were bought at a price; therefore glorify God in your body and in your spirit, which are God's.'* – 1 Corinthians 6:19-20

Do your friends lie to you when you ask them if your "butt looks fat in this dress"? Now, I showed you the indications of lying earlier, so you should be able to tell. Don't fault your friends for that lie—they were just trying to be nice. But if you think you've got junk the size of a bicycle and sleeping bag in the trunk, it may be time for some honest evaluation. Don't mistake this section for 'How to be a Stick-Insect'. We all have different bodies. Maybe you are more of a rounded figure, and that's how you will stay. You can still do things to tone what you have (though you will never—and should never—expect to be a Stick Insect), strengthen your heart and give yourself more energy. All of this directly feeds your physical and emotional health. It should grow into a lifestyle.

Here are some things suggestions to trying to get fit:

a. Don't NOT eat. Your body goes into 'starvation' mode when you don't eat or skip meals. Your metabolism slows and you will gain weight because of that and due to your body saying 'hey, we don't know where the next meal is coming from...put that there fat over on the butt shelf.' Besides...having buzzards circling you because you're about to drop over is not attractive either.

b. Don't do "fad" diets. Every few months some strange diet would sweep through a circle of women I know: 'eat only a handful of food each meal'; 'get lemons and cayenne and juice' (that one is helpful, but not as a meal!). Eating 5000 blueberries a day may keep cancer away (it will certainly keep guys away when they see your blue teeth).

Here's a good way of eating: eat what God put in front of you. Protein, vegetables (lots!) and lots of water: about eight 8oz glasses a day. It will wash fat away and your skin will look fantastic. Eating small meals five to six times a day at the same time each day keeps your metabolism going. This may seem too simple to work, but I have tried it and it does. Did the 'grapefruit diet' really do it for you? No? Eat a well-balanced meal with as many things in their natural form as possible.

c. Exercise. Meet with a doctor if necessary, but seek out a professional trainer, even if only for a few sessions, to learn the best cardio and strength training program for you. Many women like staying only with cardio, but strength training (i.e., weights and resistance) uses your muscles to incinerate fat. If you think you're straining or fatiguing a muscle group, stop. Don't overdo it, but with at least 3 days a week in the gym doing 30+ minutes cardio and doing weights, you will look and feel great! Music or audio books on your headset will help, and who knows who you may meet working out next to you!

d. Stay positive. Remember those 'Frogettes' from earlier? Stay away from them and their sisters and brothers. You will avoid wrinkles from frowning, heart problems and weight gain from stress and will feel a curious freedom.

e. Skip the sugar. Sugar is poison. 'Poison': the definition is "to exert a harmful influence on, or to pervert". Poison—I mean sugar—leaches precious minerals from the body, causing bones and teeth to become brittle. Do a search on 'sugar is poison' to see the myriad of other harmful benefits of this pure, refined carbohydrate. If it's bad for your dog and destroys your gas tank, why would you eat it?

f. Cancel the carbohydrates. Complex carbs (fruits, vegetables, nuts, seeds and whole grains) are good. Simple carbs (processed foods: white bread, baked goods, candy and sodas) should be avoided like the plagues they are. There are already books out on what aspartame and high fructose corn syrup do to you. Read them. It may not be so hard to reduce or eliminate these things after that.

Is there something you want to improve about yourself? Do it! There's no reason you can't fix the things you want to fix—just be sure you are doing it for yourself and not to please a man. I'm not talking about surgery, just that if the barn needs painting, paint it! Get that third eye removed from your forehead. Learn to speak without firing food schrapnel out of your mouth over dinner. Be more interested in others and practice asking them their stories instead of regaling people with your vast knowledge of borscht recipes.

3. Financial: *'Be diligent to know the state of your flocks, and attend to your herds; for riches are not forever, nor does a crown endure to all generations.' – Proverbs 27:23-24*

I love going to the bookstore—a little too much—but, as of the writing of this book, I don't see finance books specifically for singles. I believe that, since money can be an emotional issue, there are different issues singles have that families do not have.

For instance, I went through a painful period in my life where I didn't want to just sit in my apartment alone. Of course, that leads to not being at my apartment; i.e., being at the mall, the bookstore, even out to dinner at one of my favorite restaurants. So where did my insatiable appetite for being anywhere but my house get me? It got me out of balance financially. You see, it wasn't a money issue, it was something deeper: the desire to keep busy—to sedate—with constant activity and shopping in lieu of quiet time, doing things at home, or even resting. Not all singles are running from their singleness through constant activity, but some are. This touches our finances. The purpose of this section on Pillars is to balance the whole structure by strengthening each Pillar. Because some singles desire marriage so much, their lack of balance in Spiritual will put too much weight on Financial, in this instance. Knowing what God says about good financial stewardship give you better knowledge of building wealth, serving the poor and seeing the 'big picture' of future plans. Gone is the need for constant filling through excessive shopping, meals out and activities with groups of people which end up denting your budget. For a single person finding spiritual fulfillment, a normal amount of activities would be within the budget, but for a single person looking to fill a need by overspending on entertainment and 'escaping' all seven days of the week, the money soon goes, as does the monitoring of it, in the search for satisfaction.

Another financial issue for singles is travel. When you get married, you may still be able to travel but you are still considering another person when you want to do so. Of course, when kids come along, I've heard, the only travel involved is to the closest grocery store, doctor or kinder-gym. So, as a single person, you may be in a financial position, not to mention having the time, to go on vacation, to a conference, on a mission's trip, to a convention, an out-of-town concert or any other place your heart desires. This takes planning in your budget. In the back of this book is a form you can copy that details your budget; complete with blanks where you can fill in monthly your expenditures, actual and planned.

The Proverbs 31 woman knew how to make the most of her money. Because she had a family to care for, she knew she had to be wise about stretching money. But this is not the only mark of her financial stewardship. It is easy as a single person to be self-focused and not have to be concerned about others financially, aside from tithing and maybe donations. That's why marriage—or any change in financial circumstance—will be culture shock if you are not prepared. Notice in verse 13 where it says the woman 'willingly works with her hands'. It's easy in our culture to buy a new thing when the old thing shows wear. We're certainly busy enough to justify it. But what if we took a few minutes, for example, to drop expensive shoes off to a cobbler for new soles, instead of tossing them and buying new? Or sewing a button on a shirt instead of counting it as a rag and buying new? I'm not saying that you need to collect loose threads and lint from your dryer and make underwear, but there are resources in print and on the web, where you can find hints on saving money, whether it is through making what you could buy, refurbishing used things or putting extra work into something to make it like new.

Verse 22 talks about how her family was clothed in 'scarlet and purple'. Purple was an indication of wealth during the time of the Proverbs 31 woman, and even in Jesus' time. Because she worked, saved, bought and sold real estate (v. 16) and did other things to make her money stretch and make a profit, she was able to afford some fine things for her family.

Your job directly affects your finances, but not in the way you may think. You may not be in your dream job now, but if you took a job simply to have more money, chances are, you are subverting yourself. When you are in a job you don't enjoy, you will tend to spend money in off hours 'blowing off steam'. If someone had told me this, I may not have believed them, had I not done the same thing myself. Friday afternoon at 5 was when my life started and Monday morning at 8 was when it ended. I actually used to lapse into depression on Sunday nights, during which time it was a waste for me to get anything accomplished. My jobs were really not that bad; except for the one where my coworkers would throw hot balls of Plexiglas at me. (One guy came in two weeks after I quit, waving a gun at the boss. But that's a whole other comic book.) No, as far as jobs go, I have been blessed. Beside the plexi-balls, the worst I have had to endure was boredom or a 'challenging' boss and coworkers, but nothing a box of Dunkin' Donuts munchkins and a box of coffee couldn't cure (yes, I said 'box'). The only way I could shake the misery of my 40-hour solitary confinement was to live it up on the weekends or at night. This included going out to dinner, shopping, traveling and, while I didn't go totally insane with my money, I certainly wasn't a very good steward. I spent emotionally, trying to make myself feel better with new clothes—even though I had gained weight from all the nights out eating. I spent money on fixing up my condo so I could hang out in my 'nest' by myself, which contributed to weight gain and not doing much for my 'relationship' pillar. I had isolated myself. I was totally self-absorbed and still no happier.

> The only way I could shake the misery of my 40-hour solitary confinement was to live it up on the weekends or at night.

It was actually a blessing when everything crashing down—I got involved with a Frog who broke my heart (I know; you wouldn't think that was a blessing, would you?). I sold my condo for much less than I could have because I had held onto it too long, and got laid off from my job. I started seeing things much differently. The dream I had of working for myself—the one I was too scared to quit a job and launch out to begin—was now a reality by default. To survive, I needed to go get freelance/contract work. The temptation to just go get 'something' did rear its head, but no 9-5 job materialized. It was a tough employment market and I was one of its victims—or so I thought. I diligently grabbed onto the Lord and His word during this hard time of heartbreak and fear and did the jobs that came to me through word-of-mouth. Slowly I healed—and prospered. But it also allowed me to value money in a whole new way.

Someone said that wealth does not come from how much money you make, but how you treat what you have. In the season of hardship into which I was thrust, I was forced to look at money in a whole new way. When I came into a little extra money, instead of going to the mall with it, I gave 10% to the Lord, as always, saved a percentage into a 'don't touch' savings account, put some toward bills and the rest into a 'liquid' savings account for emergencies. As the Lord saw how I handled little, He gave me increasingly more. When emotions threatened to overwhelm me, I still didn't give in to my spending craving, but ran to Him to fix my anxiety, depression, or whatever else was going on.

'You will show me the path of life; In Your presence is fullness of joy; At Your right hand are pleasures forevermore.' – Psalm 16:11

The season of singleness is the perfect time to not only create good financial habits, get out of debt (and not back in!) and start a savings, but to learn how to budget and reap the resulting rewards of financial freedom and the ability to help others. Learn to live on less so you will be able to go do more.

4. Vocational: *'For we are God's workmanship created in Christ Jesus to do good works prepared beforehand that we should walk in them.'*

– Ephesians 2:10

We are all wired to do something. Can you say, right this minute, as you work at your job that you are happy being there? I don't mean that you should imagine it to be heaven. No situation on this earth is perfect. You may have a coworker with a penchant for throwing plexi-balls, or some job that could probably be done by a goat. Do you enjoy your job? If so, great! If not, are you doing something to change your circumstances? Obviously you need an income, and should stay at your job until you find one which suits you better, but if you're not happy, are you taking the actions you need to get out? Are you moving toward starting the business you want to, or getting the education to move to a different department or different job? In some cases, no job comes, and no opportunities open. In other circumstances, especially as single parents, you must work anywhere you can to feed your child(ren). What do you do in that case?

   a. Pray. Tell God you would rather eat glass than go into work again today if that's how you feel. He knows what you're thinking anyway; you may as well be honest. He also put the desire in your heart for something more, whether it's within that job or in something else altogether. Be sure to listen after you pray, keeping your eyes and ears open in the coming hours, days and weeks for indications of what you should do. He will make it clear. Whatever you do, don't quit your job on a whim. There's a reason you have it, and there will be obvious open doors when it's time to leave.

"YOU REALLY SHOULD COME OUT OF YOUR SHELL."

- **b. Evaluate.** My favorite 'thinking place' is a coffee shop—preferably in a bookstore. It's there that I can make notes and plan, which is what I did after I was laid off. You can surf the web looking for jobs, education, business ideas and asking yourself: if I never got paid, what would I love doing all day?
- **c. Be active.** Now that you've found some information and leads, follow up. Sometimes it's paralyzing to think of stepping out and doing a new thing, but you won't get anywhere unless you do.

Something happens when someone stays in a job which is not suited to their gifts and talents. Once the newness wears off the worker finds herself going through the motions. Because there is a steady paycheck, she becomes comfortable and she can't quit until she finds something else. But in looking for something else, she thinks, it will just be the same thing all over again. 'May as well stay where I am.' No! God did not create us just to have us sit in cubicles breathing re-circulated air waiting for 5:00 to roll around so we can rush home, eat, watch t.v., go to sleep and do it all again the next day, if that's not a desire you have in your heart.

The first thing you need to do is pinpoint your gifts. What are you good at? Where are your natural gifts? Cooking? Drawing? Arguing a case? Take some time and think, experience, go and do those things where you are gifted. There is a site where you can actually go for a week or long weekend and try out your dream job: search the words 'vocation' and 'vacation' online and look at some innovative ways of exploring a vocation you've always thought about, but were too timid or time-pressed to try. What better way to find out if you want to be a ranch hand, actor or pastry chef than to do it! It costs a little money, but your future is worth it! There are other ways of determining where your gifts lie. Is there something people say you're good at? Do they ask you to do that thing? The next question is, "what is your passion?" If you're good at doing something, it doesn't mean that is the career you should be doing. You have to want to do it.

A woman I know loves drawing, but as a career, she flies military aircraft. She also loves writing. Because she wants to shift gears now, she is preparing to write full time. In a few years, when she leaves the military, she will be able to write about all of her adventures flying recon missions in 'hot' zones. That drives her.

What drives you? On the other hand, that passion should have to do with something you are good at. I would love to be a rock star, but I have neither planned (I've never taken guitar lessons) nor do I have the talent to be one. I can't do splits and my throat hurts when I try to hit anything higher than a middle C.

I knew early that I liked drawing. I loved creating characters and telling stories. In high school, when things had to get serious, I figured I would be an architect. It was something I had NO passion for, but it was the only 'drawing' job I could think of. Rather than painting myself into a corner and declaring a major right away, I went to art school and took the wide range of classes the first year that were designed as a program to let a student experience everything. By the final year, I knew I wanted to be an illustrator. Unfortunately, I was not prepared for the fact that illustration was not a 9-5 job, so when I got out of school, I got a job at a t-shirt store doing graphic design; not drawing, but setting type and images for reproduction on shirts. Not my dream job, but the training I got at jobs through the years enabled me to be computer literate to the point where I can do anything I want with my illustration. One job, at a county sheriff's office, led to training at the FBI's Forensic Lab in Quantico, Virginia where I learned how to interview witnesses, sketch composites of law-challenged people on the loose (and dead people) and help catch criminals. My point to all of this? A talent which I couldn't imagine would amount to anything but sketching caricatures at carnivals or inventing buildings I had no interest in creating, has evolved into projects I could never have imagined. I even helped solve a traffic homicide within two days, that had detectives had no leads on for over a month! My interest in characters was fruitful. My interest in relating stories has created this book, which hopefully will help countless people to recognize and avoid deception and find their value and purpose.

Don't put yourself in a box and say 'I can only do this because it's what I've always done', or 'I can't do that because I'm not getting paid' or 'people will think I'm crazy.' You never know what adventures there are in store for you if you will just take the first step and start investigating.

Here is the most important thing: If you don't talk yourself out of your dream (and you shouldn't! You only get one life!), don't let others talk you out of your dream. You will come across naysayers who are either scared of your success or convicted about the fact that they aren't embracing their dreams. Smile and ignore them. You have an adventure to start! Here are some things to consider when trying to find your 'fit' in vocational life:

> **a. What's your passion? What do you like to do?** Many times this shows itself in hobbies or groups you belong to, but it could be something that's been in the back of your mind for some time. Nothing is too crazy (as long as it's legal).

b. **What's your gifting? What are you good at doing?** Don't shrug this off and say 'I'm not good at anything', as I've heard people say before. Everyone is good at something! If you think you're not, then it's time to explore! Go do stuff! Even if you're not good at something but have an interest in it, you will grow in it! I wasn't always good at art, but I practiced and now I do it full-time. You may be surprised at what you learn about yourself.

c. **What's your burden?** What fuels you? bothers you? What do you want to fix? Who do you want to help? It could be starving children or human trafficking or healing people. God didn't give you a gift to keep it to yourself. It is for other people.

d. **What resources do you have?** Do you have computers? Money? Materials which would suit that industry? A certain education? Access to certain real estate, vehicles, staff or training?

e. **Where are you?** Geographically, are you in the right place? Could you take advantage of your surroundings to do your vocation or to train for it?

f. **Who do you know?** Everyone knows someone, and they know someone else. It's called networking. Make the most of it.

5. Recreational: This is very important for a balanced life. I will admit, it is something I don't do enough. Recreation includes hobbies. It is said that if someone has a physical job, like lifting, loading, driving, etc., they may be happy doing a cerebral hobby, like drawing, building electronics, playing on the computer, reading or other right brain-focused activity. Likewise, a cube-dweller may find softball or other sports more interesting. Whatever your poison, pick it. You need it. Lately I have wanted to go to the zoo. I have no idea why. I thought I had outgrown it, but apparently not. The idea is stalking me like a cheetah…or a bad metaphor. I work by myself all day, so the thought of seeing creatures who don't drive or yell at me is probably what attracts me. I think it's cool, all the things God thought up. Being an artist, it just blows me away that He could use the media of fur and teeth like He has.

Don't know what to do? Don't settle for lumbering around the mall or going to a restaurant all the time. There's a big world out there. Where I lived, there were airboat rides. Get a few people together! It's a great way to meet new people and have an adventure you can talk about. And maybe it will ignite the dream you didn't know you had, to be an airboat captain. Worst case scenario: you'll have fun you didn't know you could have, you'll get a little scared in a thrilling way, and your brain will be well rested! Just keep all your limbs inside the vehicle.

6. Relational: *'A man who isolates himself seeks his own desire; He rages against all wise judgment.' – Proverbs 18:1*

People are very important to God. It's why He put them on earth. He put them in your life for a reason and He put you in their lives for a reason. In Proverbs 18:1, 'isolates' means also 'divides' or 'separates'. It is never a good idea to separate yourself from other people as a lifestyle. A person who declares himself a 'lone wolf', like our lovely examples in the Frog lineup in Part I of this book, are usually isolating for a reason. People who don't like being around people could be acting out of fear, or have something to hide, such as a double life or criminal habit. For some, they are just depressed. I've been there. At the very least, these people live by their own rules and don't let change and growth happen to them through the sometimes uncomfortable contact with other people.

'As iron sharpens iron, So a man sharpens the countenance of his friend.'
– Proverbs 27:17

The Hebrew word for 'iron' has, in its definition, the words 'harshness', 'strength' and 'oppression'. God knew that we would sin (rebel, or miss the mark), try to do things our way, and clash with our neighbors. But even that, He uses for good. When we have differences with someone we will usually come away having learned something, even if it is sometime down the road and even if it has been painful. Often only pain will bring about the growth that is most effective and beautifies us. It's like the grain of sand in the oyster. Only through the painful irritation has the oyster been prompted to solve the problem, coating the irritant in *nacre*, which is the same material out of which its shell is made. Without the irritant, there would be no pearl. Just remember that about the irritants in your life. And also remember that you are probably someone else's irritant. We all are.

The harshness of others serves to sculpt you into the work of art God desires you to be. Sometimes He uses mean tools sometimes, and they are painful. But don't give up on God or think He doesn't care about you. He is closest to you in the fire, just as He was with Shadrach, Meshach and Abed-Nego. Don't be angry at the tools God uses to sculpt you.

'And we know that in all things God works for the good of those who love him, who have been called according to his purpose.' – Romans 8:28

God can use 'informational' teaching with you too, that is, seeing someone else going through trouble, and you learning from it. But you have to be around people to learn this way. I would definitely prefer that 'informational' teaching so I don't have to go through it, rather than 'experiential' teaching, where I actually have to get slapped in the face by life in order to learn something. The strange thing is, the latter does seem to be more effective. It also makes further experiential teaching less necessary for me. Thank God.

7. Rest: *"Then God blessed the seventh day and sanctified it, because in it He rested from all His work which God had created and made."*

– Genesis 2:3

Rest is not the same as recreation. I don't want to get legalistic, but rest, especially Sabbath rest, is something that should recharge you. Literally, it means 'cease' and 'desist', which are legal terms. It doesn't mean mowing the lawn or doing the bills or having a highly-charged day of shopping, running errands and doing. It means resting—being still. The problem with resting is that, although we say we long for it, many people have a hard time sitting still. But God won't compete with your activities. I believe once I heard His impression on my heart: "Christine, I won't talk over the t.v."

Uh oh.

And during that 'being still' time, He longs to make contact with us, whether it is to guide or direct us or just to bless us with His peace. That is invaluable. I know many times when my mind is at rest, I get my best ideas. I believe it is because all the other events and issues of the day are not competing. But rest starts in the mind. When your mind is running, your body soon follows. When your mind is at rest, it is an open vessel for God to speak to, and while your body is resting, it is mending.

Some people debate over what day a Sabbath should be. In the scripture it says that on the seventh day God rested. Did God need rest? No. He did this to show us that rest is important, no matter on what day you do it. Pastors, police officers, nurses and doctors often work Sundays—the day most people use as their Sabbath—so the point is, whatever day you take, take a day out for yourself and the Lord. You won't be disappointed, and your life will be blessed (happy) because of your decision to put God first and set everything else aside for the moment.

Organizing Your Life: Achieving Balance

Achieving balance—strengthening your Seven Pillars—is an ongoing process. It is a process of maintaining, but you should always be sure, once you have put a plan in place for overhauling, reworking, or maintaining each of these seven aspects of your life, that you don't fall into a rut. During devotional time, are you reading the same chapters over and over again, not challenging yourself by asking what areas you need to change in or work on? In finances, are you giving in the same areas without asking God if He wants to change things up? You wouldn't stay with the same physical workout so, while the workout itself is good and beneficial, it is important in life to keep running the race and, as you grow, adapt aspects of your Seven Pillars to grow with you.

Goal setting is encouraged by many corporate consultants and life coaches. But they were not the first to create the concept of having goals:

'The plans of the diligent lead surely to plenty, But those of everyone who is hasty, surely to poverty.' – Proverbs 21:5

God wants to be involved in your plans. Ask Him to direct you.

Consider your gifts and talents, and the people and situations He has put around you.

'A man's heart plans his way, But the LORD directs his steps.'
                                                            – Proverbs 16:9

Following are some sheets which can help you to balance your life. Use them as guides, copy them or customize your own; whatever it takes to put your 'house' in order.

Schedule: Instead of re-creating the wheel, I'll suggest that there are companies that put out great scheduling layouts. Franklin Covey is one of my favorites, and Daytimers can be found at office stores. Of course, you could do it electronically, but for me, personally, I like writing things down.

Budget: This will help you figure things out on paper and keep stock of your assets and debts each month so things don't get out of hand. Again, go online or to a bookstore for proper guidance on this. Don't think you can skip it. Having a monthly budget will save you time and money.

Gifts: This is something that can disturb your whole budget, if it sneaks up on you. This sheet allows you to remember people you may not normally give a gift to, and sort out your Christmas list. If you take care of Christmas throughout the year, you won't be financially surprised at the end of the year.

Groceries: Another budget-eater. Always go into the store with a list. It's another form of boundary that will keep you on track.

Dreams: This is the most fun page. Let yourself go. List those things you never dared to do, that have been tugging at your heart, or, make a life change by putting down goals to get you to your dream job, investment, or life!

Part III
Chapter 17

The Perfect Relationship

You won't find a perfect relationship this side of heaven. God is the only one who can fulfill all your needs. As you've read, that relationship is important during singleness and marriage. While you're single, making the most of that time includes being ready, so when that Prince shows up, you'll be at your best. That said, there are some things you can do to increase your chances of meeting a Prince instead of being stuck with a Frog.

Places you won't find a Prince

If you're trying to get out and meet more people—namely men, there are great places to go, and places from which you need to steer clear. You shouldn't expect to meet a Prince:

At bars. Alcohol blurs the senses. Many guys count on that. Sure, some may be there just for a drink, but others are casting lines to see what they can reel in. If you don't want to deal with anything having to do with a hook, line or sinker, avoid bars as places to meet a Prince.

In jail. I was about to delete this section, because, what normal woman would try to meet a man from jail? So I did a web search on 'how to meet men' and what was the second item on the list? You guessed it: 'how to meet men in jail'! Please don't do this unless you want your incarcerated courtship reenacted on of one of those grainy reality crime shows.

At a police station. Unless you work at a law enforcement agency and know the heroes from the villains, don't agree to have dinner with any guy who approaches you while you're downtown waiting to pay your parking ticket. You have no idea where he's been...or where he's going.

In a marriage. I can't believe I even have to clarify this. After hearing the occasional selfish woman's excuses, though, I felt it necessary. The phrases "I thought it was God's will that we (she and the married guy) be together," or "His wife doesn't understand him," or the myriad other feel-good excuses we mentioned earlier from the mouth of a Frog, somehow find their way out of the mouth of a Frogette too. If you are dating (i.e., having sex with) a married man, or even contemplating doing so, stop now. There is still time for you to grow brain cells. Your tryst with Mr. Tall, Dark and Spoken For will not end well. If he does it with you, he'll do it to you. It is wicked to step into a marriage, where two people have committed to each other, and become 'the other woman'. I don't care what the circumstances are; there are no good married men…for you.

So you're looking for a Prince...

Here are some places you may find one, while you're busy living your life and doing your purpose:

- at the gym
- at church
- at a class
- at a singles' group
- yoga
- at a sporting event
- at an acting class
- in a community volunteer group
- at a garage
- at the beach
- at a marathon or other sport group
- at the grocery store
- on a movie set
- at the movies
- at your local coffee shop
- at a diner
- at the mall
- in an auto maintenance class
- in a foreign language class
- at a music class
- at a wedding
- volunteering for a cause
- at an art gallery
- at a Christmas or other holiday party
- ballroom dancing
- at a bookstore
- at the library
- traveling
- in a tour group
- at a dog park
- walking around your city
- in a cooking class
- at any park
- at a concert
- at a bible study
- bike riding
- running
- salsa dancing
- Bollywood dancing
- at computer expos
- at car shows
- volunteering for a political campaign
- at a tourist attraction
- at work
- at a fair
- at a computer store
- at a planetarium
- at an art museum

As you can see, with most of these places, you have to be out there doing something…so go do it!

Part III
Chapter 18

Healing, Post-Frog

Reading about how to avoid Frogs may be great for situations where you may meet a Frog in the future, but what if it is too late? What if you've already been involved with a Frog who has just broken your heart? Well, first of all, it's never too late to start over. All is not lost. If this has just happened to you and your heart is hurting, it is tempting to just ball up on the sofa and wait for him to call—or to rethink your actions, if you did the breaking up, and call him. But wait—read on, Princess...

Immediate safety precautions

My 'gut' protected me one particular Monday morning when the man I had been involved with turned out to be nothing like I thought he was. He had acted as though he had feelings for me for months. For over a year he had told me things about his past and present, all of which turned out to be lies. Finally, on a Thursday, with no prompting from me, he told me he was sleeping with his best friend's wife. He even seemed proud of it. All of a sudden, he acted shocked that he had revealed such sensitive information to me (*thank you, cognitive interview technique*). He insisted I keep it to myself. He said that the information he'd just revealed could 'destroy many people'. My heart was broken at the depth of the deception. I felt used and deceived and I cried until there were no more tears. Every day afterward for three days, he called me, asking if I was okay. I was touched at his concern until I realized what he was doing—checking to see if I had told anyone. I stopped answering the phone. I needed to get strong and to heal. I knew now that there couldn't be even a friendship. I could have no contact with this man.

That was when things got bad.

He text messaged me that if I wanted it this way, he would 'make things ugly'. He was two miles away and was on his way to my house, having called me names I had never been called before.

I come from a family of military people, namely Marines. I don't scare easily. I had never felt like a victim before, but this was as close as it came. The day before, an impression came heavily upon my heart: *pack a bag and put it into the car*. It was a strange thought, but I did so, grabbing the computer and toiletry bag and putting them into the car the previous day. After the phone call the next day, sure enough, I fled my house, driving to another lot in the apartment complex. I didn't know where to go and I was shaking badly. I called two friends, neither of whom answered. The third one, my friend Lisa*, did answer. She happened to be a mile away in her car with her 14-year old son. I watched from a distance, hunkered down in my car, sobbing to the point where I was hyperventilating and barely able to speak, watching as this man's telltale black sports car sped through the parking lot past my hiding place toward my building. My friend Lisa kept me on the phone, notifying me that she had just entered the complex, and then that she was pulling slowly toward my building. I followed her and together we faced this man.

God has all kinds of ways of protecting his children. Sometimes he sends armies. Sometimes he sends horses. And sometimes he sends fiery blue-eyed blondes with the life experience to stand up to bullies.

Lisa hadn't needed to flex any muscle, couldn't have anyway. The guy was bigger and stronger than she. For over half an hour, he tried to charm her, and I was sure she was falling for it, as she blinked her baby-blues at him. I felt even more helpless at the thought of my so-called smart friend melting from this guy's saccharine words. However, when he roughly tried to grab my phone to erase his enraged text messages, she stepped in between us, her blue eyes blazing and her voice sharp, and said 'I know you! You just showed your true colors!' It was as if Lisa were waiting for him to do just that so she could nail him. You see, Lisa has been through more difficulties in life than you and I may ever see. She was kidnapped and held prisoner by a gang in South America when she was younger.

After a few weeks she was able to escape. She had dealt with much worse than this guy. That was why she was able to handle him and see exactly what he was about. And is why now I can see the same thing: *'We comfort others with the comfort we have received.'* Lisa's comfort came to me that day in protection. Later she was able to give me counsel, when my world seemed to be crashing around me.

God's protection is there for us at all times. My hope is that in reading this section, you will not need the kind of protection I did, and that you will avert incidents before they occur. There were things I should have done differently in the face of an enraged Frog. These are steps that would not have needed to happen, had I extricated myself from the situation when I saw the first red flags. Let's say you're reading this book or this part of the book after the fact. You have already been involved with a Poison Frog—a dangerous man—and things have gone bad.

If you know are NOT in immediate danger:

If you are getting red flags and just want out of the relationship, but you do NOT feel you are in immediate physical danger (i.e., you don't believe at that moment the Frog will do you physical harm), you should still take steps:

1. Have NO contact with the Frog

This means NO contact...not just physical proximity, but no calling, email or texting. NONE. Forget about being afraid of appearing rude or heartless. You are protecting yourself. He does NOT have your best interest at heart. Allowing him to converse with you and manipulate you will weaken your resolve, and you will go back with him repeatedly, not letting yourself heal and move on from what you have decided is a dead-end or unhealthy relationship. Any contact on your part lets the Frog know he still has a crack through which he can crawl and have access to you. He will not change for you and he has *nothing* you want.

2. Take threats seriously. File a police report.

Even if he has never threatened you before, if he starts now, it is serious. Take the time to file a police report with your local police or sheriff. Don't tell the Frog you are going to do this, just do it. If you tell him, it will give him a chance to convince you not to or, worse, will make him angry and could escalate things. The existence of a police record will help you, should you have to call police to your house in the future, or should you end up having to testify in court.

3. Keep a paper trail

If he is not leaving you alone and you think things may take a bad turn, take physical notes of any strange behavior or interaction, with the time and date and, as exactly as you can, what was said. Write it down and keep it in a safe place. This will also help if police need to be called in the future.

4. Inform close friends and neighbors

It is always good to have someone checking on you, aware of the situation, and praying for you. You will feel better having a support system, as well.

5. Make sure your home is secure

Many law enforcement agencies have home safety checks as a free public service. You can arrange to have an officer or deputy can come to your house and show you all the non-secure areas in and around your home (i.e., overgrown foliage where an assailant can hide, windows or doors that don't lock, etc.). Use the department or agency's **non-emergency** number for this, not 9-1-1. The number is usually on their web site or at the front of your phone book.

If you feel you ARE in danger:

If you are getting threats of physical harm from the Frog, overt or veiled, and you feel that your safety or life is in danger, do all of the steps above, and:

1. In immediate danger, call 9-1-1

If the man is present or says he is coming to where you are, do not hesitate to call the police. Don't think you are bothering them, or that you are making a big deal out of things. There is a reason you feel your life or safety is in danger, and you need to pay attention to that. You only get one chance to protect yourself. Many times when I rode along with the sheriff, we got calls that turned out to be nothing—the assailant never made good on his threat, or he left when he saw the call being made. Our arrival helped the caller to feel safe, and it is part of law enforcement's service to the public. It also made a record of the aggressor's actions. It only takes an irreversible moment for someone to harm you.

2. Stay at a friend's house for a while

If you are afraid to stay in your house, find a friend to stay with, preferably one whose address the Frog doesn't know. Don't tell anyone—even other friends—where you are staying until the situation can be resolved. Your friend is putting her neck out there for you and you don't want to endanger her or her household. Make absolutely sure you are not followed by changing your route and turning frequently so you are sure you are not followed. If you think you are being followed, drive to a police station or hospital emergency room and go inside. Don't park somewhere back in the facility's lot and walk to the door—pull right up to the front and go inside.

3. Be aware of your surroundings

You should be doing this anyway, as a normal course of life. During this difficult time, your awareness should be heightened, especially if you will be going anywhere alone or alone at night. Try to have a friend or group of friends walk you places that make you uneasy. Police and security guards are usually willing to walk you to your car in public places, too.

4. Notify neighbors

If you are concerned about being home alone but must stay or insist on staying in your home, tell some of your neighbors to be aware. You don't need to tell them all about what's going on, just that you're having trouble with someone. You don't want your neighbors to be alarmed or feel unsafe, but they do have a stake in your situation, considering that you live in the same area.

5. Pack a bag and keep your gas tank full

It sounds extreme, but it's a good idea to be prepared for all circumstances during this time. Put the bag, with clothes and other non-valuables, out of sight in your car. Have a plan for where to go. It is a good idea to keep your phone charged, too. If you think the man is outside, stay in your house and lock the doors. You are safer inside than trying to get to your car, unless you know without a doubt the man is nowhere on your property. This doesn't mean he calls from a cell phone and tells you he's on the other side of town. Make sure you can see from the safety of your house that he's not on your property. Still, try to stay inside.

6. If you make contact

If you are on your way out of your house, or are any other place where the Frog confronts you, do not engage him in conversation. He has already proven he is a danger to you. Leave as quickly as you can. Do not let him pull you in with guilt or use your compassion to get you close to him. Do not answer questions or verbally defend yourself. It is a good idea before any of this transpires, to take a self-defense class. You may not think you need to…you know the guy, right? But if you knew him, you would not be in this situation. Besides, self-defense classes are a good idea in general. Make sure the class is run by a present or former law enforcment officer or military, someone trained in martial arts or someone with a track record in professional security. This will boost your confidence, too, in how you appear, and will make you less of a target. The important thing to remember if you mistakenly come in contact with the Frog is to get away. Do not start a physical fight. You will most likely not win and will probably be injured or worse. He can also sue you for assault. Just get away *fast*.

What not to do, once your relationship with the Frog is over:

1. Do not have contact with the Frog

I say it again: You will either be sucked into the relationship again, or you could be physically hurt. Have no contact. The manipulations some Frogs use at this time can harm you emotionally. You are not clear-headed now, and must wait until time has passed to encounter him again, if ever. There is no reason to talk to him again. Forget about that sweater you left at his house. It is not worth your emotional health or physical safety.

2. Do not try to confront the Frog yourself or 'reason' with him.

This will only prove dangerous. If you wanted out of the relationship and try to reason, you could be drawn in again, as mentioned above. If he has anger issues, you could be harmed physically, or worse. You have to realize that Frogs don't change overnight, so don't fall for the 'I've changed' line if he does end up talking to you. If he tells you that, tell him you're glad for him, but not to contact you again. Don't use too many more words than that. Extricate yourself as soon as possible and do not answer any subsequent calls, emails or texts, no matter how tempted you may be to do so.

3. Do not backbite

I know this is difficult, especially if he has slandered you, physically or verbally abused you or is telling an untrue account of what happened between the two of you. You feel like spreading the news to everyone of what he did to you. This includes social networking sites. Don't do it. Take the high road. People may believe him, and they may not. You are not in charge of what people believe or what people think of you. This is a time when your true friends, as well as people of low character, will show their true colors: your friends as the true friends they are, and the others as people better left out of your life. The truth will come out in time. A deceiver will ALWAYS be shown to be what he is. God promises this in Psalms 5, 109 and all over the Bible. I have seen it happen. If you must talk to someone, make it a trusted female friend and/or a counselor. You can get as ugly as you want with them because you know your words will go no further. Keep any communication to anyone else about the matter short and neutral. No one needs to know anything about it. By the way, warning the Frog's new girlfriend or someone else directly connected with him that he is an imminent danger does not fall under this category. It is biblical and a righteous move to warn someone about a dangerous man. Do so, then move on, no matter what her reaction to your news. Don't expect her to throw roses at you and thank you, though. Women can be very mean when they want what they want. More on that later.

4. Don't seek news

You don't need to know how your Frog is, where he's working now or who he is dating. Such knowledge does not help in your healing. It reopens your wounds. You don't want to give the Frog the satisfaction of your concern or, if he is more troubled, the encouragement that you still want a connection with him. Social networking sites have ways of allowing you to block your ability to see his posts and his ability to see yours. Make use of them.

5. Don't keep it

The gum wrapper he left in your car after the Phillies game, the t-shirt he left at your house when he helped you wash your car that day, his chinchilla's studded collar—these things do not get you to your goal of healing. If there is something you absolutely must get back to him, like a valuable item, give it to a mutual friend to give to him, or have one of your own friends—preferably male, drop it off to him. Keep #4 in mind, and don't ask the friend how he was or what he was doing. Tell the friend not to be forthcoming with any news about you, as well.

6. Don't do a drive-by

This should fall under 'no contact', but I wanted to be more specific, since this is technically not contact. There is no reason, unless you live next to the Frog, that you need to drive by his home or work to see whose car is in the driveway, to see if he's home, or for any other reason. This also doesn't help your healing and if you're caught, *you* will be branded as the stalker.

7. Don't plot his demise

Lighting a bag of fiery poo on his doorstep...slashing the tires on the car he called 'his other girlfriend'...most people won't do the vengeful things they dream up, but the best thing to do is focus your mind on things other than how his car would look with four flat tires. You may want to play film director in your mind just to feel better, and have entire dramas in your head of what you'll say if you happen to see him, or how you would like to get back at him. This not only steals your peace and delays your healing, but it actually trains your mind to do the very things you're thinking of doing, even if it's just yelling at him when he's in your view again. Negative thoughts don't benefit anyone. Redirect your thoughts. Renew your mind. Ask God to help you and He will.

8. Don't jump into another dating relationship

It may ease the pain for a while, but it's not fair to you or your new male friend. You need to heal and be the best you can be for your future mate. Using another person as a sedative or 'upper' is not respectful of him and is downright mean. It also delays your healing. You need time alone with close friends and by yourself.

9. Don't beat yourself up

So you messed up. You went too far. You missed the warning signs. You used bad judgment and now the relationship is all over. But think of it this way: this is the beginning of your new life of wisdom, making right choices and the potential of finding that amazing man who will know how to love you. Your life is not over. Now is the time to work on yourself and pour your energy into family and friends. The most important thing is to get close to God by reading his word and being with positive, healthy friends who love you. This happened because you moved away from Him, but He is waiting for you to come back. Do things for *you*—including helping others.

10. Don't do the unthinkable

You may think there's nothing to live for. Or, maybe your thoughts aren't clear, and you just want the pain to go away. But the pain is temporary, believe me, I've been through it. After my Frog, I could barely move on the sofa. I was in too much pain to sleep, but had too much pain being awake. I was frozen for an entire day.

Then things started getting better.

I decided to hang on. I didn't know what I would do, but I did know that as each day went on, time would heal my injured heart, day by day. I still have scars, but am much stronger, and I'm alive! Pain is temporary. Suicide is permanent. You are precious and a Frog is not worth your life. If you are really contemplating suicide, call someone, even if you don't feel like it. Reach out. Make a deal with yourself: that if you still feel like ending your life in a month, you'll call someone again. But stay alive for that month. And keep calling people and your counselor until you don't need to anymore. You are far more important than a stupid reptile.

Healing steps

For the present time, your life has to be all about you: about your relationship with God, about your friends, about reclaiming your peace and joy and about balancing your Seven Pillars again. In an unhealthy dating relationship, one or all of these things have suffered. Now, it's time to take some steps toward healing. Time will heal you, but there are proactive things you can do now:

1. Get involved in a Bible study

God's word is a healing balm, and you may be surprised at the other women you meet who have been through what you just were, and worse. God uses people who have been down similar roads to heal others who are have just traveled a difficult one. These people will all be praying for you, and soon you will feel the warmth of community around you like a hug.

2. Spend alone time with God

There is nowhere else on earth where peace can be found. It is tempting to anesthetize with alcohol, drugs, t.v., internet or other diversions, but don't. God's peace is the only thing that will truly heal you. It was made for your heart. Read His word. This is an opportunity for growth and to get you past whatever had allowed this to take place. Take advantage of it. You don't want to go through this again. Go for a walk in a sunny, grassy park or by the rolling blue ocean with its spray and look at what he made for you.

3. Focus on someone else.

There are lots of hurting people in the world and people who need help. They are waiting for someone just like you to listen to them, to help them with errands, single moms who need help with their kids and home, elderly people who need company and little kids who have no one to hang out with them, people with AIDS and cancer who are lonely and depressed need someone to visit them. You will be amazed at how your own efforts at helping someone else will minister right back to you.

4. Date yourself

Get to know yourself, without hearing a man's opinion or interests. Take a class, a trip, start a project, write that book (that's where this book came from!). There is a whole world out there waiting to be grabbed. All you have to do is pick the one thing you have desired to do, and do it! And when you're done, pick another thing! Before you know it, you'll have photos of yourself climbing the Alps, a title on the NY Times Bestseller list, and the curious knowledge of how to make vegan sushi. Well, at the very least you'll have fun.

5. Seek counseling

Getting help doesn't mean you're a weakling or crazy. All of us need help at one time or another. Counseling based in scripture is strong medicine on your road to healing. Friends are helpful, but often a 'disinterested' other party will counsel you with pure motives and an objective ear. It's not forever; just to get you over this rough patch. Many churches have counseling services for free. Just be sure they are counseling based on biblical principles, otherwise it's just someone's opinion helping you 'cope' (i.e., 'struggle').

6. New boundaries

Boundaries are empowering, as we discovered earlier. Like the rules of a game, there is freedom in dictating to others where the buck stops… in a nice way, of course. Think of your downfalls with your Frog. Did you spend too much time alone with him? Put up with abusive or disrespectful talk? Allow your schedule to fall by the wayside while your Frog insisted you live by his late hours and unannounced appearances at work and at home? It's time to rewrite the rules of your game, as mentioned in Chapter 8.

Time boundaries should be set and remain even when you meet the most adorable man in the world. Again, he will respect and be more attracted to a woman who has her own life and knows she doesn't need him to 'complete' her. Don't linger on the phone. There is no need for eternal conversations that last until sunrise and make you feel like you've met your 'soul mate'. Tell Romeo you'll speak with him when you see each other. Even out on a date, set a time limit. You'll have all the time together you'll want when you're married. This way, you haven't wasted your time, bonded your heart with him (this is the same kind of oxytocin bonding that happens with sex) and ended up brokenhearted, should things not work out. This works to keep your heart intact. It may seem cold to come up with a time limit for the phone and stick to it, but you will remain honorably detached and he will respect you for it...and will either chase you or give up because he's lazy. Either way, you win.

7. Forgiveness

This is difficult and takes time, but it is essential for your healing. Your wrath does nothing to the Frog who hurt you. Let him go. Mark my words, God has seen what happened. The Frog will not get away with it. Forgiveness is something which releases *you*. You may never get an apology, but decide to release him from your anger. You need to be free to start your new life!

Are you the friend?

Maybe you're not the Princess who has encountered a Frog. Maybe you already have, but you see your friend following the same path you did, before you were subsequently hurt and are now wiser. What do you do?

I can say from experience that when you try to warn any woman, friend, acquaintance or otherwise, that they are dealing with a Frog, you can get one of three reactions:

1 - Wise. She takes your advice and moves on. After my Frog, I had no problem (and still don't!) taking a woman's warning about a dangerous man, and moving on. If this has happened with you, kudos! You have helped a woman avoid certain heartbreak and thwarted the plans of a Frog.

2 - Hearing-impaired. She hears your advice and moves ahead anyway. This is very common. Don't be discouraged. Though you may be able to discern better in this situation than a woman who is losing her heart to a Frog, you can't make someone do what's best for them. You've done your duty, now move on. She will learn in her own way, in her own time, how to recognize and avoid a Frog.

3 - Wants what she wants (i.e., Foolish). She lashes out at you and moves ahead anyway. I have seen a few friendships between women end because a woman won't listen even to her friends. Remember 'Girl's

Gotta Have It?' Some women repetitively indulge Frogs, and will stop at nothing to get what they want, even if it means scolding you, ending your friendship and even gossiping about you to try to make themselves feel better. Again, kudos for doing your duty. You have told her the truth, and she must learn on her own the things that you already know. You must trust God through the possible loss of a friend and know that He will heal things in His time. The results of telling the truth—or the fear of doing so—should never stop you from telling the truth, if you are trying to help another person. Just think about later, if you didn't tell the truth, the relationship with the Frog tanked (which it will, inevitably), and she wonders why you didn't even try to warn her. I know, it seems unfair, but by giving a warning at least you are offering a gift which could save her mental and emotional health and, possibly, could protect her physically. If she throws that gift back in your face, it is at her own risk. You have done your due diligence.

You may also encounter leadership in some form: at church, school, work, law enforcement, who either can't or won't do anything to reprimand the Frog, or to provide justice or protection. They may even believe the gossip about you and be suddenly 'unavailable' to you.

Fear not. Your Heavenly Father sees what this man did, and there will be a day when your reputation is restored, and this man is dealt with. But remember, it's not your place to play Chuck Norris and rescue anyone or set anything right.

God has greater plans for your situation than you can imagine.

If you are the friend, it may look now like you have lost your friend—the woman you warned—or that people look at you as a troublemaker because you tried to protect someone. Don't worry—all will be revealed.

If you are the woman who has fallen for a Frog's lies and have realized your mistake only to be judged and given the cold shoulder by those who you thought cared about you, take heart—the truth will be revealed. This is the time to draw close to God. His opinion is the only one which matters, and He will never give you the cold shoulder.

Go back and read Part III about your purpose and vocation, if necessary. Waste not one more acre of brain real-estate on this Frog or on those who would believe him. You have fun and important work to do, a glorious life to live, and you are going to be your fun and fabulous self once again!

You are a beautiful creation of God. This was just a pothole. Jump over it. Get on down the road. Time is short. Love God and live your life.

Helpful Tables

Years ago, I found that part of ordering my life included keeping a monthly budget. It helped me when I knew what costs or bills were coming down the road. There are comprehensive budget sheets you can find in books or online. I would suggest either printing one out for each month, or getting a *portable document format* (PDF) of one to fill out for every month.

One list I add in my life is for birthdays, Christmas, anniversaries, and other events that need gifts, 'chipping in', a lunch, a dinner, food and favors for a party or any other expenditure that seems to creep up during the year. You may not be able to plan for every 'gift' event, but by listing and setting aside money for the ones you know come up each year—and some extra for those unexpected ones—you can better shield your budget against the financial surprises that surface. This is just a short example, but feel free to make your own.

Gifts Budget

Month/Day/Year	For whom	Gift	Cost
_____	_____	_____	_____
_____	_____	_____	_____
_____	_____	_____	_____
_____	_____	_____	_____
_____	_____	_____	_____
_____	_____	_____	_____
_____	_____	_____	_____
_____	_____	_____	_____
_____	_____	_____	_____
_____	_____	_____	_____
_____	_____	_____	_____

Groceries

Fresh Fruits
_____
_____
_____
_____
_____
_____

Vegetables
_____
_____
_____
_____
_____
_____

Frozen
_____
_____
_____
_____
_____
_____

Meats
_____
_____
_____
_____

Drinks/Coffee/Tea
_____
_____
_____
_____

Snacks
_____
_____
_____
_____
_____
_____

Canned/Boxed Foods
_____
_____
_____
_____
_____
_____

Spices/Condiments
_____
_____
_____
_____
_____
_____

Bread
_____
_____
_____
_____

Pharmacy
_____
_____
_____
_____

Goals

The following list is a 'memory-jogger' for goals that may coincide with your dream, or things that may get you closer to determining what your dream is! The list is divided into the Seven Pillars which make up a balance in your life. Of course, the most important pillar is the spiritual. Without a relationship with God, everything else is futile and ineffective (*John 10 - 'Without Me you can do nothing'*). Go to a quiet place with your Bible and a notebook and ask your Creator to bring to mind His plans for your life. Don't worry; He won't ask you to go to Africa and live among spiders...unless that's something you already want to do. Chances are, those things you already love doing are on that path down which He wants you to walk with Him!

Sometimes thoughts and daydreams need to be written down for the first step toward achieving them! Write small and dream big!

Things I want to do before I die (just some suggestions; add your own.)

Physical
- ski in the Alps
- run a marathon
- get in shape (specifically, toned)
- lose ____ pounds
- ice skate at Rockefeller Plaza in NYC
- start running
- start working out
- get a personal trainer
- get toned
- surf in Hawaii
- _____
- _____
- _____
- _____
- _____

Spiritual
- have peace
- pray more
- start memorizing bible verses
- apply one bible verse a week to my life
- volunteer at _____
- find a spiritual mentor
- find ways to have more peace
- change up my devotional time
- choose a book of the bible to study
- pick a subject and find out what God says about it
- _____
- _____
- _____

Vocational

- ❏ have an art show
- ❏ get training in
- ❏ make a movie
- ❏ be in a movie
- ❏ write a screenplay
- ❏ learn a language
- ❏ get my degree in
- ❏ breed dogs
- ❏ start a _____ company
- ❏ take a business class
- ❏ get a business mentor
- ❏ take one step a week toward my new vocation
- ❏ _____
- ❏ _____
- ❏ _____
- ❏ _____

Financial

- ❏ buy a house
- ❏ get out of debt
- ❏ start an investment portfolio
- ❏ learn more about real estate
- ❏ commit to start saving
- ❏ sell belongings and save the money or pay a debt
- ❏ set up a budget
- ❏ learn more about money management
- ❏ give
- ❏ _____
- ❏ _____

- ❏ _____
- ❏ _____

Relational

- ❏ help someone do their dream
- ❏ listen more to friends
- ❏ be more aware of people who are hurting and help them
- ❏ give out random, encouraging notes
- ❏ help a new mom once in a while
- ❏ cultivate at least one close friendship in the coming year
- ❏ meet someone I have admired
- ❏ _____
- ❏ _____
- ❏ _____
- ❏ _____

Recreational

- ❏ write a book
- ❏ ride a horse
- ❏ drive a car valued over $500K once
- ❏ paint a picture outside
- ❏ visit the city of _____
- ❏ visit the city of _____
- ❏ visit the city of _____
- ❏ visit the city of _____
- ❏ travel the world
- ❏ see the Grand Canyon
- ❏ build a car
- ❏ drive across the country
- ❏ herd cats

- ❏ sail in the Caribbean
- ❏ take a boat around the world
- ❏ _____
- ❏ _____
- ❏ _____
- ❏ _____

Rest

- ❏ go camping
- ❏ spend a few hours alone at the park
- ❏ get a massage
- ❏ practice being still for longer than usual
- ❏ watch a sunset on the beach
- ❏ go to bed earlier
- ❏ go fishing
- ❏ walk in the mornings
- ❏ _____
- ❏ _____
- ❏ _____
- ❏ _____

Add your own dreams!

And attach a time deadline, so you actually plan to do them! You may want to do these in a notebook so you can expount on them and get detailed.

Dream   *Time goal*

Dream 1: _____ _____
First step: _____ _____
Second step: _____ _____
Third step: _____ _____
(you can add steps) _____ _____
Cost: _____
Need to save $ _____ per week by _____

Dream 2: _____ _____
First step: _____ _____
Second step: _____ _____
Third step: _____ _____
(you can add steps) _____ _____
Cost: _____
Need to save $ _____ per week by _____

Dream 3: _____ _____
First step: _____ _____
Second step: _____ _____
Third step: _____ _____
(you can add steps) _____ _____
Cost: _____
Need to save $ _____ per week by _____

Dream 4: _____ _____
First step: _____ _____
Second step: _____ _____
Third step: _____ _____
(you can add steps) _____ _____
Cost: _____
Need to save $ _____ per week by _____

Dream 5: _____ _____
First step: _____ _____
Second step: _____ _____
Third step: _____ _____
(you can add steps)_____ _____
Cost: _____
Need to save $ _____ per week by _____

Dream 6: _____ _____
First step: _____ _____
Second step: _____ _____
Third step: _____ _____
(you can add steps)_____ _____
Cost: _____
Need to save $ _____ per week by _____

Dream 7: _____ _____
First step: _____ _____
Second step: _____ _____
Third step: _____ _____
(you can add steps)_____ _____
Cost: _____
Need to save $ _____ per week by _____

Dream 8: _____ _____
First step: _____ _____
Second step: _____ _____
Third step: _____ _____
(you can add steps)_____ _____
Cost: _____
Need to save $ _____ per week by _____

Putting a time deadline to your goals

Again, this is just a guide. One financial advisor suggests opening a 'Freedom Account' (you can name it what you want). It's a savings account where you deposit a certain amount per paycheck, record it in a notebook or on your computer, and mark the account just for _____ (whatever you are saving for). This isn't your main savings account, which you use for retirement, or the secondary one for 'emergencies'. This account is specifically for your dreams and goals. For instance, if you have three dreams: 1) to write a screenplay, 2) to visit Paris and 3) to get a personal trainer, the amount of money you put in per week (say, $25) will be divided three ways. You'll need money to write a screenplay, to purchase the software, for editing or to account for a trip to Los Angeles or New York City when the time comes to pitch it.

It's good to try not to 'borrow' from your other categories, but if you need to, it's better to borrow from other categories in this account than to borrow from one of your other accounts. For instance, if you put four weeks of money in for these three goals, you will have $100 in a month. If a trainer costs $50/hour, you have the option of either paying him the whole $50 now (even though you only have 1/3 of that accounted for him: $33), or just waiting another couple of weeks to start with your personal trainer so the other two categories remain untouched. It depends on the urgency of each goal.

I can't tell you how many times my own Freedom Account assisted me in remaining financially free while using this 'extra' for these goals.

As far as steps, yours (for, say, 'writing a screenplay') may look like this:

Step 1: Read/study screenplay formats and storytelling.

- go to a bookstore or library and read how-tos and actual screenplays (WHEN will you do this? Always attach a time goal)
- attend a media conference; specifically sitting in on the breakout sessions and classes on screenwriting (WHEN will you do this?)
- watch films with your 'screenwriter' hat on. Take notes. (WHEN?)
- find out the physical format your screenplay needs to be in. (WHEN?)

Step 2: Write!

I could tell you what all of this entails—character arcs, creating a character, the 3-act structure—but there are people with much more experience and work under their belts who can help you better. The only way you get better at writing is to write and be open to learning.

- Make a writing schedule. You may think you can do this in your head. Don't. You will never do it. Treat it like a doctor's appointment, or somewhere you have to be, because you do—if you want to get your screenplay finished.

Step 3: Edit

- A bestselling author recommends letting a month go by after finishing your script before starting your editing, to let things settle, get your mind involved in other things, and come back at it with a fresh eye. I've tried it and it works. You will see glaring errors, inconsistencies and mistakes and be able to tighten your script.

- Find an editor. This step can be a 'cost' point. It is best to pay a real editor (one who does it as a business, not one of your friends…unless they do it as a business and you pay them).

Step 4: Contacts

- Go to film festivals (When will you do this? Write it down.)

- Work your network. Remember the 'vocation' section, where you may have provision? Maybe you don't know people in the film industry. That's ok. You can still go and make contacts. Go to 'meet up' groups. Go to your local film commission. There are many ways to get in front of people in the industry. But don't use people. Get to know them. Form professional relationships. Learn from them. It will make you more well-rounded in the industry. (When will you do this?)

- If you have the savings, go to Los Angeles. Do you have friends there? I went there alone one year, not knowing anyone. I met a waiter as I was eating lunch on Ventura Blvd. He was a friendly guy just starting out in the industry. Today, we are still friends, having kept in contact for years. Now he is a successful actor and director in network t.v. and films and has appeared on shows like *CSI: Crime Scene Investigation*. You never know who you will meet or what it will become. (When?)

You may think this is overkill, showing a list this way. After all, this isn't a book about screenwriting. The reason I did this is to show how detailed the goal list needs to be, and how each goal needs a deadline. I have heard so many people say 'I wouldn't even know where to start' regarding a dream or goal they have. Well, here's where to start! Without detail and a time goal, your list will just be a list.

Devotions

When you read God's word, it enters through your eye gates and is stored forever in your mind. When you read it often, it is easier for the Holy Spirit to bring to you the truths and direction you have read in scripture and store them in your heart, where they will be effective.

There are a few good books by authors like Kay Arthur or Elisabeth Elliott, about having a quality time with God. Below are some additional suggestions:

1. **Rise early.** I know. I don't like getting up early either, but you would be amazed at how this changes your life. If you work really early in the morning and are still comatose when you get to work, you may find that lunch time or evening time is best, but mornings are recommended. The influences of the day have not yet hit you over the head and you are, basically, a blank canvas.

2. **Find a quiet place.** Devotional time won't fly at a crowded restaurant, the monkey house at the zoo, or at preschool. It's also difficult if you're in a room in your house that's screaming to be swept or is piled with wash. If you're good at ignoring that kind of thing, you're ok. A park, your bedroom, backyard or anywhere else where you won't get distracted by people or work is idea. Clue family or roommates in, that this is your quiet time and to leave you alone until it is done. If they don't respect it, tell them to do the wash and sweep the floor. Trust me, they'll make themselves scarce.

3. **Use your Bible.** Sounds obvious, but you don't want to rely solely on a devotional book for your time with God. His word is living and active.
4. **Have a journal and pen/pencil.** This is for writing out your prayers, desires, and whatever you feel God is telling you. No one will read it. Be transparent.

There are several ways you can approach your time with God.

Prayer: First always is prayer. I like to just pour out my heart to Him, adoring who He is and what He's done, confessing any sins I may have done or thought, thanking him for what He's done in my life and what He has provided, and asking him for requests for my friends, family, country, situations and for me. After that, I sit still, pushing outside distractions from my mind, and listen.

Sometimes you feel like reading a devotional book, sometimes you have a desire to study God's word, and sometimes you just want to be still and drink in God's creation around you. This list is not meant to be followed to the letter, but it provides some starting points for your own time with God. There are different ways to study, or to just have time with Him:

Reading the Psalms. This book is uplifting, especially when you are going through trials. You can read 5 Psalms a day to total a whole month.

Reading Proverbs. Proverbs is split into 31 chapters, which also stretch for a month, making for a Proverb-a-day reading, if you choose.

Inductive Bible study. This is an easy and exciting way to study God's word. It consists of 3 simple steps:

1. Take one scripture and write down exactly what it says.
2. Write down what the scripture means, in your own words.
3. Read the scripture again and write down what it means to you specifically.

This is not something to zip through. Be still and really think about what the verse speaks to you, personally.

Devotional books: As mentioned before, you can search online.

One book of the Bible: There are books and online guides which help study one book of the Bible at a time throughout a month or more. It enriches your knowledge of and intimacy with God to study His word this way, and you learn how people in the Bible dealt with some of the things you go through.

Bible in a year: You can read the entire Bible in a year, and then start all over again. Because God's word is living, you will be changed and will grow each year that you read it.

༺

It is my hope that this book, while not perfect and not an exhaustive authority on how to spot and avoid a Frog, at least gives you some insight on how to see and hear in a dating situation, how to take the initiative with healing, and how to make choices in your own life which lead you closer to being whole as a human being. I have had to live the lessons in this book more than once. I learned my way wasn't working, and that I needed to change the way I did things—and asked God to help. That's when things started getting better.

Nothing will change until you make the decision to change poor decisions into wise ones. You are precious and one-of-a-kind and deserve a man who treats you so!

In the meantime, don't let anyone (namely yourself) steal your dreams. You were meant to do something. Go find out what it is, then do it. Most importantly, stay close to God. He knows the beginning and the end, and is eager to walk the path with you, if you let Him.

Epilogue:
Happy Endings

You didn't think I could write a book on how to spot a Frog and not give you real-life examples of Princes, did you? Well, here are some real-life examples of women who waited for their Princes (and yes, they had their share of Frogs!), who learned how to keep the treasure of their purity intact during their courtship (no, they're not perfect, and have their histories too!), and married their Princes.

Happy ending #1: Belinda and Paul

Belinda met Paul at work when he moved there from Europe. She was attracted to him immediately, but did nothing about it but pray. Another woman stepped forward to 'stake her claim' in that subtle way women have, clearly stating her interest in Paul to Belinda. In her mind, Belinda shrugged. If Paul and the woman were to be together, that's the way it was. Paul, a painfully shy photographer, made no moves toward either of them. He and Belinda got to know each other at work and became friends.

Fast forward to weeks later, when Belinda, Paul and several others were to go on an outing up the coast to another beach. Everyone cancelled but the two of them. They didn't want to simply go home, so they continued the trip up the coast, watching the weather get more foreboding. When the rains unleashed, they took cover in the car, waiting for the storm to subside. Belinda wanted to express her interest in Paul, but remembers telling God: If you want me with this man, he's gonna have to make the first move. And he did.

After some conversation, he asked her if she could see marrying someone like him. She returned the question. They were engaged soon after. That was over a decade ago. Now they have two beautiful boys. This author still visits them for card games and great fellowship.

Happy Ending #2: Jane and Tim

Tim was a hot commodity in the New York fashion industry. He had been shot by some of the top fashion photographers. He partied like it really was 1999. He bought and sold clubs and dated beautiful women. And then the phone call came: one of his ex-girlfriends had died. When Tim asked how, the caller said it was AIDS.

Panic seized Tim's heart. He went to the doctor and found out the worst: he was HIV positive. He went home stunned, not knowing what to do about the tragic news. He turned on the t.v. and saw a local pastor talking about Jesus and His love for mankind. He give his life to the Lord. He experienced the comforting joy that came with a loving God inhabiting his heart. He continued to model, but gave up on a future: he could never get married now. Who would want him?

He got an assignment in Europe and started going to a Bible study there. It happened to be that he met a woman named Jane, who was also a model. They became friends. Tim told Jane his whole story. Jane wasn't particularly attracted to Tim, but God was working in her heart. She felt that He was telling her she was to marry this man. Tim was amazed that his disease was not an issue to her, and they got married.

Jane remembers the day after their wedding. She woke up and looked at her new husband, the scales* removed from her eyes: she could see… she had married a gorgeous man! Even better was that he was a Prince—and still is today.

Today, Jane and Tim actively serve in church. Both are vegetarians and prefer a raw diet. Tim's T-cell count, even over two decades later, is still good and he is still healthy. Jane is also HIV-negative. The two are still very much in love.

Happy Ending #3: Trish and Brian

Trish was the very definition of a Southern Belle…only she was from Austin, Texas. Soft-spoken, well-mannered and blonde, she also loved God with all her heart and was involved in her church. She had prayed for a

---

*Scales' in the bible indicate blindness. They were literal in Paul's case, but also describe spiritual blindness.

husband for so long, that at 52 years old (still looking like a svelte 36 year old) she thought maybe it wasn't what God had planned for her life.

Then one day, for no particular reason, she decided to move from the location she usually sat in at church, to a seat across the room. That was where she met Brian. Now, Trish was and still is a Princess; not only in the 'identity' sense of the word, but in how she carried herself. Brian was most definitely—and still is—a workin' man. But something about his gentleness and kindness drew Trish and they began courting. They prayed about their future together and, with green lights from their prayers and from wise counsel, they are now married.

Happy Ending #4: Beth and James

Remember Beth, who had dated Joe the deceptive man/woman? Well, while I was in the middle of writing this book, Beth went to do her dream: serving in a foreign mission field. It was something she had always wanted to do. It happened that a God-loving man named James was also serving in that same country. Beth and James became friends and…you guessed it…they are now married.

There is something I can't help noticing about these stories; something that can also be found in the Bible. In these stories, you may see a 'then one day' or a 'and it happened'. In the Bible, usually after a time of trial or hardship, we see 'and it came to pass'[1] in Joseph's case, when his release from prison was imminent and he would soon meet his future wife and be placed second in command of Egypt. In Ruth's case, right before she met her husband to be, it says 'And she happened to come to the part of the field belonging to Boaz'[2]. Coincidence? I think not. Just like God had a plan with the ancient peoples, He has plans for you. He is the same yesterday, today and forever. Know Him. Do your purpose. And don't rush to be married. You may be surprised at the adventure he has for you, if you'll just let him surprise you.

---

1 - Genesis 40:1, 20, 41:1
2 - Ruth 2:3

www.ingramcontent.com/pod-product-compliance
Lightning Source LLC
Chambersburg PA
CBHW022354040426
42450CB00005B/176